Speech

The Power of Persuasion

Selected Speeches of Brendan Nelson

Edited by
David Furse-Roberts

Jeparit Press

Published in 2024 by Connor Court Publishing Pty Ltd under the Jeparit Press Imprint.

Jeparit Press is an imprint of Connor Court Publishing in conjunction with the The Menzies Research Centre and The Robert Menzies Institute.

Connor Court Publishing
PO Box 7257
Redland Bay QLD 4165
sales@connorcourt.com
www.connorcourt.com

ISBN: 9781923224186

Cover Design by Branded Graphics

Printed in Australia.

Contents

To my parents for the gifts of communication and emotional intelligence

To the Jesuits for an ethic of service to others

To the medical profession for its belief in me

To the Liberal Party of Australia for allowing me to serve and shape our nation

Hon Dr Brendan Nelson AO

'Put your heart in it!' – The craft of speech

Hon Dr Brendan Nelson AO

Politics ultimately rests on the power of persuasion. Until you learn to communicate effectively, whether to small or large audiences, it is difficult to achieve your own full potential. It is even more difficult to challenge and change the attitudes and outlook of those whom you lead – or wish to lead.

The most fragile yet powerful of human emotions is hope. Speech has the power to inspire, to motivate others to believe in a better future and to build it.

When I look back on the speeches profiled by the Menzies Research Centre, I appreciate just how privileged I am to have played a role in shaping our nation. I have been able to do so through leadership of the medical profession, the Liberal Party, diplomatic service, the Australian War Memorial and the Boeing Company as its global leader.

It began in Hobart. A young firebrand doctor with a reform agenda for both health and the Australian Medical Association (AMA). I found myself sitting in audiences listening to speeches delivered by my colleagues. I have not ever had training in the craft of speechmaking and delivery, but I knew what I liked listening to and what I didn't. I found myself looking around me to see the reaction of others to what we were hearing.

Early on, I wrote speeches, but soon realised that I didn't have time to do so. Although I was grateful to those who helped research and gather material I asked of them, I refused to deliver a speech written by someone else. People wanted to know what I thought and I was determined that is what they would hear. I learned also that audiences would always remember how you made them feel, but less often what you said. The ambition of a good speech is to offer context and meaning, evoke emotion and impart three key messages.

Like leadership, crafting and delivering a speech is not something that can be taught – but it can be learned.

It is learned through observation of, reflection upon and absorption of the substance and style of those who clearly communicate effectively and persuasively. Tone – *how* you say something is as important as what you are saying. In this, authenticity is essential. You must believe in what you are saying if you are to persuade people to go where in their best selves they know they need to be, but are reluctant to do so. In this, the key is to engage the audience first, taking them to a place where they will be willing to listen to what you have to say. Essentially, you need to have them with their arms not folded across their chest before you present your central argument. From humour to a simple story, the audience needs first to be disarmed. Hopefully then, they will come to accept if not embrace the substance of your argument.

Unfortunately, most of the speeches I have delivered were done without a written document. I always thought carefully beforehand what I would say, structuring it in my own mind. I start with a blank sheet of paper, recording the flow and inserting factual information I want to impart. The most difficult task is how to begin and to end. Once I have done this, it is in my head and I am prepared to speak having run over it several times internally.

From observing and working closely with John Howard, I realised that firstly, position gives you authority and a willingness on the part of an audience to listen. Howard rarely used a written speech, whether a formal event or a dinner. He spoke 'off the cuff'. I knew he had prepared himself but I could also see that even if a speech did not flow as well, audiences are much more engaged if they know you are looking and speaking directly to them. The added advantage is that you can assess the reaction to what you are saying.

I am proud of all the speeches profiled here. All in their own way were important at the time and played a role in shaping me and those to whom I spoke. But a number are particularly important.

My first address to the National Press Club in 1993 as President of the Australian Medical Association played a significant role in reforming the AMA as I confronted my profession with its own failings. It also directly delivered the first visible, explicit health warnings onto cigarette packets and turned the government and medical profession's attention to Aboriginal health. AMA membership surged on the back of that speech.

As Education and Training Minister in 2005, I delivered an impromptu speech to the Liberal Party Federal Council articulating our vision for education and the inherent worth of every human being finding and achieving his or her full potential. Constantly challenging a societal attitude that spoke to young people in terms of university education being valued above all else:

> *The Menzian vision is equally if not more important, because of all of the things we have achieved as a country of which we can be extremely proud. One of our failings is that over the last two generations, we have created a country in which young people feel that their lives are valued by the educational choices that they make …*
>
> *… no matter how hard I try, I cannot see Australia through their eyes. But if I did, I could be forgiven for thinking that if I don't get an outstanding year 12 result, and a university education, a BMW and a mobile phone and fashionable clothes, then maybe perhaps, my life is of lesser value to my country than those who do. Every single thing that we are endeavouring to do in policy is about challenging and changing that cultural orthodoxy.*
>
> *For many young people, apprenticeships and training and moving into TAFE is as equally valued as a university education. And for some young people, just getting from school to a job emotionally intact is a far more significant achievement than anything that any of us here have ever been able to do.*

Perhaps the most difficult but important speech of my life is the 2008 formal Apology to forcibly removed generations of Aboriginal children. In government we had opposed an Apology since the recommendation to do so was delivered with the *Bringing Them Home* report in 1997. A small number of backbenchers had argued against John Howard's opposition to a formal Apology, but most had either supported his position or gone along with him given the significant response to other recommendations it contained.

But Australia had changed in the decade to 2007. It was clear we had to support the Apology, morally and politically. This was going to be hard for us. Support for it could not be imposed on the Party Room, nor on the National Party. The process of arriving at support for it, I believed, would be critical to not only the outcome but the stability and future of the Liberal Party.

About half the Liberal Party room was supportive of an Apology. About 30 per cent had reservations through to outright opposition. The remaining 20 per cent, as is often the case, were prepared to back the leadership.

I was conscious of the suppression of dissent to which MPs had been subjected in the final two years of the Howard Government, in the interests of discipline. I knew it was important that the decision be one of the Party room and would be settled once we had all met and had an opportunity to listen to one another's point of view. This would be important to holding things together, well beyond the issue at hand. Each one of them needed and deserved their 'day in court'.

The language of 'Stolen' Generations was offending the sensibilities of many of our supporters. Though recognising in hindsight the devastating impact of removal of these children, they resented the imputation of universally bad motives. Many younger Australians especially, were enthusiastic in support of the Apology but less aware of the history.

One of the devices I learned over the years in bringing people to where they don't want to get on difficult issues, is to make sure they know that you understand and respect their view. In their heart of hearts, I knew most of my colleagues opposed to an Apology, also knew it was the right thing to do. What upset them was the seemingly shallow nature of the debate which reduced it to slogans, running roughshod over their perspective.

What I did was publicly present the concerns of those within our ranks opposed to the Apology. "We look back now on these events over six decades with a sense of shame, but can our generation be held responsible for these forced removals? We are proud of what our ancestors did at Gallipoli, but we cannot claim responsibility for sending them. In many cases, the motives for removal were decimation and elimination of Aboriginal culture, but in others, the motives were to remove children for their own welfare in the belief they would have a better life."

I went to Cape York and asked respected Indigenous intellectual and advocate, Noel Pearson for his views. He said, "Well Brendan, I worry a bit about it. I worry that white Australia will tune in for the Apology, tick that box and move on." Of course he was supportive of it, but I shared his concerns. The nation would largely support the symbolism and feel-good dimensions of the Apology but neglect the substance.

On the plane back to Canberra, I decided I would do what I had done before as AMA president. On the day, I would confront Australia with the reality and existential challenges of Indigenous Australians. It would be a 'feel good' event. But it should be one to also jolt us into a project of national importance to improve the lives of the first Australians.

When the joint party room finally convened in early February to consider the Apology, the relieved gratitude from many that they could finally have their say, was palpable. I put the arguments before the room. The case for supporting the Apology and the case against. I then told them that my strong recommendation was that we must support the Apology. Failing to do so would, in my opinion be morally reprehensible and politically unthinkable. There would be no 'free' vote. We would adopt a position as a Party and as a coalition.

The debate and contributions were thoughtful, respectful and often emotional - from both sides of the debate. After almost four hours, it was clear that an overwhelming majority supported it. Some did not and a handful said they would reserve their position. I knew who they were and would speak to them privately.

When I stood to sum it up, I said in part that I would write my speech over the weekend. When I rose to deliver it the following Wednesday, every one of them would hear something of their view and perspective on this. I would do my utmost to see that in turn, all Australians would not feel 'excluded' from this event of national significance.

Just before we broke to leave, Bill Heffernan stood and said, "This is the best meeting I've ever attended. I'm proud of the bloody lot of you."

As they left, I quietly agreed with Bill. I was proud of them also. Even those opposed to it accepted the outcome with grace.

The galleries were packed and filled with many from the 'stolen generations'. Unbeknown to me, Kevin Rudd had earlier met and been photographed with former prime ministers, including Malcolm Fraser. John Howard of course was not among them.

The Great Hall was filled with people and large screens had been erected in public spaces throughout the nation.

Kevin Rudd spoke to the Apology and spoke well. As he did, I saw the emotion of many in the galleries and the meaning it held for them.

My turn came. What I didn't know then, but discovered the following day from ABC Canberra, was that two of Kevin Rudd's staff were in the Great Hall urging people to turn their backs from the screen before I had uttered a single word:

> *In rising to speak in support of this motion, I recognise the Ngunnawal, first peoples of this Canberra land.*
>
> *Today our nation crosses a threshold.*

We formally offer an apology to those Aboriginal people forcibly removed from their families through the first seven decades of the twentieth century.

In doing so, we reach from within ourselves to our past, those whose lives connect us to it and in deep understanding of its importance to our future.

We will be at our best today – and every day – if we pause to place ourselves in the shoes of others, imbued with the imaginative capacity to see this issue through their eyes with decency and respect.

This chapter in our nation's history is emblematic of much of the relationship between indigenous and non-indigenous Australians from the arrival of the First Fleet in 1788.

I went on to describe the Australia of the decades through which these removals occurred, its values and motives. I used the words of those who had been removed, the deeply traumatising impacts and consequences. From the National Archives oral histories, I quoted directly from those who had been removed.

Controversially – and I knew it would be – I described the circumstances in which too many Indigenous people and their children find themselves today. I pointed out that more Aboriginal children are being removed today – tragically – than ever were through the period of the forced removals for which we apologised.

I also reminded the parliament and those listening, of Neville Bonner, of his life and journey. An early pioneer in the journey of reconciliation.

When I finished, an awkward silence. Joe Hockey started applauding as he stood. The entire chamber followed his lead with few exceptions. I stood looking at Kevin Rudd. We both simultaneously reached out over the dispatch boxes to shake hands. That image spoke to what had been achieved. I was proud of my party. I was proud of the Nationals. I was proud of what we had been able to achieve, notwithstanding the damage to me along the way.

At the morning tea that followed, one of our conservative Liberal Party members, a woman not known for ever supporting me, clutched my elbow. "Brendan, thank you for what you did today. You apologised for these past wrongs and you defended our dignity. Thank you."

Each anniversary of the Apology, I receive a handful of letters and emails, similar to one that arrived in 2013 from a South Australian primary school teacher.

> *Dear Dr Nelson*
>
> *I decided to talk to my year six class about the parliamentary Apology to the stolen generations on the occasion of the fifth anniversary. In preparing for the class, I read Kevin Rudd's speech and I read yours. I am writing to apologise to you. I was one of the people turning my back on you the day you delivered your speech. In reading it carefully, I now appreciate the power of your words, what you said and why. It is in fact, the better speech.*

The 2008 Budget-in reply address as opposition leader was another landmark for me. The Rudd Government towered over the political landscape at that time. My objective in the speech was to 'frame' the Government as being like the set of a western movie – facades being held up by sticks. Much style but little substance. I further wanted to announce some policy and finally, remind and enunciate to our Liberal Party members at a time of political adversity, what it is in which we believe.

The centre-piece was a cut in petrol excise. The Rudd Government had promoted 'Fuel Watch' as a solution to crippling petrol prices. As I announced our policy, I said "Watching the price of petrol does not make it come down."

Late that evening, three Labor backbenchers congratulated me on a "great speech".

The most emotional speeches I have ever delivered are those that speak to our military history, devotion to duty and individual sacrifices made in our name. The 2017 address to the National Press Club, *Triumph and Tragedy* brought me to tears delivering it. So too the audience was visibly moved.

The key to these speeches is to take the audience on a journey that offers them a sense of what it means to be an Australian. A combination of facts, battles and the stories of individuals in their own words. The key is to bring the dead to life and in doing so, enable people to see something of themselves in not only what they are hearing, but what they are feeling.

Another powerfully emotional speech through which I struggled to maintain my own composure, was the UN Holocaust Remembrance Day address delivered to 2,000 members of Sydney's Jewish community in 2018. A potent reminder of the depths to which human beings – educated people – can descend in certain circumstances. That speech also speaks to my own journey of discovery in relation to values, character and moral courage.

It was a true privilege to deliver the John Howard Lecture in his presence in 2021. Liberal philosophy, national values, a transformational geopolitical realignment, Australian history, military sacrifices and an idea to create a resting place for Indigenous remains before the Australian parliament and the restructuring of Australia Day that should remain 26 January and why. It is a speech of which I am proud in paying tribute to those who made us who we are and gave us what we have. Foremost amongst them, John Howard.

It was said of Sir Winston Churchill that he had "weaponised the English language in the defence of Great Britain". So too anyone wanting to change a world that yields so painfully to it, needs to master the crafting and delivery of a speech. Within these pages lies my own attempt to do so.

Introduction

Simon Berger

Assembling a collection of speeches for Dr Brendan Nelson is not without challenge.

For a start, he almost never read from a prepared text.

Instead, he relied on his extraordinary memory and ability to read a room.

Furthermore, there are no former speech writers to consult.

Brendan had many fiercely loyal staff. However, he held the view that ultimately "I was elected to offer my own thoughts and ideas, not those of a staff member or public servant".

When an important speech warranted meticulous research, he usually did this himself.

In doing so, he not only sought to broaden his already considerable knowledge. He sought to really understand and empathise with people he was speaking about.

The words reproduced on these pages are powerful. However, it was Brendan's passionate delivery that often left audiences mesmerised.

The range of topics of Brendan's speeches is as diverse as his career.

While most parliamentarians held a different job before or after politics, Brendan Nelson's career path would confound any career counsellor.

In three decades he has been: a general practitioner; President of the Australian Medical Association; a parliamentarian; Education and Defence Minister; Liberal Party Leader and Leader of the Opposition; Ambassador; Director of the War Memorial; and President of Boeing Global.

In each role, his calm demeanour belied the sense of urgency with which he tackled problems and implemented change.

As AMA President, he brought into sharp focus the unacceptable state of Indigenous health, long before the Closing the Gap framework.

He staunchly defended the medical profession from a Labor Government that invoked class war rhetoric against doctors and was openly hostile to private health.

As Education Minister he championed standards and values in schools and the right of parents and students to make their own choices in education.

He delivered substantial reform of universities. Importantly for a generation of Liberals, he also delivered Voluntary Student Unionism.

In 2006 John Howard appointed Brendan Defence Minister, saying the portfolio required somebody who "would burn the midnight oil" and that "Brendan is your man".

With the War on Terror raging and great instability in our region, he presided over ten deployments, mounting a strong moral case for them.

He also drove major investments in our capability, including two new army battalions and new heavy air lift capability, air warfare destroyers, amphibious ships and Super Hornets.

Brendan became Leader of the Liberal Party and Leader of the Opposition in 2007, following the defeat of the Howard Government.

At that time, morale was low, internal debate was rife and Kevin Rudd was the most popular Prime Minister in Australian polling history.

Well documented disunity added a further degree of difficulty.

As Brendan would later reflect, his role was a "poisoned chalice".

Using the doctor's bedside manner, Brendan stabilised our Party.

He navigated important policy changes. These included dropping WorkChoices and supporting the apology to stolen generations, the

Kyoto Protocol, the abolition of the wheat export single desk and law reforms for same sex couples.

While there was pressure from some quarters for greater changes, Brendan embraced the Howard legacy that Liberals celebrate today.

As Brendan began to frame the Labor Government and lay out an alternative vision for Australia, his time as Leader was cut short.

His departure from parliament leaves us to hypothesise about one of the best Prime Ministers Australia never had.

As a Liberal, Brendan Nelson was difficult to pigeon hole.

His paths into parliament and the Party leadership were unconventional.

Brendan was the son of a maritime unionist and grew up in a Labor voting household.

He established a medical practice in Hobart's northern suburbs with David Crean – a future Labor Member of the Tasmanian Parliament (and brother of future Labor Leader, Simon).

Brendan was a Labor Party member. At one point, he was approached to run as a Labor candidate.

He says: "I came to my Liberal belief through life, absorbing it through reflection upon and familiarity with the hard work, self-sacrifice and idealism of just everyday people. I am a better person and a stronger Liberal for the path that I chose."

In 1995, he challenged a sitting Liberal Member for preselection in Bradfield – winning by just three votes.

As a backbencher, he spoke out on social policy, sometimes challenging prevailing orthodoxy.

For example, he advocated for a trial of safe injecting rooms and methadone treatment, to work alongside the Howard Government's "Tough on Drugs" strategy which put significant investment into policing, enforcement and education.

He also opposed the Government's then position on relaxing cross media ownership rules.

He later recalls:

> *Although I wanted to be a minister and to drive policy, I had all but given up believing it would ever happen when, in December 2000, John Howard asked me to be Parliamentary Secretary to the Minister for Defence.*
>
> *I was surprised because I sensed that John believed me risky, with an earring and a questionable background for Liberal politics. But I learned of John Howard that he respected people who challenged him provided they had an intellectually sustainable basis for their argument and refused to parade it through the media.*

In articulating his vision of Liberalism, Brendan very much emphasised economic policy as a means to an end, rather than an end in itself.

He drew a distinction between value and values.

He invoked examples of people who inspired him – none more than former Liberal Senator, Neville Bonner, who in 1971 became the first Indigenous federal parliamentarian.

In Brendan's words, Bonner's life was "a study of not only courage, conscience and compassion in the face of extraordinary adversity, it is also one of personal and national reconciliation".

Brendan spoke often about the importance of living one's life in the service of others.

Nowhere did he invoke that theme more than in the way he commemorated the sacrifice of our service men and women.

Our ANZAC legacy is something Brendan continued to speak about with passion in his roles as Ambassador (where he visited the Menin Gate 74 times) and Director of the Australian War Memorial.

In his Budget Reply speech as Liberal Party Leader and Leader of the Opposition in 2008, Brendan articulated Liberal beliefs in the following way:

Our beliefs are in the individual, in the encouragement of, and rewards for, hard work and self-sacrifice in everyday life.

We believe very strongly in the family as the bedrock of Australian society, while respecting and reaching out to every other Australian, whatever their economic or personal circumstances.

We believe in choice. We believe Australians should be encouraged and supported in choice in health and education.

Equally, they should be free to join a union or not to join a union.

We believe strongly in defence and security and investment in it for the protection of our nation.

We believe very strongly that small family businesses are the lifeblood of our nation and its economic prosperity.

We believe always in lower taxes, once our obligations to society in health, education, road infrastructure, defence and other requirements have been met.

We believe ultimately in the individual. We believe that the inherent worth of every single Australian is paramount and that our task as Liberals and as Nationals is to stand against oppressive bureaucracy and governments that too often – and under this new government – appear to think that they know what is best for Australians, instead of leaving choices and freedoms in the hands of individuals who actually make this country work.

We believe we will be at our best as a nation if we see ourselves as and strive to be an outward-looking, highly competitive and compassionate people, reconciled with our Indigenous history and imbued with fundamental values of hard work, self-sacrifice, courage, tolerance and a determination to see that we support one another, that we respect our freedoms and stand up for the rights, values and freedoms of not only all Australians but all people throughout the world.

The last paragraph is adapted from the "Vision for Australia" he articulated at the start of his parliamentary career, along with a motto for his electorate: "Put your heart in it".

Putting his heart in it is something Brendan Nelson has always done and always will.

Simon Berger is Deputy Federal Director of the Liberal Party of Australia and a former senior adviser to Brendan Nelson.

Chronological List of Speeches

Address at the National Press Club as AMA President, 29 September 1993

Australia Day Address for the Australia Day Council of NSW, 25 January 1995

Bradfield Preselection Speech, 13 May 1995

Leadership in Politics and Integrity, 1996

First Speech to Federal Parliament, 20 May 1996

Drugs: The Doctor's Dilemma, 27 April 1999

Menzies' Spirit Still Guides, *North Shore Times*, 8 December 1999

Neville Bonner Tribute, 31 May 2000

The Vision for Education, Address to the Sydney Institute, 10 April 2002

Voluntary Student Unionism, 16 March 2005

Dame Pattie Menzies Oration, 18 April 2005

Values, *North Shore Times*, 3 May 2005

Valuing Vocational Education/Plain Language Report Cards, Liberal Party Federal Council, 25 June 2005

The facts eventually added up, *North Shore Times*, November 2005

Defence Minister Address at the Dawn Service at Gallipoli, Turkey, 25 April 2007

Apology to Australia's Indigenous People, 13 February 2008

60th Anniversary of Israel, 12 March 2008

Budget Reply Speech, 15 May 2008

Suspension of Standing and Sessional Orders (Aged Pension), 15 September 2008

Leave of Absence, 4 December 2008

Valedictory (Final) Speech, 16 September 2009

1. Australian National Identity

Australia Day Address for the Australia Day Council of NSW, 25 January 1995

> Addressing the Australia Day Council, Dr Nelson speaks of the core human values that should define us as Australians. He envisions an Australia that esteems the health and integrity of every human life no less than the economic goals of growth and prosperity.

I was both humbled and honoured when I was approached by the Australia Day Council of NSW to be an Australia Day Ambassador for the city of Manly when I know that there are many of you here who would be far more worthy than I to speak of the virtues of our great nation and its people.

On Australia Day we not only celebrate our growing sense of national spirit and pride but we also should reflect upon and discuss our national identify and direction. It is a time to think of who we are, where we have been and the direction in which our nation should head.

1995 is the year of tolerance and I can think of few human and national characteristics more important than tolerance toward one another whether it be in culture, religion, values, beliefs or ideas.

At this time of year there seems to be no shortage of people criticising the choice of our newly announced Australian of the year – "too much media", "never heard of her", "used to be a pom", "too black", "too white".

Success is not measured by the number of degrees you have, the wealth you accumulate, the spectrum of people you know, nor by the accolades and publicity you might attract. If we look throughout the Australian community and society, those for whom we have the highest regard are people who have fought for things in which they believed. Facing adversity, hardship and criticism in their chosen field, these are people who persevered in seeking to make the lives of all of us that much better.

The strength of this nation and its people can be measured in our compassion and tolerance toward other human beings. The ability to express emotions, challenge the thinking of other people and place the interests of others ahead of your own are the virtues by which human achievement should be measured. When he was Australian of the Year, the late Professor Fred Hollows urged us to engage ourselves in what he called "human caring" in which our own vocation should be of service to others.

Everything this country represents today has evolved out of hardship, sacrifice and determination. Whether it has been in war, natural disasters, scientific discoveries, sporting achievements or economic risk, the sacrifices and vision of those who came before us today have made us what we are.

In looking to the future, let us be seen as a nation that values our responsibilities of its people as much as our rights, an intelligent yet compassionate leader in international affairs and a country in which constraints on investment and wealth generation are seen as the enemy of effective social reform and policy. These are the characteristics that should typify Australia's progress through the early part of the 21st century, where the past sacrifices of its people, indigenous and non-indigenous, are as important in our day to day lives as our ambitions for future prosperity and peace. Any consideration of our future must deal with the failures of our past, notable amongst which is the health status and despair of Australia's indigenous people. In striving for a single national vision of our future, the first step is concluding a meaningful reconciliation with Aboriginals and Torres Strait Islanders that embraces not only symbolism but also substance. If Aboriginal children continue to have life expectancies 15-20 years less than the rest of the country, whatever else is achieved we will have failed.

Although there are tragically many examples of our poor treatment of Aboriginal people, two that I have encountered are important to consider as we reflect on the year of tolerance and the future of our country.

There is a place called Mapoon, 80 kms north of Weipa, on the Cape that was home to a large Aboriginal community.

In 1963 the Queensland Government moved in with the police to clear the land for use by mining companies who had leases over it. Aboriginal people and their families were forced at gun point into boats from where they were dispersed to Bamaga in the north and as far south as Cairns. Homes were then bull dozed and burned. There is an Aboriginal woman there, who along with other people and descendants of Mapoon have returned to rebuild their community but this time with the support of the Queensland Government. Constance Cooktown told me that on that day in 1963 she was returning from a fishing trip with her husband only to find the homes burned and her children gone in boats taking some months to find. This was 1963.

Only last week I took the Human Rights Commission and the Deputy Leader of the Democrats, Senator Meg Lees, to Old Burnt Bridge which is only four kilometres out of Kempsey here in the State of New South Wales. Some 110 Aboriginal people live without sewerage and sanitation, dwellings are corrugated iron and pieces of timber, rubbish is not collected by the Shire Council, only half of the dwellings have electricity usually by extension cords travelling very large distances and not surprisingly only 10 percent of the community live beyond the age of 45 years.

I raised these important issues because if we are to have a certain confidence in ourselves, our nation and our future in the same way that individuals do, we must confront our own failures nationally.

Today young Australians search for a sense of fulfilment in a climate of uncertainty in employment, technological change and environmental sustainability. The challenge for us, our community and political leaders is to transmit a meaningful sense of belonging and purpose to young people who, uncharacteristically as young Australians, face a future that does not guarantee greater prosperity than that endured by their parents. We must demonstrate by our actions that we understand the problems faced by young people and the solutions that are needed.

Hope and confidence can be instilled if young people feel they are active participants in decisions made about our future, if their voices are heard in the corridors of power and, most importantly, if they know that their future health and integrity is not now the subject of political exploitation.

At the other end of life, we are rapidly increasing the proportion of our population that is aged. The effect of the aging of Australia on our health care system, economy, social priorities and political agenda is likely to be significant. We can no longer pay simply lip service to the burgeoning and frequently unmet need for community and residential care for elderly Australians. Demographics demand also that we turn our attention now to lifelong planning for the care of older Australians.

The intrinsic worth and value of older people may well also be linked to securing the uncertain confidence of youth. Societal acceptance of aging in which older people should be venerated and respected, can if we choose it, facilitate an improved emphasis on families. Generational love and nurturing so characteristic of family life in those cultures that now comprise our multi-cultural society where both children and aged parents are loved, respected and wanted is something from which we can all learn.

Australia needs urgently to change its attitude to older people who, too frequently, are marginalised, trivialised and forgotten other than for the incorrectly perceived cost they may pose. The teaching of life skills to young people by older people would transmit a mutual sense of respect and understanding to both groups.

Already in Australia our expectations of employment are changing. There is a growing realisation that full employment in the future will have, perhaps, a different meaning than it has in the past. As such we need to implement strategies that will change the attitude of a nation to unemployment and unpaid work. Australians engaged in voluntary work, those who are unemployed and those caring for families at home should not feel demeaned to be participating in unpaid work. We define ourselves through our work. Self-esteem is vital and can be assured if we work to change our national attitudes to those in unpaid work. Terms like "dole bludger" or "just a housewife" should be expressions of a bygone era.

The important role of voluntary work needs much more emphasis, not only for its benefit but also for the contribution it can make to our economy and the effort required to care for our ageing population. Governments, unions and local communities must consider the role of voluntary work in contemporary Australia where programmes should be optionally available for the unemployed who seek to maintain structure in their day. We should see ourselves as being valued by one another.

On Australia day, we look toward our national symbols such as our Constitution and flag. Although other Australia day Ambassadors will possibly be promoting republicanism. I would like to give you an alternative view …

The lesson that I have learned is that whilst some people tell me that I ought to "get onto the Republican cause with everybody else", we should recognise that there is a generation of Australians for whom the Constitution and flag mean much much more than we younger Australians will ever understand. I have yet to hear anyone pushing a republic tell me that they would rather be dead than continue under the status quo.

Australia will eventually become a Republic but let us face it with slow earnest deliberation. Let us educate ourselves about what we have, why we have it and the sacrifices of our ancestors. Let us instead show a bit more enthusiasm for teaching our children about the nature of our constitution and how precious it is, before we rush changes that few understand.

Unfortunately we live in a selfish world where rights seem more important than responsibilities and value more important than values.

This, more than anything else we must change and in doing so we should be listening to the nation's youth whilst respecting past sacrifices of older Australians. Our past tendencies to worship at the altar of growth and development leave us a legacy of air, water and noise pollution, deforestation, land degradation and ozone layer depletion that will impose on us economic and ecological restraints to which we must now begin to adjust.

This country is at a turning point in its history and those with vision have a unique opportunity and a great responsibility to see that it becomes one that values the health and integrity of human life as much as it does achieving our economic goals...

We are proud to be Australians because our national identity has been based on "mateship", born out of a selfless concern for the welfare of those whom we might barely know – to the point of laying down a life. This is our defining characteristic – not the colour of our skin, place of birth or cultural background. We celebrate today our concern for one another and our willingness to show it. This country, each and everyone of us *can* make a difference – in our homes, local communities, schools and national arena – don't ever stop believing.

Defence Minister Address at the Dawn Service at Gallipoli, Turkey, 25 April 2007

Representing Australia at Gallipoli on Anzac Day 2007, Dr Nelson pays homage to the ANZAC spirit of "endurance, courage and selfless determination to help others".

Australians all let us rejoice, for we are young and free.

Our anthem is a national epitaph to those whose sacrifice in peace and war, gave us that freedom.

Family epitaphs to the dead, in so few words, say so much – of love, life, loss and us.

Private C.V. Hamilton

23rd Battalion 29.11.1915 (age 20)

HE DIED THE WAY

HE WISHED TO DIE

FOR HIS COUNTRY

(Lone Pine Cemetery)

Private R.J. Oliver

4th Battalion 27.4.1915 (age 18)

MY SON, WOULD THAT

I COULD HAVE DIED FOR THEE

(Lone Pine Cemetery)

Private John Simpson Kirkpatrick

3rd Field Ambulance 19.5.1915 (age 22)

HE GAVE HIS LIFE

THAT OTHERS MIGHT LIVE

(Beach Cemetery)

With awkward humility, we pause here at Gallipoli, free and confident heirs to a legacy born of idealism and forged in self-sacrifice. We do so in renewed commitment to one another, our nation and the ideals of mankind.

At this hour ninety-two years ago, ANZACs were on the cusp of giving our nation its identity and place in the world, not only by what they would do here, but how they would do it.

By first day's end were two thousand Australian and New Zealand casualties.

Courageous New Zealanders gave us that first ANZAC day and forged in bloody sacrifice the bond within which our two nations live.

At its end eight months later, 8,700 Australians would be dead and 19,000 wounded, but with abiding respect for their Turkish adversaries.

Charles Bean's account of a digger arriving at the front trench before the Australian assault on Lone Pine, says it all:

"Jim here?" he asked.

A voice in the fire step answered, "Right here, Bill."

"Do you chaps mind shiftin' up a piece?" said the first voice. "Him and me are mates, and we're goin' over together."

Each of them had only one life – only one chance to use life in a selfless way for others and our nation. They chose us.

From the safe distance of this century, it is tempting to settle for the broad brushstrokes of history in neglectful ignorance of individual sacrifices made in our name.

To understand what happened here, to feel a connection with this place, is to be fully Australian.

No group of Australians has given more, nor worked harder to shape and define our identity than those who have worn – and now wear – the uniform of the Australian Navy, Army and Air Force.

They forged values that are ours and make us who we are, reminding us that there are some truths by which we live that are worth defending.

Let us recommit ourselves to that which Gallipoli asks of every Australian, whether by birth or immigration.

Our Australia – their Australia – is a nation in which our values are etched less in granite and marble than they are in our flag, a slouch hat, rising sun, and a smile that says, "G'Day mate. Can I give you a hand?"

Our responsibilities to one another transcend and define our rights. We salute principle before position and honour values, not value.

We will be at our best in facing different, threatening horizons, if we triumph as they did, over fear.

The bedrock for our most fragile, yet powerful of beliefs – hopeful confidence in the future – is the gift given us by generations of servicemen and women.

Precious Australians, who lie here, and in distant places of the world, do so as silent witnesses to the future they have given us. We honour them by the way we use our lives and shape our nation.

The sun will soon pierce the night sky.

Let us shine that light into dark corners of the world as an outward looking, compassionate and confident people imbued with the ANZAC spirit of endurance, courage and selfless determination to help others.

Robert "Mac" Calder of the 14th Battalion heard a voice calling from no man's land, "Have you forgotten me Cobbers?"

He didn't. We won't. We never will.

We are young and we are free.

Lest we forget.

The August Offensive: The Last Gasp, 6 August 2015

Speaking in August 2015, Dr Nelson recalls the August Offensive, which he describes as the "the largest and most costly of the Gallipoli campaign". He emphasises that some truths "are worth fighting to defend".

With a sense of awkward humility, abiding reverence and infused with overwhelming pride, 128,000 Australians paused at the Australian War Memorial in the pre-dawn darkness of Anzac Day this year. So too did several million others at the cenotaphs, memorials and places of commemoration throughout the nation and places throughout the world…

Charles Bean was Australia's First World War historian. Bean landed at Gallipoli with the troops on 25 April and stayed with them at the front through the entire war. He was witness to it all. Wounded at Gallipoli during the August offensive, he refused to be evacuated. It was said of Bean that no-one risked death more often than him.

He would then, over almost a quarter of a century write and edit the twelve volumes of the official history.

Finally, in searching for the words to type onto the blank page before him, to summarise it all, he wrote this:

> *What these men did, nothing can alter now. The good and the bad, the greatness and the smallness of their story ... it rises, it always rises ...*
>
> *above the mists of ages, a monument to great hearted men and for their nation – a possession forever...*

Australia had to form the Australian Imperial Force (AIF), for which General Sir William Throsby Bridges is owed a great debt. We sent Australians overseas in an Australian uniform with an Australian flag.

Aboriginal and Torres Strait Islanders living in a desperately unequal Australia and though prohibited from doing so, only four to five generations after the arrival of the First Fleet, enlisted to fight for the young nation. In doing so they found equality in the AIF. There was no 'black or white', only 'shades of grey'.

A series of largely catastrophic military battles ensued until the stunning leadership of General John Monash of the Australian Corps in 1918.

Australia has never been more divided than it was during the period of the First World War, principally but not only around the conscription referenda. Whether Tasmanians, Victorians or Queenslanders, people looked to the federal government for answers to increasingly difficult questions.

From a nation of 4.5 million in 1914, 1 million men were of an age that could volunteer. Of those, 417,000 died and 330,000 were deployed overseas. Four years later would be almost 62,000 dead. Another 60,000 would die within a decade of returning to Australia. Such was the impact on our young nation. We emerged from the war proud of what had been achieved but a generation inconsolably mourning its dead and dying.

Though public discourse was deeply embittered, we remained true to our democratic principles.

Every nation has its story. This is our story.

There is no more powerful or poignant chapter to that story than the 'August Offensive' one hundred years ago. By early August, three months after the landing, a stalemate enveloped the Gallipoli peninsula. The Anzacs were contained within a 160 hectare beachhead. British commander, General Ian Hamilton wanted an all-out attempt to break the deadlock. A 'last throw of the dice' was conceived and planned to seize the high ground north of the ANZAC sector. It would be the largest and most costly of the Gallipoli campaign.

A complex series of offensive attacks requiring precise timings were planned involving British, Australian, New Zealand and Indian troops. All would end in heartbreaking failure.

Success depended on the Allies seizing three high points – Hill 971, Hill Q and Chanuk Bair.

Birdwood failed to appreciate the rugged, twisted folded terrain. He ignored the poor physical condition of troops worn down by constant artillery fire and fly-borne diseases spread from dead corpses.

Even had the Allied Commanders' actions and questionable tactics succeeded, there would still be many more ridges before reaching the Kilid Bahr plateau overlooking the Dardanelles.

On the evening of 6 August, two columns of allied troops headed for key features on the Sari Bair Range – Hill Q and Hill 971. The objective was to advance to the hills to the north and link in a pincer with the Light Horse assaults at dawn the next day. The Australian attack on Lone Pine was to be a distraction for the Ottoman forces.

At the same time, 20,000 British troops in five divisions started landing at Suvla Bay, eight kilometres to the north.

Simultaneously the New Zealand and mounted brigades began their advance to Chanuk Bair, one of the highest points of the Sari Bair ridge. They were to capture it in support of the dawn attack by the Australian light horse at the Nek. The depleted 6th Battalion was to take out the enfilading machine guns at German Officers Trench at midnight, essential to the success of attacks the following morning. They failed. The 1st Light Horse attacked at Pope's Post. Of the 200 in the attack, 154 were killed and wounded. At Quinn's Post, Major George Bourne stopped the attack when most of his men of the 2nd Light Horse were killed in the first wave. New Zealand's finest moment at Gallipoli was also its most costly – 900 men died at Chanuk Bair. The undermanned New Zealand mounted brigades suffered 100 casualties capturing the outposts. By 4.30 am, three of the four battalions had reached the apex, 400 metres below the summit. The Canterburys were lost on the southern side of the spur.

Brigadier General Francis Johnson who was described as ill but 'fighting drunk' that day, made the fateful decision to halt the attack at the apex and wait for the Canterburys. In doing so, he further sealed the fate of the Australian 3rd Light Horse who were about to attack at the Nek into withering Turkish machine gunfire. Johnson's delay gave the Turks time to be reinforced. Johnson ordered the Auckland battalion to attack into fierce rifle and machine gun fire. Of the 400 who attacked only 100 reached the pinnacle.

Finally, after a naval bombardment and followed by two British battalions, the Wellingtons reached the summit almost unopposed at 3 am on 8 August. The Turks counterattacked and fought desperately all day. The dead New Zealanders clogged the trenches.

By evening when the British relieved the Kiwis, only 49 of the 760 Wellingtons who attacked that morning were able to walk off the hill unaided. Corporal Cyril Bassett was awarded the Victoria Cross for keeping communication and phone lines open under intense fire. On 10 August, Ataturk launched a heavy counterattack, annihilating Chanuk Bair's British defenders. As the British fled the pinnacle pursued by the Turks, the New Zealand machine gunners restored order at the apex firing into the surging humanity.

Almost 100 years ago to the hour, the Australians attacked at Lone Pine in a battle of epic, senseless savagery. At its end four days later would be 2,300 Australian casualties, 7,000 Turkish casualties and seven Australians would be awarded the Victoria Cross – two posthumously.

Lone Pine was a frontal assault over 100 metres, but the fighting and dying was by bayonet and bombs in the Turkish trenches, galleries and tunnels. The network of Turkish trenches at Lone Pine constituted the strongest part of the Turkish front line in the Anzac area. At the southern edge of the feature known as 400 Plateau (from its height above sea level), the ground was bitterly contested and changed hands repeatedly shortly after the Landing. A single stunted pine tree grew there, so the Australians called the area 'Lonesome Pine' from a popular show song of the day. To the Turks, it was simply Kanlisirt (or 'Bloody Ridge') after their heavy losses from the 19 May attacks.

By early August the Turkish trenches at Lone Pine were protected by barbed wire and a heavy overhead cover of pine logs and earth. No man's land between the Turkish and Australian front lines was relatively wide and the Australian line formed a salient around the feature known as the Pimple. The original Lone Pine tree had long since been destroyed.

Brigadier General Howard ('Hookey') Walker commanded the 1st Australian Division. He had serious reservations about a frontal assault in broad daylight over open ground. The Turks held the hill which dominated Lone Pine – baby 700, and as such 'Hookey' Walker wanted it taken out first with a full division. Birdwood would not hear of it, insisting that the continuous pressure on the Turks of fighting at Lone Pine 'must help the attack elsewhere'. The 2nd, 3rd and 4th battalions took their position in the trenches. They had sewn white patches on their backs and wore white armbands. The artillery bombardment stopped at 5.30 pm and the whistles blew. Most charged across open ground, others emerged from the tunnels in no man's land. It was over in a minute.

The Australians had to fight through the pine logs and earth covering the Turkish trenches. By 6 pm the main trench network was captured and cleared. In a corner of one trench, eight Turks and six Australians lay enjoined having bayoneted each other. Eight isolated defensive posts were established in broken trenches at the centre and long Turkish communication trenches were blocked with sandbags. Sergeant Laurence, a tunnelling engineer, stood atop the captured Turkish trenches looking back to the Australian lines and observed the carnage: All the way across is just one mass of dead bodies.

> *Beside me I count fourteen of our*
>
> *boys – stone dead. It is a piteous sight.*
>
> *Men and boys who yesterday were full of joy and life, now lying there cold, lifeless ... glassy eyes, sallow, dusty faces. Soulless ... somebody's son, somebody's boy.*
>
> *The Major standing next to me says, "Well, we have won". Won – that means a victory, and all these bodies within arm's reach. Then may I never see a defeat.*

The worst was yet to come. The Turks counterattacked the next day. Bullets, bayonets, bombs, clubs, fists, feet and teeth were the weaponry used in this most intense battle of subterranean anarchy of the entire war. Private Cecil McAnulty of the 2nd Battalion recorded a diary of sorts:

> *Frank and I were on the extreme left … there was a clear space of 100 yards to cross without a patch of cover. I can't realise how I got across it. I seemed to be in a sort of trance, the rifle and machine gun fire was hellish. I remember dropping down when we reached the trenches, looked around and saw Frank and three more men alongside me … I yelled out to the other four chaps, This is only suicide boys. I'm going to make a jump for it I thought they said alright we'll follow. I sprang to my feet in one jump.*

The diary stops dead.

McAnulty died at Lone Pine between the 7th and 12th of August. Private John Gammage of the 1st Battalion wrote:

> *The moans of our own poor fellows and also Turks as we tramped on their wounded bodies was awful … the wounded bodies of both our Turks and our own … were piled up three and four deep … the bombs simply poured in, but as fast as our men went down another would take his place.*
>
> *We had no time to think of our wounded … their pleas for mercy were not heeded … Some poor fellows lay for 30 hours waiting for help and many died still waiting.*

One thousand corpses were dragged from the Australian trenches for burial. Many more were left to rot in the captured Turkish trenches as the Australians prepared to defend against an expected counter-attack.

An incident just before the assault observed by Charles Bean, perhaps says it best. An Australian soldier leant over the forward trench and to the men in it asked,

> *"Jim here?" A voice rose from the fire step, "Yeah, right here Bill" "Do chaps mind movin' up a piece?" asked the first voice, "Him and me are mates, and we're goin' over together."*

The first Allies returned to Gallipoli in December 1918 and said of the plateau around Lone Pine:

> *It (Lone Pine) was covered with a thin scattered whiteness not unlike the sprinkle of melting snow.*
>
> *Over the former trenches lay the bare white bones, piled or clustered so thickly in places that we had to tread upon them as we passed.*

One name inscribed on the Lone Pine Memorial is that of Private Mark Smith of the 4th battalion, killed at Lone Pine. He was 21 years old. Benjamin Smith had gone into the attack with the 3rd battalion. Having heard of his brother's death, he spent three days trying to find Mark's body. He couldn't, but retrieved a pine cone from a log in the Turkish trenches and sent it back to their mother, Mrs McMullen. From it she grew a seedling which she sent to the Yarralumla nursery in 1929.

Every six months she would write to the Memorial's director, John Treloar asking of the status of 'her son's tree'.

In 1934 when only the foundations of the Australian War Memorial had been laid, the Duke of Gloucester ceremonially planted that sapling. Today it is the magnificent Lone Pine tree honouring one Australian son, but honouring them all…

At 11.44 pm last Tuesday night, 4 August, seven letters a metre high were projected onto the horizontal concrete beam immediately below the dome above the Hall of Memory at the Australian War Memorial. They read one name – WHITE A. H. – Alexander Henry White.

His name along with almost 62,000 others who gave their lives for us and our nation is being projected on thirty occasions for thirty seconds through the centenary of the First World War.

It is being projected for two reasons.

Each one of us needs constant reminder not to settle for the broad brushstrokes of history. It is easy, human beings that we are, to settle for headlines and in neglectful indifference to allow the past to be a distant stranger, to forget individual sacrifices made in our name and devotion to duty.

Second, it is to remind us that in the end, there are some truths by which we live – and they are worth fighting to defend; politically, diplomatically and at times – militarily.

This is our history, but it has much more to do with our future.

We are Australians not only or so much because we have a constitution and the machinery of a democracy given us by the British. We are defined most by our values and our beliefs, the way we relate to one another and see our place in the world. We are defined by our triumphs and failures, our heroes and villains; the way as a people we have faced adversity and as a nation how we face the adversities and emerging horizons before us. As the world moves from one age to another; as the tectonic plates shift with the re-emergence of China and as we face a generational struggle against resurgent totalitarianism in the form of Islamic extremism, we must be clear about who we are and in what we believe. Until his death leading his men at the Nek, Alexander White carried with him two precious items. He wore a locket within which was a photo of his wife Myrtle and infant son, 'young Bill'.

He also carried in his bible a poem he had cut from a newspaper:

Let me be a little braver
When temptation bids me waver
Let me strive a little harder
To be all that I should be
Let me be a little meeker
With the brother that is weaker
Let me think more of my neighbour
And a little less of me.

The Hall of Memory at the Australian War Memorial within which since 1993 has been interred the Unknown Australian Soldier, has standing as silent sentinels above him, fifteen stained glass windows. Each depicts a serviceman or nurse from the First World War. And at the base of each is a single word. Charles Bean, John Treloar and the Army historian asked themselves – what were the qualities, the values seen in these men and women which we regard as essential not just for victory in battle, but for depth and breadth of character? …

A century after the August offensive, young Australians looking for values for the world they want, as distinct from the world they think they are going to get, need look no further than these.

The world loves talent, but it 'pays off' on character …

At Pozieres, France in 1916, Australia sustained 23,000 casualties in just three weeks.

In late July Charles Bean recorded this:

> *Many a man lying out there at Pozieres and in the low scrub at Gallipoli,*
>
> *With his poor tired senses barely working through the fever of his brain*
>
> *Has thought in his last moments, well … well … it's over. But in Australia – they will be proud of this.*

We are.

We are damned proud.

We are proud of what they gave us – belief in ourselves and the gift of knowing that ultimately a life of value is one spent in the service of others and our nation. That sentiment of Alexander White's poem, '*Let me think more of my neighbour And a little less of me,*' is what most strengthens and sustains the most fragile, yet powerful of human emotions – hope.

Like them, what we need most is one another.

Currie-Monash Commemorative Dinner Address, 8 August 2017

> In this speech, Dr Nelson reflects on the invaluable relationship between Australia and Canada with "histories bound in common values and aspirations". These commonalities, Dr Nelson states, is reflected in the legacies of General Sir John Monash of the Australian Corps and General Sir Arthur William Currie of the Canadian Corps, who each led their respective troops with honour and bravery to deal "the greatest blow against the Germans of the First World War".

Australians all let us rejoice, for we are young and free.

O Canada!
Our home and native land
True patriot love in all thy sons command.
With glowing hearts we see thee rise,
The True North strong and free.

Two anthems, two nations, two histories bound in common values and aspirations.

Canada, Australia – strong, young and *free*.

We pause here at the Australian War Memorial where our nation, Australia, reveals its soul, its character.

Australian and Canadian, we do so as free and confident heirs to a legacy born of idealism, forged in self-sacrifice and passed now to our generation.

We gather in renewed commitment to one another, our two nations, the values that bind us and the ideals of mankind.

As US President John F. Kennedy observed at the ground breaking for the Robert Frost Library at Amherst College in 1963, a nation reveals itself not only in those whom it chooses to lead, but those it chooses to honour.

On this day we honour two men who by their leadership gave us a greater belief in ourselves and a deeper understanding of what it means to be Australian and Canadian.

General Sir John Monash GCMG, KCB, VD commander of the Australian Corps and General Sir Arthur William Currie GCMG, KCB who commanded the Canadian Corps.

On this day in 1918 each man led our respective troops in what would be the greatest blow against the Germans of the First World War.

The Battle for Amiens was famously described by the German Army's commanding officer, General Erich Ludendorff in his 1919 memoirs as:

> *… the black day of the German army in the history of war … the worst experience I had.*

'Amiens' lent its name to the decisive defeat delivered by the British Fourth Army and the French First Army on 8 August 1918 against German forces in northern France.

There were twin objectives – to finally and permanently break the German lines driving a wedge between them, and then to protect Amiens, its railway station, rail lines and critical infrastructure.

The British part of the operation – aimed at driving the Germans east, away from Amiens, for a distance of up to eleven kilometres – was launched by three corps: the British 3rd Corps north of the Somme River (50 divisions); the Australian Corps south of the Somme River and north of the Amiens-Chaulnes railway line; and the Canadian Corps on Australia's right, between the railway and the Amiens-Roye road.

Twenty-five French Divisions were on the right flank.

The Canadians were brought down from Arras in great secrecy, while the Australian Corps was augmented by the return of its 1st Division from the Lys front.

Guns silently registered onto their targets rather than ranged by firing a few rounds.

Into the attack were brought 430 British tanks under the cover of masking aircraft noise – a device successfully employed by Monash at Hamel.

Monash addressed his troops on the evening of 7 August:

> *For the first time in the history of this corps, all five Australian Divisions will tomorrow engage in the largest and most important battle operation ever undertaken by the Corps. They will be supported by exceptionally powerful artillery, tanks and aeroplanes on a scale never previously attempted.*

The battlefield was thickly covered in fog when massed British guns brought down the creeping barrage signalling the start of the advance at 4.20 a.m.

In the pre-dawn on 8 August, Monash wrote:

> *In black darkness 1 million infantry are deployed over 12 miles of front … with a mighty roar 1,000 guns begin in symphony and a great illumination lights up the eastern horizon and the whole complex organ began to advance.*

Sergeant Walter ('Jimmy') Downing of the 57th Battalion wrote:

> *The waiting men fidgeted … As though a flaming dawn had been flung into the sky, the whole world flared behind us … a titanic pandemonium of ten thousand guns. We shouted to each other, but we could not hear our own voices, buried beneath colossal ranges of sound … The hoarse and frantic rumbling of the sixty-pounders, the long naval guns, the great howitzers, was like the rapid burring of a thousand drums…*
>
> *…Then a rattling of machine-guns told us that the lads in front were at grips with the enemy …*
>
> *… We hurried forward fearful lest we should be late at our places as bullets zipped among us …*
>
> *… the Canadians took Marcelcave, immediately across the railway from where we were, and all was ready for us to go forward.*

> *We had watched them at work – encircling villages, storming strong posts and fighting through woods.*
>
> *They (Canadians) had a rough time, for the difficulties of their terrain were often great, but they were good men. In the ancient Homeric style they were led in person by their colonel, accompanied by their chaplain. We were often able to assist them when we were farther forward than they, by firing into the backs of the enemy across the railway line.*

Barely three hours later the German front line trench system had been overrun.

In the Australian sector, the 4th and 5th Divisions passed through the 2nd and 3rd Divisions, who had led the assault until then, pushing ahead to the second line of objectives another three kilometres on. By mid-afternoon, these too had been taken.

Gunner Helmore reported from deep into enemy territory:

> *Entering Fritz's land with mixed feelings … abandoned gun positions, corpses littered about, blankets strewn everywhere … we could not repress a shudder at the gruesome sights we saw.*
>
> *German trenches ploughed up by shells and a few still shapes in grey uniforms told the tale of our big barrage … there was no barbed wire; no support or reserve trenches, just a small shallow front line as if the enemy feared no offensive from our side or was planning an advance himself … very different from the German defences at Ypres.*

The RAF provided strong aerial support and improved techniques for co-ordinating with ground forces. Allied aircraft circled above the infantry when not in the multiple dogfights.

Canadian air ace Raymond Collishaw wrote:

> *The fighter Squadrons suffered heavily … the whole Roye road was strewn with hundreds of aircraft and derelict tanks. Each time the fighter pilots were launched to assault the infantry, they could see the aeroplane graveyard beneath them, and one was*

> *conscious, while passing through a hail of fire, that at any moment the frail shell, in which the pilot felt poised precariously, might join its kind below.*

George Maxwell of the Canadian 49th Battalion observed the human toll on the ground. He found a group of dead machine gunners from his Battalion, none bearing visible wounds, killed by the concussion of a high explosive shell.

> *Some were in a crouching posture, as if tending their guns. They looked as if they were still alive, some resembled wax figures. One ... was caught in the act of lighting his pipe, his hands still cupped around where the match had been ... and there he knelt, stone dead.*

For a time the British corps in the north had fell behind the required rate of progress, thereby exposing the 4th Division's left flank to fire from German troops north of the Somme around Cérisy.

The Australians still pushed on to the second objective – catching in the process hundreds of German support and reserve troops in the Morcourt Valley – then continued on with the third and final stage still with the Germans firing into their flank and rear.

On reaching the ridge overlooking Morcourt, a Company with its left flank exposed saw Germans preparing to escape from the Australian advance. The OC of A Company boldly decided to attack the village without the other two companies, although it was reduced to half strength.

Whilst two small groups flanked the village, the remainder, led by Captain Norman Wilson, entered the village from the south headed by one tank, machine guns and a six pounder in rapid action.

The early vigorous German defence was quickly defeated in ferocious fighting and the village captured along with many machine guns and 200 prisoners.

For his leadership and courage, Wilson was awarded the Military Cross.

The 116th Battalion was the least experienced of the Canadian units deployed on 8 August. But it was led by one of Canada's bravest and most competent soldiers – LTCOL Georges Pearkes VC.

Pearkes had been awarded the Victoria Cross in the bloodbath of Passchendaele, but at Amiens he valiantly led the 'Umpty Umps' as the Battalion was known.

Pearkes had trained his unit in the new Canadian and Australian techniques of assault. Under Currie, they no longer moved en mass. Men now dashed from position to position under cover fire from other small units and then in turn covering their advance.

The unit's cohesion was shattered in an ambush at Hamon Wood. Suffering many casualties the Battalion wavered. But Pearkes gathered up his scattered men and drove them on towards their objectives, the 116th taking more than 400 prisoners.

Pearkes' adjutant noted:

> *The dash of our men was marked, showing a marvellous difference from the old staid method of following the barrage shoulder to shoulder.*

By nightfall, both the Allied armies had reached their final objectives south of the Somme.

A shattering blow had been dealt to the German Army, which sustained 27,000 casualties – 16,000 prisoners of which half were taken by the Australians, another third by the Canadians.

Among the 450 guns captured was the 11-inch German gun mounted on a railway platform, which had been shelling Amiens from the village of Harbonnières.

Attacked by British aircraft, then British cavalry, the gun was finally secured by Australian infantry. Its barrel is displayed here today at the Australian War Memorial, a powerful reminder of the brutal industrialised killing of the First World War.

Three days later, on 11 August King George V arrived at Amiens and Knighted Monash, the first battlefield knighthood in 100 years. It would also be the last.

Monash and Currie, in the perfection of teamwork, gave us a war winning combination.

Both were meticulous planners who developed reputations for the clever application of firepower.

Each was a Corps commander of genius, co-ordinating infantry, tanks, artillery and air support.

Both men had been in a business before the war that almost went broke.

Both were pre-war members of the militia who rose through the ranks to become corps commanders of their respective national military forces.

Both are subject to popularly-held views that their achievements as military commanders have not been given 'proper recognition'.

Of John Monash, his biographer Geoffrey Serle wrote:

> *... he had the first essential qualities, the capacity to bear great strain and to make quick and clear decisions. His sheer intellect, breadth of grasp, his articulateness especially, together with his forceful personality, induced respect and confidence among his juniors ... in 1918 the men in the line knew that all was right behind them.*

Arthur Currie is widely considered one of the ablest generals of the First World War. He had executed the heroic Canadian victory at Vimy Ridge that would give his nation its 'story'.

Among his strengths was his emphasis on meticulous planning and preparation, and recognition of artillery's importance to trench warfare.

Canadian Prime Minister Borden held Currie in high esteem.

Britain's wartime Prime Minister David Lloyd George called him a "brilliant military commander."

There is even evidence to suggest that Lloyd George at one

point had considered appointing Currie commander of all British forces.

But like Monash, he courted controversy and criticism.

Australians and Canadians have served, fought, suffered and died in almost every major conflict from the Anglo-Boer War, two World Wars, to Korea, Iraq and Afghanistan. In peacekeeping – including East Timor, counter piracy and disaster relief, we have been there together.

We have each paid a similar price in casualties and our combatants have been awarded a similar number of Victoria Crosses.

We are Pacific nations who know there are truths by which we live that are worth fighting to defend – politically, diplomatically and militarily.

We are nations motivated to defend these truths in the belief that our interests are our values, and our values are our interests.

We are nations whose citizens enjoy political, economic and religious freedoms.

We are nations that uphold a free press, an independent judiciary, free academic inquiry and are societies in which faith coexists with reason …

What is most important in all of this is for us, Australians and Canadians, to be confident about whom we are and in what it is that we believe.

It is not for us to lecture other nations about their values, but we must be very clear about our own.

And upon this bedrock must be a clearly articulated vision for our nations that is economic, human and social.

Canadians and Australians – we are defined less by our respective constitutions, flags and machinery of democracy given us by the British than we are by our values and our beliefs, the way we relate to one another and see our place in the world.

We are shaped most by our heroes and villains, our triumphs and failures, the way as a people we have faced adversity and how we face the inevitable adversities coming and respond to threatening, new and emerging horizons.

Two heroes, two leaders of men who shaped not only victory in war but confidence in ourselves and our two nations have brought us here.

We best honour them and those whom they led by the way we live our lives, shape our nations and world.

Inspired by them we are strong and we are *free*.

Battle for Australia – Commemorative Address, BAE Theatre, 6 September 2017

> Dr Nelson commemorates the Battle for Australia beginning in 1942, which he describes as Australia's "next most important year" after 1788.

To the young people who are here I say you don't realise what you're learning when you're learning it. It's often in random moments of quiet revelation that the most significant things that will shape and influence your thinking and attitudes will come, when you least expect them …

We are young. And we are free. And we are free in no small way for the events that bring us here today, to commemorate what is broadly known as the Battle for Australia…

If 1788 is the most important year in this nation's history - the British First Fleet arriving and all of the devastation that would bring for millennia of rich Indigenous custodianship, culture and history, and from it the origins of the Australia we would become and the people we now are – the next most important year was 1942.

The Second World War was no mere extension of the First. This was not about emerging national identity or Australia's place in the world. Our vital interests were at stake. The Japanese landed on the Malaya Peninsula on the same day they attacked the US Fleet at Pearl Harbour.

We were, when the war had been declared in September 1939, seven million people. One million Australians mobilised, including 70,000 women who did much, much more than the important task of nursing.

We would, over those six years that would ensue, send half a million Australians overseas. Thirty thousand would be prisoners of war. Eight thousand would die in captivity, in the most brutal and most unimaginable of circumstances.

And we would emerge from the war victorious, uncertain of our future and inconsolably mourning our forty thousand dead, living with the one hundred thousand physically wounded and an indeterminate number, as is the case today, of those bearing psychological traumas.

Once the Japanese had landed in December 1941 they rapidly advanced through South East Asia. Nine hundred and twenty five Australians died in the defence of what the British called 'Fortress Singapore'. And then twenty two thousand young Australians of the 8th Division, fit, young, healthy volunteer Australians went into captivity.

On the following day, 16 February 1942, our then great wartime Prime Minister John Curtin described this as "our nation's gravest hour". He addressed the nation on that day and he said,

> *The fall of Singapore can only be described as Australia's Dunkirk for in it lies not only the future of the Commonwealth of Australia but the frontier of the United States of America, indeed of all the Americas, and the peoples of the British speaking world.*

He said,

> *The protection of this country would no longer rely of that to a contribution to a world at war, but rather resistance to an enemy threatening to invade our shores.*

Only three days after that speech two hundred and fifty two Australians, military and civilians, and some Americans, were killed in the bombing of Darwin by the Japanese, the first of 63 attacks on the Australian mainland in 1942. There would then be a series of critical events and battles that would occur through that momentous year, 75 years ago.

The strategic defeat of the Japanese by the United States Navy and the Royal Australian Navy in early May at the Battle of the Coral Sea was the origins of the alliance between Australia and the United States which endures today and has been the bedrock of security in the Western Pacific ever since.

And then the defeat of the Japanese at Midway the following month that forced the Japanese to get to Port Moresby, having planned it to be a seaborne assault, across the hinterland to the north.

And hence the gripping struggle at Kokoda, at Isurava in late August, the pivotal battle at Milne Bay – the first defeat inflicted on the Japanese Imperial militarist army on land.

What the Americans did, supported by us and others, at Guadalcanal.

Three Japanese midget submarines entered Sydney Harbour in late May, but there were five mothership submarines just 80km off the coast of the headlands of Sydney Harbour.

There was every reason for Australians to believe that Japan was coming and that this nation, as it's Prime Minister had said to them, was now resisting an enemy threatening to invade our shores.

It is very tempting, human beings that we are, to settle for headlines, settle for some of those broad brushstrokes I just outlined, popular imagery and mythology of our history. Our comfortable lives, 75 years on, breed easy indifference to these individual sacrifices that have been made in our name, devotion to duty and to our country.

Many of you, much younger than me, would not know of some of these events but just before the fall of Singapore a ship, SS Vyner Brooke, embarked a range of civilians including 65 nurses to get them out of Singapore before it fell. It was strafed from the air by Japanese fighters on 14 February 1942.

Of the 65 nurses on-board 25 managed to get to Bangka Island. And then, on a place called Radji Beach, with machine guns pointed at them the 25 nurses walked into the water. Only one, Vivian Bullwinkel, would survive.

Her uniform and medals are proudly displayed here at the Australian War Memorial. She spent three and a half years in captivity.

And she recorded Matron Irene Drummond as these young nurses walked into that water before being machine gunned from the back.

Matron Irene Drummond said,

Chins up, girls. I'm proud of you … I love you all.

There was a small Royal Australian Navy ship; HMAS *Perth* that had already been lost in the Sunda Strait, a ship called HMAS *Yarra*. It's a sloop, for those of you unfamiliar with the navy it's a smaller version of a fighting ship.

It was escorting a small merchant convoy back to Australia, after the fall of Singapore, from Java and the young commanding officer, Lieutenant Commander Robert Rankin, encountered five Japanese warships. Three heavy cruisers, two destroyers.

He made the decision to disperse the convoy, put out a smoke-screen and turned that little Australian ship headfirst into those five Japanese warships. Having taken multiple hits he gave the order to abandon ship and he and those on the bridge were hit moments later when a salvo hit it on 4 March 1942.

Leading Seaman 'Tubby' Taylor went back to his gun and kept it firing until the ship went down.

The captured British merchant seaman, Joseph F Murphy, was witness to it from the Japanese Cruiser, Maier and he said,

Silently we stood and watched the little sloop, white ensign flying and guns blazing against the hopeless odds … hers was a gallant death and one of which Australia should be proud.

We of a younger generation hear the word Kokoda often. And often it's regarded as a place where one goes to find strength and inspiration. Perhaps at times to deal with all sorts of traumas in our lives.

But in 1942 on the stepping stones of courage and despair a small group of Australians, young Australians, defended our country and stopped the enemy from getting to Port Moresby.

One of them who did survive, a member of what was called the 39th Militia Battalion – these were members of the militia, they were either conscripts or too young to get into the professional army and they were what stood between us and the Japanese – and one of them, Sergeant Jack Simms, he'd been a shop assistant from Ballarat, said to us in the year 2000, clearly struggling with his own psychological traumas.

> *Some prayed, some swore with fear, but you wouldn't show it in front of your mates. One of the boys got shot fair between the eyes, right alongside me. It was a perfect shot. Terrible to be afraid, but it's the brave ones afraid that still kept going, that's what they did you know. Scared bloody stiff and they still kept going.*

In Anzac Hall here you will see now, just in front of the Lancaster bomber, a small tank. It weighs just eight tons. It's a Japanese Ha-Go 95 tank.

The Japanese landed 2,800 Marines and those two tanks at a place called Milne Bay on the south east corner of New Guinea in late August 1942 in an attempt to get to the airstrips and then provide air support for their attack along Kokoda to Port Moresby. On 27 August a 27 year Australian pilot of 76 Squadron, Squadron Leader Peter St George Turnbull, was killed flying at treetop height strafing that tank.

There are four words up there in New Guinea, at Isurava, enshrined into granite. Four words of values that were seen in these young Australians.

Courage. Nothing of value in life is achieved without taking a risk.

Endurance. You never give up.

Sacrifice. In order to achieve the objectives that we've set for ourselves we have to make sacrifice, we have to give things up and often with immense physical and or emotional pain.

And mateship. That in the end what we need most is one another.

There are a small number of veterans here today, I say to young people, who fought in these campaigns that I'm referring too, and they're old. But once they were young. They were young like you.

And today, and for the rest of your lives, when you sing our National Anthem, just think of them, because that is why we are free.

They are the best generation this country has ever produced.

They were born in the aftermath of the First World War.

They grew up through what is called the Great Depression, and may God grant never you ever experience one.

They then came to their teenage years under the shadows of a war that was coming.

They mobilised to defend our freedoms and vital interests.

They then set about the economic and social reconstruction of our country, Australia, and gave us the prosperity that too often we have taken for granted.

So always remember them.

They put principle above position, values ahead of value, they regarded their responsibilities to one another and our nation and its future as transcending and defining their rights.

We will always remember them.

We remember them here every day, for we are young and we are free.

Tragedy and triumph – 1917, National Press Club address, 19 September 2017

Dr Nelson reflects on our nation's "most tragic, damaging year", 1917. He reminds his audience that, despite emerging victorious in the following year, Australia had lost and was mourning 60,000 dead. He notes that our nation has been shaped by how we have endured and responded to such adversity, and that from our nation's worst year, ultimately, we emerged with a "deeper understanding of what it means to be – Australian".

... at least they'll remember me in Australia
Australians all let us rejoice ... for we are young and free.

We pause here 'in the heart of the land they loved', free and confident heirs to a legacy born of idealism, forged in self-sacrifice and passed now to our generation.

We do so a century from our nation's most tragic, damaging year – 1917.

It was the worst of times ...

Barely a year later we emerged victorious – but inconsolably mourning 60,000 dead. Yet from this wrenching cataclysm, embittered, deeply divided – we remained true to our democracy.

We had our story.

We were Australians.

Our young nation's innocence was brutally lost in the bloodbath at Fromelles and hard-earned victory of Pozieres in 1916.

The bitter conscription referendum rendered us a deeply divided people facing the new year of 1917.

The AIF began in the snow of Bullecourt and finished in the quagmire of Passchendaele, the cost – 77,000 casualties; 22,000 dead and missing.

We were three years into a war in which victory seemed an ever receding horizon. No solace to anguished families in humble homes where telegrams and letters spoke to suffering, death and lives given.

The harsh realities of British military leadership were revealed to the man who was witness to it all – Australia's official war correspondent, Charles Bean:

> *Bullecourt, he said, more than any other battle shook the confidence of Australian soldiers in the capacity of the British command.*

He saw the struggles of the ordinary soldier, men simply 'flicked aside'.

Aghast, he watched in April the 4th Australian Division torn to pieces attacking into a hail of machine gun fire and German artillery at Bullecourt.

Of the 3,000 men from the 4th Brigade, 2339 were killed, wounded or taken prisoner.

In May, Bean returned to Pozieres where a mortally wounded Australian had asked him: *Will they remember me in Australia?*

Here he collected the first artefact for the Australian War Museum he had conceived – The 'Centre way' trench sign.

These were the sacred relics of triumph and tragedy, of heroism and bloody sacrifice.

As Bean searched amongst the detritus of the Pozieres battle, the Australian War Records Office was established at AIF Headquarters in France. Birth had been given to what would become the Australian War Memorial.

The Americans joined the war in April, but not the battlefield for another year.

Russia was seized by a Bolshevik revolution. Lenin would rule by year's end.

Prime Minister Billy Hughes left the Labor Party, splitting it asunder to triumph in an electoral landslide. Australians wanted a wartime leader.

Ireland's independence revolutionaries stirred negative Catholic opinion led by Archbishop Daniel Mannix.

Months of Industrial warfare broke out in August, 97,000 striking workers crippling transport and industry.

Hughes crushed the unions with sweeping powers. Cynicism and anger spread.

Recruitment stalled. Hughes ran a second pre-Christmas conscription referendum. Again, a majority of Australians voted No.

But it was the events in Europe that would weigh heaviest on any residual Christmas cheer.

One word from 1917 would describe inconsolable grief and mourning for an entire generation of Australians.

Hell on earth now had a name – *Passchendaele.*

The 'suffering of Christ' – and suffering it was.

This small Flanders village – lent its name to a series of battles that would epitomise the war of brutal attrition, of suffering inflicted on so many for so little.

For purists – the Third Battle of Ypres …

The Passchendaele campaign began on 31 July.

The Germans had seven weeks after Messines to fortify their defences in the Ypres-Salient. They built concrete pill boxes, bloc houses, machine gun nests, barbed wire and fortified field artillery batteries.

Over 15 days in late July, the British fired 4.3 million artillery shells from 3,000 guns into the north, attacking on 31 July with a creeping barrage in front of troops with tanks – 27,000 casualties in a day.

Then it began to rain.

With the intricate drainage system of the Flemish lowlands destroyed, the battlefield was a quagmire.

The weather improved in early September as the five Australian Divisions were brought together in support of the imminent battles.

General Herbert Plumer's 'first step' on the road to Passchendaele was the **Menin Road.**

Side by side, the 1st and 2nd Australian Divisions attacked in the centre flanked by 11 British Divisions.

It went to plan, the advancing barrage winning ground occupied by the infantry.

In less than three hours across a 12 kilometre front, all objectives were taken.

Another 5,013 Australian casualties, two Victoria Crosses awarded.

Clinical enough a description, but the 'mad photographer', Frank Hurley wrote:

> *The way was gruesome, awful beyond words ... the dead and wounded lay about everywhere, the ground had the appearance of having been ploughed by a great canal excavator and then re-ploughed ... through this the wounded had to drag themselves – and those mortally wounded pass out their young lives ...*
>
> *... the battlefield on which we won an advance of 1500 yards was littered with bits of men ... literally drenched in blood.*

Charles Bean described the men coming out of the line on the Menin Road:

> *... looking like a dead man looks. A man of the 20th Battalion had a wound inside the thigh still bleeding ... passing, he grinned, "We got the bastards good on the second ridge".*

Plumer's second 'step' was at Polygon Wood on 26 September. The 4th and 5th Australian Divisions attacked with the British.

The intensive artillery preparation and the 'creeping barrage' was the best ever. The infantry came in behind five layers of bombardment described by Bean as:

> *... roaring, deafening, it rolled ahead of the troops like a Gippsland Bushfire.*

Of the 55th Battalion, Bean wrote:

> *Captain Cotterell led its advance, walking easily, cigarette in mouth, map in hand, behind him the thick line of "worm columns" each led by an NCO. All pillboxes were immediately outflanked ... from some came whimpering boys, holding out hands full of souvenirs.*

Walter 'Jimmy' Downing of the 57th battalion was in the thick of it:

> *... We were caught in the barrage ... no time for caring as we stumbled past reeking bodies ... heads down as though in a hurricane of rain, not ripping steel.*
>
> *... men running, staggering, bent low ... dropped into shell holes, tautened faces ... crouching as they burrowed for dear life ... on all sides the groans and wailing of mangled men.*
>
> *A sergeant ran around his platoon ... the top of his skull was lifted from his forehead by a bullet, as on a hinge, and his body fell on two crouching men, washing them with his blood and brains.*
>
> *... bodies, living and dead were buried, tossed up, and torn fragments buried again ... the most awful sound, the muffled voice of a man buried under three feet of dirt, was heard ... dig me out!*
>
> *... relieved, we were a pathetic band ... all hysterical to varying degrees, the strong supporting the weak, we walked through Polygon Wood ...*

Sinclair Hunt of the 55th Battalion was a school teacher from Croydon, Victoria:

> *... though we suffered much ... the capture of Polygon Wood was a most difficult operation brilliantly executed ...*

The exhausted and demoralised Anzac Divisions were finally relieved on 18 October by the Canadians who made the final assault on Passchendaele.

They clawed forward to capture the Passchendaele Ridge on 6 November.

For Haig, no more could be achieved in Flanders. His breakthrough had failed – miserably.

After three months the British line advanced 8 kilometres, only to expose it to German artillery. British losses stood at 275,000 dead, wounded and missing.

Thirty-five Australians had been killed for every metre of ground taken.

Nine of 61 Victoria Crosses awarded, were to Australians.

Barely five months later, in three days the Allies lost Passchendaele and all the ground won in the Third Battle of Ypres.

Mounted on the German concrete blockhouse at the centre of the Tyne Cot cemetery today, is the cross of sacrifice. Amidst manicured lawns and 12,000 graves, including those of 1369 Australians, it bears a plaque:

This was the Tyne Cot Blockhouse
Captured by the 3rd Australian Division
4 October 1917

… The daily Last Post Ceremony at the Australian War Memorial is our offering, to give meaning where there is none.

This simple gesture, including reading of the life, love, service, suffering and loss of just one of them, is our national tribute.

It is an expression of loss, suffering and love reaching into us all.

Pilgrims bound by a single, reverent emotion pause with awkward humility as stillness descends.

The Last Post sounded in the commemorative area, cloaked by the Roll of Honour, arrests the soul.

The silence that surrounds it is the most powerful sound heard.

In that silence, I always look up to the names of these young lives – silent witnesses to the future they have given us.

I am reminded that we are all equal in death.

I am reminded that we are Australians, that there are truths by which we live that are worth fighting to defend.

As the doors of the Tomb of the Unknown Australian Soldier close, we are stirred by the most fragile yet powerful of human emotions – hope.

We are all driven to believe in a better future. Sustaining that precious belief, we honour them best by the way we live our lives and shape our nation.

Sarah Morley and Fanny Seabrook, in their despair and inconsolable grief, asked, '*why?*'

In the tragedies of 1917, the Seabrook brothers, Robert Morley made their *"willing sacrifice for a better world' and 'the love of friends"*.

A century on, they ask of every Australian, are we prepared to make our sacrifices for others and for a better world?

In reflection Bean wrote:

> *Wherever they fought – the Australians were sustained by a belief in their worth.*

We are Australians defined less by our constitution than we are by our values and our beliefs, the way we relate to one another and see our place in the world.

We are shaped most by our triumphs and our failures; our heroes and villains; the way we have endured adversity and how we will face adversities coming, responding to new, emerging and unseen horizons.

From this worst year, we emerged with a greater belief in ourselves and a deeper understanding of what it means to be – Australian.

For we are young, and we are *free*.

2. Liberalism and Enduring Human Values

Menzies' Spirit Still Guides, *North Shore Times*, 8 December 1999

> Marking the 50th anniversary of the election of the Menzies Government, Dr Nelson describes the foundational principles of the Liberal Party including "an open mind, hard work, self-sacrifice, idealism and concern for other human beings", which are as relevant in modern times as they were in the time of Menzies.

This week marks the 50th anniversary of the election of the Menzies Government. For 16 years this remarkable man towered over Australia's political and economic landscape.

But this is also the 50th anniversary of the proclamation of the electorate of Bradfield. Named in honour of arguably Australia's finest engineer, Dr John Job Crew Bradfield, this unique area has been represented first by former Prime Minister Billy Hughes followed by Harry Turner and David Connolly, each of whom served for more than two decades.

His biographer described Jack Bradfield as a classic example of the spirit which built Australia – a man who communicated equally at all levels, from the workmen to the Governor. This extraordinarily gifted and visionary man's greatest achievement was the construction of the Sydney Harbour Bridge.

The electorate of Bradfield has developed an electoral division synonymous with the finest ideals and traditions of the Liberal Party. In forging post war liberalism, its party members and elected representatives have moulded and enunciated principles of enduring value.

An open mind, hard work, self-sacrifice, idealism and concern for other human beings have been the philosophical foundation taken to Canberra by its elected representatives. As the Liberal Party rebuilds itself in NSW, and federally ponders the year ahead in which social policy has been emphasised by the Prime Minister, there are guiding principles from the past as relevant today as they were then.

To the 1944 Canberra meeting called to form the Liberal Party, Robert Menzies said this:

> *We took the name Liberal because we were determined to be a progressive party, prepared to experiment and in no way reactionary.*
>
> *What we must look for is a true revival of Liberal thought which will work for social justice and security. True Liberals have great and imperative obligations to the weak, the sick and the unfortunate. They must give them all the sustenance and support they can. To every good citizen the State owes not only a chance in life, but a self-respecting life.*

To ignore these words is to court irrelevancy.

Dame Pattie Menzies Oration, 18 April 2005

> Speaking in 2005, Dr Nelson honours the legacy of Dame Pattie Menzies. He pays homage to her as a "woman of substance" who led from both position and from principle throughout her life. Dr Nelson also iterates her significant contribution to the Liberal Party, to her country, and to her family throughout her life.

… Today, in this, the inaugural Dame Pattie Menzies oration, we seek in our own inadequate way to honour a remarkable Australian, woman, mother and wife.

A political movement reveals itself – its values and beliefs, not only by those it elevates to lead in its highest offices, but by those whom it honours.

Some people lead from position, others by principle. Pattie Menzies did both. The debt owed her legacy by the Liberal Party of Australia and the country we serve, is one we can barely understand, let alone repay.

Born in Victoria in 1899, she married Robert Menzies in 1920 at the age of 21. Given the immediate and amiable rapport established between her father and Robert on political matters, Pattie questioned whether his interest was in her or her father!

She would give birth to three children and support her husband through 18 years as Australia's Prime Minister. Sixteen of those were of course consecutive years as our nation's first – and still longest serving, Liberal prime minister.

In 1995, death robbed her of the opportunity to see the return of a Liberal government led by arguably her late husband's greatest admirer.

Today is not a day for a lengthy biography. But we should not ever settle for the broad brushstrokes of our party's history, passing over pioneering sacrifices made in our name. Today is one to reflect on our past, this woman whose life helped make us who we are and, therein our approach to the future.

She was a woman of substance where it is a much abused term.

Dame Pattie was in the parliamentary gallery when in 1939 Earl Page accused Menzies of cowardice in World War 1 and disloyalty to Joe Lyons, She neither forgave nor spoke to Page again.

When Menzies returned to the Lodge in 1949, she insisted they give up their Melbourne home. Dame Pattie was determined that in the context of a housing shortage they should not have two. Though frequently offering her husband advice, she felt that "One politician in the family was enough".

But it was she that first proposed to Sir Robert that the Commonwealth subsidise accommodation for the aged, having regard to the "companionship of husband and wife". Menzies later said, "The effect of the legislation was quite remarkable ... I don't think any of our schemes was ever more widely welcomed by the public or gave us greater satisfaction."

Although we all admire talent, it's character that really counts.

John Bunting, who served as both Secretary to the Cabinet and the Prime Minister's department during Menzies' tenure, recounts in his portrait of him an incident that, says so much of Dame Pattie.

> *... inadequate as the (lodge) staff was, Dame Pattie made things just a bit worse by her preference for doing things herself. I remember on a visit to The Lodge being taken through a room where floor cleaning was in process. There was due apology, but I would understand, it was said, that the household work had to go on. I did, of course understand, but what surprised me a little was that an extra staff member engaged specially for cleaning was taking it easy in one of the chairs and that the cleaner on her knees with the scrubbing brush and soap was Dame Pattie!*

She resented the enmity and derision frequently offered in the modern political era: As a guide to the Young – and not so young –

she told the National Library oral historian in 1990, that we should respect the point of view of other political parties whilst disagreeing with it.

> *That was their point of view and you respected it. Today I don't like the abuse that goes on in Parliament. I think it is quite unpleasant and belittling to both sides, people are there to set an example to the rest of Australia and if they're going to be like that, the rest of Australia is going to be like that.*

This was a woman of humility, self-deprecation, grace, determination, good humour, wit and lifelong love of one man. Her loyalty to her husband was matched only by that to her country.

Where then should the Liberal Party head in this the 21st century? Australia faces different horizons and different challenges from those of Dame Pattie's era.

There are two things we must do.

The first is that we should not ever lose sight of what it is in which we believe. Knowing what we're against is not the same as getting what we want.

The deep value system that operates in all of us as Liberals will drive our ideas, responses to events and interaction with Australians.

Ours is a philosophy that cannot be learned from a scholarly manifesto. It is one of idealism, hard work and self-sacrifice absorbed through everyday life. It is the belief in the inherent worth of every individual and the political expression of a philosophy that enables all human beings to both find and achieve their own potential.

Our real enemies are cynicism, disillusionment and intolerance of differing expressions of our Liberal inheritance. Rejection of social conservatism deeply rooted in Christian values should be as repugnant to us as ostracism of those who equally embrace injustice with liberal attitudes. What those at either end of our broad philosophical movement must understand, is that what we need most is one another.

The German physicist Bernhard Philberth in *Revelation* put it best:

> *Progress leads to chaos if not anchored in tradition. Tradition becomes rigid if it does not prepare the way for progress. But a perverted traditionalism and a misguided progressivism propel each other toward a deadly excess, hardly leaving any ground between them.*

"Progressivists" are no less essential to our party's future than its "traditionalists".

Our second imperative is vision.

Good management is essential to our nation's future. It is about getting results. Vision however is what informs leadership. Like a campfire around which we sit, the vision we enunciate on behalf of our country should warm us as we reflect on who we are, the values and sacrifices of those who gave us our economic and cultural legacy and most importantly, where we want to go.

We ignore such thinking at our peril …

My generation was born into an Australia with a well-defined mesh of values loosely defined as God, King and Country.

From the early seventies however, we saw churches and ethics based organisations progressively marginalised from public debate. The value of parenting as a fulltime occupation was diminished, volunteering was considered the domain of the "do gooder" and young people felt they were being pushed to the "zeniths" of educational achievement – frequently beyond their natural abilities and heartfelt preferences.

In elevating gambling to the status of a religion and having some arguing euthanasia on the basis that death is an acceptable escape from insufferable physical and emotional pain, we saw by the mid-nineties the price paid by young Australians.

It wasn't so much the peak in young male suicide at 27 per 100,000 nor illicit drug use by teenagers approaching a majority experience.

We had reduced the toll taken by disease and car accident, but failed to have any impact on that exacted by despair.

When John Howard came to government a culture had emerged in which many young people felt that they had little to believe in other than themselves. The mesh of values enshrined in Dame Pattie's "God, King and Country" contained more than a few gaping holes.

No society can flourish so long as it defines freedoms in terms of rights rather than responsibilities. To do so demeans and devalues the individual. Nor can we allow young people to adopt values for the world they think they're going to get as distinct from the one they want. As observed by ANU social policy analyst, Richard Eckersley, young Australians frequently think that cynicism, mistrust, impatience, materialism and detachment are the values likely to ensure success.

I was told by my father in the 13th year of my life that in the absence of family wealth and influence, the only way that I would live in a better house than the one in which I was growing up, would be to work hard at school.

The aspirations they had for us – to have a better job, live in a better house and drive a better car – have become for the next generation cruelly oppressive expectations. Still largely tethered to those ideals, young see parents' accumulated wealth and doubt they will ever match it, let alone exceed it.

When 2,600 year eight students were surveyed for the Victorian Centre for Adolescent Health's "Gatehouse" longitudinal study in 1999, the results were disturbing.

Only 40 percent could identify a person whom felt knew them well – favourite music, best friend, dreams and deepest fears. However, only a quarter could name a single adult whom they felt they could trust. Not a parent, teacher, neighbour, doctor. No one.

The problem perhaps is not that many young Australians have not learned our values. It is that they have.

So what does all this have to do with articulated national vision? Everything.

Resilience building in young lives requires three things.

Young people must have a stable and loving relationship with at least one adult, preferably a parent.

They must secondly be part of a school community in which identity is built. It is important they are known and understood as individuals.

But thirdly, young people must grow in community that gives meaning and purpose to their lives. The growing pilgrimage by young Australians to Gallipoli is but one manifestation of their search for meaning.

Our vision for our country must be one which embraces broad economic, human, social and cultural objectives. Subtle but powerful forces influence not so much what we think, but how we feel.

Young Australians understand the central importance of progress and economic growth, but to what end? Towards what we are striving to grow.

Fiscal consolidation and sound economic management over the past nine years has allowed a generation to escape the single biggest lifelong cause of poverty – unemployment. Gun control, the emancipation of East Timor, taking up arms against terrorist fundamentalism, defining clearly which side we're on in the war on drugs, determined efforts to practically address the existential despair that is much of Aboriginal Australia, Tsunami relief – these things send powerful subliminal messages to young people about the future we want.

We should not ever lose sight of the fact that if all our economic and scientific problems were ever solved, all important questions would remain unanswered.

As many Australians embrace with enthusiasm the share market, broadband, the Republic, engagement with the rest of the world and multiculturalism, others feel a detached sense of grief. John Howard's great strength has been to not uncritically bow to the ambitions of the former whilst respecting the rights and legitimacy of fears held by the latter.

We should in all we do, show that we value the health and integrity of human life as much as achieving our economic objectives, strive to be an outward looking, competitive yet compassionate country with its indigenous history, imbued with the values of hard work, self-sacrifice, tolerance and courage …

Dame Pattie Menzies, her life and that of her husband, have given us a legacy upon which we must build the foundation for our future. Thank you for giving me the undeserved privilege of being able to honour it in some small way.

Values, *North Shore Times*, 3 May 2005

Speaking in 2005, Dr Nelson speaks of the importance of instilling values within our young through education. He emphasises the importance of education as a "guiding story that leaves a moral imprint" which enables young people to live responsibly and morally. Dr Nelson remarks that "a values free education risks the production of a values free adult".

In January 1942, Reinhardt Heidrich, SS Ruler of the "protectorate of Bohemia and Moravia" called a meeting that would change the world. To the Berlin suburb of Wannsee he summoned 13 German ministers and senior public servants.

At its end two days later, the meeting would resolve to implement what would become known as the "final solution". A year later, almost 90 percent of the Jews who would be exterminated under this heinous policy had lost their lives.

Of the thirteen who devised this despicable attack on humanity, nine had the best university education Europe had to offer. It begs the question as to what values had informed that education.

As parents, grandparents and imperfect human beings, there are many ambitions we have for our children and grandchildren. Of course we want them to be clever, articulate, to acquire a thirst for learning and to finally leave the education system with the prerequisite skills for life and work.

But above all these ambitions, we want most for them to be happy, well-adjusted adults who go into the world imbued with human values by which they and their actions will be ultimately judged.

Though schools and employers love talent, in the end it is character that pays off. As Ralph Waldo Emerson said almost 150 years ago, "character is higher than intellect". This aggregate of qualities distinguishes each person from one another. It defines moral constitution and is the intangible product of education increasingly sought by parents and demanded by the world in which the next generation will live.

Parents remain the bedrock of character formation in children, but increasingly we want school to be an extension of the values taught at home, whatever the many imperfections we bring to the task of parenting.

Today's society is a product of decisions taken twenty years ago. It appears something has happened that now requires special police units to supervise certain schools.

One member of the federal parliament defended his aggressive behaviour on the basis that he could "take you to any sports ground any Saturday and show you parents abusing the ref". We were told that this is "the Australian way". So concerned is it by this very behaviour that the Victorian government is legislating to ban parental abuse.

This is the point. When governments have to regulate behaviour that would otherwise be socially acceptable, the price we all pay is loss of freedom. The failure of individuals to make sacrifices in the name of civility restricts ultimately the freedoms of us all. Benjamin Franklin and Edmund Burke both recognised that in order for "men to enjoy freedom – they must be virtuous". Each must have strength of character.

Some teachers have argued to me that their (difficult) role is to be neutral. As one irately said, "Students need the necessary information to make decisions from a variety of choices. My job is to see they understand the consequences of the choices they make".

But how can anyone be really neutral when dealing with young people? These are life choices – drug use, exploitation of others, relationships with authority or sexual activity. As such, it is surely the responsibility of key adults to take a stand, to abandon the pretence of neutrality but not in a judgemental way.

If key adults suggest young people have only choices and not responsibilities, they do so to send a powerful subliminal message that 'anything goes'.

Education needs a guiding story that leaves a moral imprint on our children, one which shapes and reinforces values enabling them to live responsibly.

A values free education risks the production of a values free adult.

Surely we want young people to be responsible, accountable and trustworthy? They should be fair, tolerant, caring and compassionate. It is not just government values or religious values that should inform education, but also the values of communities within which schools are based.

Is it possible that one of the factors driving the movement of students from government to non-government schools in the burgeoning outer suburbs of our large cities is a perception of values-based education?

These and other contentious issues will be considered at the Values Forum. All are welcome. It is difficult to think of a more important issue.

800th Anniversary of the Sealing of Magna Carta, 15 June 2015

Dr Nelson describes the significance of the principles enshrined in the Magna Carta. Dr Nelson notes that it is on this foundation that our entire nation has emerged, and therefore that these principles should be defended.

The Runnymede Memorial is in Englefield Green, Surrey. It overlooks the River Thames and Runnymede Meadow.

Known as the Air Forces Memorial, it commemorates 20,456 men from across the air forces of the British Commonwealth killed in operations during the Second World War.

Inscribed onto the memorial are the names of 1,382 Australians who died fighting with the RAF while serving in the Royal Australian Air Force.

None has a known grave.

They died in defence of the truths upon which we pause here to reflect.

We do so as free and confident heirs to a legacy conceived in a document signed 800 years ago, shaped in free democratic debate, forged in bloody self-sacrifice and passed now to our generation.

One Australian commemorated on the Runnymede Memorial who died in the struggle to defeat Nazism is Flight Lieutenant John William Yarra DFM. A decorated Spitfire pilot who had flown in the defence of Malta, Yarra was killed on 10 December 1942 attacking a German convoy and a flak ship off the coast of Holland.

He was 21 years old.

Months earlier, John Yarra had written a letter to his mother, Harriet, to be sent to her in the event of his death:

> *My Dear Mother ... I entered this war with the knowledge that I had a rather small chance of coming out of it alive. I was under no false impression – I knew I had to kill – and perhaps be*

killed. Since I commenced flying I have spent probably the happiest time of my life ... Above all, Mother dear, I have proved to my satisfaction that I was, at least, a man.

His younger brother, Robert would give his life for us, shot down over France in 453 Fighter Squadron in April 1944. A third Yarra brother would survive the war fought in the Pacific.

One family, three sons, two Australian lives – sacrificed in the name of all we hold dear.

The Yarra brothers are just two of the more than 102,700 Australians who have given their lives in defence of the truths by which we live.

Each lies as a silent witness to the future they have given us.

We honour them best by the way we live our lives, shape our nation and resolve to be steadfast in defence of those truths.

Whilst democracy might be regarded as a 'work in progress', those truths have their origins in Magna Carta, signed in 1215 at the place where John Yarra's name is now, and will forever – be remembered.

When serving as Australia's ambassador to the North Atlantic Treaty Organisation (NATO), I was invited to deliver an address in honour of NATO's seventh Secretary General – the reformist visionary, Dr Manfred Worner.

I used the opportunity before NATO's leadership across twenty-eight nations, to answer the question most commonly asked of me – why is Australia, not a NATO member so deeply and strongly committed to the Afghanistan campaign?

Australia, I said, was committed to Afghanistan and the war within it for four reasons.

Firstly, three thousand innocent civilians were murdered on 11 September 2001 – including ten Australians, in an attack on the United States.

An Alliance means something to us.

We are Australians – we value loyalty, we say what we mean and we mean what we say. Five days after those heinous attacks, Australian Prime Minister John Howard committed our nation to do whatever would come next in defence of our ally and was supported in it by the then opposition.

Secondly, a year later, 88 Australians were among the 202 civilians murdered in Bali. Death had come from three men who had trained in Afghanistan with Al-Qaeda under the protection of the Taliban.

Our direct interests of the most important kind were directly affected.

Thirdly, our generation is facing a resurgent totalitarianism in the form of Islamic extremism. An earlier generation fought to defeat fascism and militarist imperialism in the 1930s and 40s.

The next generation had stared down communism through the cold war.

We are now engaged in a generational struggle against those who have hijacked the name of Islam to build a violent political utopia. These are people fanatically opposed to not only the United States, but to nations and people of all faiths committed to the ideals of mankind, the equal treatment of men and women and the liberating power of education.

But the fourth is perhaps the most important.

It is the right thing to do.

Two years ago, the Chief of the Turkish Air force stood in the commemorative area at the Australian War Memorial. He pointed to one of the names in bronze of the theatres where Australians have fought and died over more than a century and asked of me "why were Australians there?"

"That is a very important question, General," I replied. "In answering it, your journey of discovery will lead you to an understanding of who we are and in what we believe."

To him, as to the NATO audience, I said the Australian government's decision to use the Australian Defence Force also reflects our nation's values – the belief in individual political, economic and religious freedom; commitment to the rule of law; a free press; free academic inquiry; the co-existence of faith and reason; equality; fair play; compassion for those in need and pursuit of the public good.

We regard it as both immoral and delusional to think we can leave the fight against tyranny, oppression and brutality to the United States and a handful of other nations.

The decision-making matrix of every Australian government to deploy the ADF – in peace and in war, has included that key question, what is the right thing to do?

No surprise then that the men and women who wear – and who have worn, the uniform of the Royal Australian Navy, Australian Army and Royal Australian Air Force over more than a century, are widely regarded as having given most and worked hardest to shape our values and beliefs, our nation's sense of itself and place in the world.

Much of the foundation for those values that so anchor our nation, lies in the tenets of Magna Carta.

It has as much to do with our future as it does our past.

A people that loses sight of its history and that in which it believes – is dangerous.

Winston Churchill described Magna Carta as, "the most famous milestone of our rights and freedom".

"The Great Charter" began life as a document sealed by John, King of England, at Runnymede – a meadow on the River Thames, near Windsor, Surrey on 15 June 1215. Its intent was to end the rebellion of a group of barons against the much hated, friendless and frightened king.

That charter agreed, promised much – the protection of church rights; protection for the barons from illegal imprisonment; access to swift justice; and limitations on feudal payment to the Crown.

The initial charter was a failure.

After John's death, the regency government of his young son, Henry III, reissued the document. It was stripped of its more radical content, in an unsuccessful bid to build political support for the royal cause. At the end of the first barons' war, the charter formed part of a peace treaty agreed to at Lambeth.

It would then be known as "Magna Carta".

Henry reissued the charter again in 1225 in exchange for a grant of new taxes; his son Edward I did the same in 1297, this time confirming it as part of England's statue law.

Magna Carta is one of the most important documents in British history.

Its clauses bear the principle that both king and subjects were bound together by the common law of the land.

The charter has assumed iconic status. Commonly assumed to be a law protecting individual English freedoms, it is a lighthouse for liberty.

The values of Magna Carta are enshrined in British institutions as fundamental tenets of British belief.

When Captain Arthur Phillip raised the Union Jack over the Port Jackson Foreshore on 26 January 1788, under imperialist legal theory he imported into this country as much of British common law as was capable of application to its penal conditions.

As Geoffrey Robertson QC has reminded us, whilst waiting at the Admiralty for provisioning of the First Fleet, it was Phillip who drafted what he described as the first law for a land that only **he** envisaged **might** become a nation:

> *There can be no slavery in a free land and consequently, no slaves.*

This legacy is shared across the British Commonwealth and within western liberal democracies.

In living memory these values and institutions came under their greatest threat during the Second World War in the fight against fascism in Europe and Japanese imperialist militarism in the Pacific.

Sir Winston Churchill said of Magna Carta:

Throughout the document it is implied that here is a law which is above the King and which even he must not break. This reaffirmation of a supreme law and its expression in a general charter is the great work of Magna Carta; and this alone justifies the respect in which men have held it.

Western Allies in wartime drew on Magna Carta as a powerful reminder of what was at stake.

In January 1941 when Europe and much of the world were at war, US President Franklin D. Roosevelt in his third Inauguration address, spoke of the need to defend democracy and freedom.

He evoked Magna Carta as inspiring democracy:

The democratic aspiration is no mere recent phase in human history. It is human history. It permeated the ancient life of early peoples. It blazed anew in the Middle Ages. It was written in Magna Carta.

Franklin D. Roosevelt

As leader of the Australian opposition in 1940, John Curtin said:

The things for which we are fighting in this war are surely those which are conferred in Magna Carta and the Bill of Rights.

Then as Australia's Prime Minister in October 1942 – the most important year in Australia's history after 1788 – he again drew from it to inspire and lift the nation, reminding us of the very foundations of our belief:

Today, seven centuries after Magna Carta, we are faced with the necessity to defend all that was won on the struggle for human liberty.

When war broke out in 1939, an original copy of the 1215 Magna Carta was on display at the New York World's Fair.

With Germany's crushing, early blitzkrieg successes and America neutral, the British cabinet considered gifting this copy to the United States.

The British government declared common history and shared values: "Magna Carta is a part of American, as well as English history and both peoples equally trace their personal liberties from the signing of that document."

The manuscript was found to belong to Lincoln Cathedral, returning from Fort Knox, Kentucky in 1946.

It was in the war's aftermath that the Charter inspired perhaps its greatest modern aspiration.

The Universal Declaration of Human Rights was adopted by the United Nations in 1948. The ideal was that this declaration would promise individual liberty to all and become the "international Magna Carta of all men everywhere".

That is – the rule of law is central to our democracy and is the well spring of the freedoms we so cherish. Every person – irrespective of rank, status or office is subject to the same laws, legal and judicial processes.

Just as we citizens must obey the law, so too must our governments and its officials.

No person or entity can ignore the law and act with arbitrary power. The executive government and its agencies, including the Australian Defence Force are required to follow fair procedure and respect the rights of citizens.

The Australian Defence Force (ADF) is an instrument of national power and is responsible to the Australian Government.

Australia's democratic institutions underpin our society and way of life.

We believe change to be the consequence of vision informed by persuasive debate, rejecting violence as a means to change either minds or the law...

Government is a compact between the ruler and the governed.

These are basic tenets drawn from Magna Carta.

At the conclusion of the third session of the Australasian Federal Convention in March 1898, to debate of a motion calling on delegates to take the draft bill back to each colony for the approval of the people, a South Australian delegate, Josiah Symon said this:

> *... sir, no man can remain unmoved upon this momentous occasion. We who are assembled in this Convention are about to commit to the people of Australia a new Charter of union and liberty; we are about to commit this new Magna Carta for their acceptance and confirmation, and I can conceive of nothing of greater magnitude in the whole history of the peoples of the world than this question upon which we are about to invite the peoples of Australia to vote. The Great Charter was wrung by the barons of England from a reluctant king. This new charter is to be given by the people of Australia to themselves.*

And so for our young nation, the principles enshrined in Magna Carta informed both federalism and the framing of our constitution.

Quite simply, we cannot have democracy without the guarantee of the rule of law provided by Magna Carta.

Upon that foundation, our nation's system of government has been built. This principle and guarantee needs to be defended – politically, diplomatically and at times, militarily.

As Frederick the Great observed, "Diplomacy without the sword is like music without the instruments."

To the Australian Defence Force falls the responsibility to do so when asked – at home, on our borders, in our region and in distant parts of the world.

On 23 August 1916, Second Lt Edward Lionel ('Leo') Butler wrote to his wife after the bloodbath of Pozieres in which Australia had sustained 23,000 casualties in three weeks.

> *I couldn't help wondering if it was worth it – whether there was anything gained in this war which justified such sacrifices.*

Four months later just after Christmas, a short distance from here at the Presbyterian Church in Ainslie, a large multidenominational crowd packed the church and its surrounds to honour the life of Private Malcolm 'Mac' Southwell of the 20th Battalion. Waist deep in mud, he was killed by shell fragments at the battle of Flers on 5 November 1916.

As if to answer Leo Butler's question – the very question asked by the families of every one of the 102,700 Australians listed on the Roll of Honour at the Australian War Memorial, those assembled at the church and the broader community heard these words said to Malcolm Southwell's family:

> *It must be their chief consolation to know he laid down his life in the noble cause of righteousness and liberty, and therefore died not in vain.*

For righteousness and liberty, 2 million Australian men and women serve – and have served this nation over more than a century, upholding values enshrined in Magna Carta.

Witnesses and Survivors Holocaust Exhibition, 30 November 2016

> Speaking at this exhibition, Dr Nelson describes it as a permanent reminder of "the difference between right and wrong" and the effects of allowing "political and social thought to head in certain directions". Dr Nelson also reminds us of the anti-Semitism which to this day remains a "virulent and repugnant force" in parts of the world.

Six million people.

Almost a quarter of the population of Australia, almost the entire population of Sydney.

That is how many were exterminated in the worst genocide of the twentieth century. Jews, Roma, gypsies, the disabled and political prisoners. But almost all were Jews.

Jewish identity has been shaped by three things:

- Anti-Semitism, still a virulent and repugnant force in many parts of the world
- The Holocaust or 'Shoah'
- The embattled nature of the state of Israel for whom existence is a daily struggle

Adolf Hitler was able to undertake this mass extermination for two principal reasons.

The first was that the majority were indifferent to the plight of the minority.

The second was that in Germany – as in other parts of Europe, anti-Semitism was deeply rooted – religious, secular and racial.

One observation through my own life not having ever faced nor endured even a fraction of the adversities suffered by many of you here, is that almost all of life's suffering and pain stems from people making themselves the centre of their own lives. So too, nations making their own narrow self-interest the centre of all else.

In the *Use and Abuse of Australian History*, Graeme Davison concluded that ethical and responsible citizenship demands each of us be imbued with the imaginative capacity to see the world through the eyes of others.

The Australian War Memorial is many things. But above all else is the repository of our nation's soul.

This place and the stories of two million men and women told here, reminds us that we are Australians and that there are in the end some truths by which we live. And they are worth fighting to defend – politically, diplomatically and at times, militarily.

Not everyone agrees with this exhibition.

One regular visitor to the Memorial told me emphatically that she was opposed to this exhibition. "This has nothing to do with Australia and the Australian War Memorial", she said. She told me that she would never walk through it.

It has everything to do with us, for we are a part of humankind.

In a world grappling with the mass movement of people; the persecution of political, religious and ethnic minorities; euthanasia and a generational struggle against resurgent totalitarianism in the form of those who have hijacked the good name of Islam to build a violent political utopia, we must remind ourselves of that of which humankind is capable.

Our responsibility is to stimulate and challenge visitors, Australian and international, to see the world through the eyes of others.

One of the most memorable experiences of my life – top ten, occurred here in this room in 2013. In this room we had hung the works of Alan Moore.

Alan Moore was commissioned by the Australian War Memorial as an official war artist during the Second World War. He was deployed to the South West Pacific on New Year's Day 1944, drawing and painting. He then went on to Europe and was there with the British at the liberation of the Bergen Belsen death camp in April 1945.

As I wheeled him along the wall behind me, in his late nineties he looked up at the works he had not seen for decades.

We stopped in front of a drawing of the SS guards removing the bodies of the dead women and children from the railway carriage. He whispered, "The Welsh guard … the Welsh guard. As I was drawing this, the Welsh guard told me that no one would believe it. He was right, so I went and got my camera and took photos as well."

We paused again at a drawing of clearly non-descript buildings and a perimeter fence. There were objects of some sort on the ground and a man standing in their midst. Alan said, "The blind man … the blind man with the stick. He was walking amongst the dead and did not know it."

Two generations ago, the leadership of the Australian War Memorial had refused to hang his works telling him, "No-one is interested in the Holocaust."

That has changed.

The Australian War Memorial does not aspire to be one of the best museums in the world – it is. As such, we have a responsibility to tell the story of the Holocaust as responsible global citizens with a global outlook.

The great 18th century Prussian philosopher, Immanuel Kant said;

> *Every human being is an end unto himself,*
> *and not a means to be used by others*
> *Respect for one's own humanity will be found*
> *in respect for the humanity of others*
> *and morality is freedom.*

In this exhibition – this permanent exhibition will be found our own sense of morality, to be reminded of the difference between right and wrong and the consequences of allowing currents of political and social thought to head in certain directions.

Not a single person lobbied us to present this exhibition.

We are doing it because it is the right thing to do.

We still have seven objects and artefacts and story board in the World War Two galleries. There are now eighty-five here.

We are proud to tell some of the stories of the 30 to 35,000 Eastern European Jews who migrated to Australia after the war from 1945 to 1960.

We are proud of this, Witnesses and Survivors exhibition.

The Power of Speech: UN Holocaust Remembrance Day, 28 January 2018

> Speaking on UN Holocaust Remembrance Day, Dr Nelson reflects on the horror faced by Jews under Nazi Germany. He reminds us that in the "stories of these survivors", powerful values such as courage, honesty and love can be a valuable guide to our common future.

It is a humbling privilege for me to address you here, especially in the presence of survivors of the Holocaust or 'Shoah'.

We pause here on the occasion of the 73rd anniversary of the arrival at Auschwitz of the Soviet forces from the 60th army of the First Ukrainian Front.

The liberators would find some 7,650 barely living survivors, hundreds of thousands of personal effects, items of clothing – including shoes, and 700 tonnes of human hair.

This was the place where as many as 1.5 million people – mainly Jews, had been murdered by the Nazis.

In November 2005, the United Nations General Assembly proclaimed 27 January 1945, the day on which Auschwitz was liberated, as international Remembrance Day to mark the Holocaust.

With awkward humility and abiding reverence, we gather here to reflect upon, remember and honour them all.

In commemorating the dead, we are inspired by the triumph of the human spirit given us by those who survived …

The power is in the story …

In January 1942, a world away in the outer lakeside Berlin suburb of Wannsee was a meeting convened by Reinhard Heydrich.

Heydrich was the Reich Protector of Bohemia and Moravia. He commenced by reiterating his appointment by Reich Marshal Goring as the plenipotentiary for the "Preparation of the Final Solution of the Jewish Question in Europe".

Responsibility for handling the final solution would lie with him and Himmler, 'without regard for geographic boundaries'.

In total, 11 million Jews would be targeted for extermination. Without a whimper, the thirteen officials signed off on the "Final Solution". The minutes would record their decision to "cleanse the German living space of Jews in a legal manner".

This marked the darkest seminal moment in a series of events that would see the murder of six million Jews, abhorrence beyond the comprehension of our modern, comfortable lives.

It was also in 1942 that British poet, T. S. Eliot wrote these prophetic words:

> *A people without history is not redeemed from time*
> *for history is a pattern of endless moments.*

A nation that does not know – nor understand its history, is dangerous.

The events that bring us here tonight and upon which we reflect, have everything to do with our future and the people we strive to be …

Nations like people, face "moments of truth".

Moments in history which challenge our very survival and values. Well led, we emerge stronger, more resilient. But if not, they may do us lasting damage.

Those who survived, fled and found their way to Australia in the aftermath of the Second World War and Holocaust, made our nation.

More than simply help our economic and social reconstruction, they nourished our better instincts, gave a greater belief in ourselves and a deeper understanding of what it means to be an Australian.

I first visited Washington in 1999. I have since done so in various capacities on more than thirty occasions.

Irrespective of time constraints, there are two places I always visit. One speaks to the ideals of mankind, the other to the evil darkness into which we are capable of descending.

The first is the Jefferson Memorial.

Thomas Jefferson was first Secretary of State and third president of the United States – a giant of man, notwithstanding his views on slavery.

Enshrined in marble, I look up to the words he crafted for the American Declaration of Independence:

> *We hold these truths to be self-evident: that all men are created equal, that they are endowed by their creator with certain inalienable rights, among these are life, liberty, and the pursuit of happiness, that to secure these rights governments are instituted among men...*

From Jefferson I always then go to the Holocaust Museum.

There is a sinister sense of foreboding walking into the building which immediately evokes a large railway station or prison.

Some exhibits in particular stand out, such as the thousands of shoes – including those of children.

The video footage of Nazi doctors experimenting on the insane and physically disabled. Highly educated professionals who crossed the threshold in 1930s Germany, believing some people's lives of so little value they could be ended with state sanction.

Then there are the photographs. Hundreds and hundreds of black and white photographs of men, women, adolescents and children looking out from lives never lived.

High up on the second floor is a photograph of Rosa Goldenzeil.

A Hungarian woman of advancing years, Rosa arrived with her daughters at Auschwitz in the spring of 1944. As selection commenced on the rail platform, she quickly grasped the situation. Rosa turned to her daughter holding her baby – "they are saving any women with children, give me the baby".

Rosa knew by her own age that she was already dead as was the baby.

What moral courage did she draw upon to make the decision to save her own daughter and in doing so give up her own life and that of her cherished grandchild? In this, Rosa was like so many others.

Six million Jews were murdered in an act of unspeakable genocidal barbarism. So too were homosexuals, Roma, gypsies, the disabled and political dissidents …

The Holocaust: *Witnesses and Survivors* opened late in 2016.

The exhibition presents the Holocaust through the stories of survivors who made their new lives in post-war Australia.

We present the rise of Nazism, the Wannsee Conference, transportation, the horrors of the gas chambers, ghettos and persecution.

The raw, powerful drawings of Bernard Slawik when he was interned at Janowska, depict death. They present a harrowing and deeply personal account of the callous, bureaucratic killing of the Jews of Lvov. He would eventually escape and make his way to Australia in 1948 with his wife Alma who had also escaped independently.

Of the Bunk Beds he drew in the Janowska concentration camp, reflecting on those incarcerated before their transport to the Belzec gas chambers near Lublin, Bernard Slawik wrote:

> *Three-high, the bunks. Two to a mattress – 400 souls in one barrack. Like logs they lie, exhausted. To sleep, sleep, sleep ... rest, forgetfulness.*
>
> *400 broken people. Not father, not wife, not child, not brother, not sister; just 400 broken beings ... some screaming wrench themselves from sleep.*
>
> *Nightmares? Memories? Surely it is all one fantastic nightmare.*

His drawing of the naked women before their murder by camp guards hangs next to another of begging children brutally forced into cattle cars for the journey to the Belzec gas chambers.

Artefacts, documents and relics from the Jewish Holocaust Centre here have enabled us to bring individual stories of suffering and survival to life.

Finally, Alan Moore's works at the Liberation of Bergen-Belsen are now permanently and proudly displayed …

Anti-Semitism is far from a feature of modern history.

The Roman Empire embraced Christianity. In doing so, anti-Semitism played a catalytic role in building the foundations of the religion that would supersede Judaism. European and western civilization was largely defined by Christianity which at various times used anti-Semitism to meet its political and theological objectives.

Anti-Semitism at different times has been seemingly ubiquitous, found in major religions, the political left and the political right, educated classes and amongst the illiterate poor.

It was into this context that the 19th century arrived.

Scientists drove a fascinated culture of order and control. Race emerged as a feature of the nation state along with nationalism. Populist perceptions rooted in race ran in parallel with social Darwinism and eugenics. The First World War would herald the introduction of industrialised killing on a scale never before seen.

Then, the bitter hardships experienced by Germans after the First World War radicalised anti-Semitism. The Weimar Republic from 1919 to 1933 legitimised violence as a form of control that was acceptable to the educated, upper classes.

Hitler was able to take advantage of two key things.

The first was that the majority were indifferent to the plight of the minority.

The second was that in Germany, as in other parts of Europe, anti-Semitism was deeply rooted – religious, secular and racial.

Anti-Semitism did not end with liberation of the death camps, nor with the end of the war, the Nuremberg trials and nor even formation of the United Nations.

Anti-Zionism, Holocaust denial, distortion of truths, glorification of Nazism have all featured at different times in the world since.

As we gather here today, troops are deployed across Europe protecting synagogues and Jewish places of congregation. Fire bombings, desecration of cemeteries and other violations of freedom are real and present dangers.

In recent years, crowds in some circumstances have even chanted "Gas the Jews" and "Death to the Jews".

Only three years ago the United Nations General Assembly debated anti-Semitism.

In Plato's republic in 400 BC, Socrates concluded that the root of all evil is – ignorance.

Jefferson in nominating "Education as the defense of the nation" echoed a similar sentiment.

Who am I to argue with either?

But of the thirteen German Ministers and senior public servants assembled at Wannsee, nine had PhDs, Masters Degrees and the best university education Europe had to offer.

Adolf Eichmann – Heydrich's henchman in charge of implementing all this, said at his trial that Heydrich had expected opposition to the plan from the bureaucrats. Not only did they not resist, they embraced the heinous idea with enthusiasm.

It is more than education. It is character.

The Greeks called it "the stamp of personalit".

In my opinion, ethical and responsible citizenship relies on three things.

First, a minimum level of education – including scientific literacy, is required for people to understand and be resilient to change in society, including the technologies upon which it increasingly is built.

Second, we all need to be imbued with what Professor Graeme Davison described in *The Use and Abuse of Australian History* as, the imaginative capacity to see the world through the eyes of others. Almost all of life's pain, suffering and misery in my experience stems from people and nations making themselves the centre of their own world.

Third, people need to be imbued with a deep value system that informs character. As both Benjamin Franklin and Edmund Burke observed, 'Men must be virtuous and have strength of character to enjoy freedom'.

As Education minister, I oversaw the introduction of Values Education into Australian schools. Teachers would not only teach a set of values derived from wide, national consultation, they would also act them out. At the end of the initial trial in twelve schools, one teenaged girl remarked as a result of the programme, "We now have more freedom".

One secondary teacher critical of the initiative said to me, "You don't understand. My job is not to tell these kids what to do or not do. My job is to present them with choices and allow them to make their own decisions". My response was in part to say that in the end, we have to tell them what we think is the right thing to do.

Imagine being a teenager growing up in western society today, including Australia. It must be very tempting to embrace values for the world you *think* you are going to get – impatience, materialism, detachment, cynicism and mistrust, as distinct from values for the world you want.

The stories of these survivors, the qualities embodied in their humanity and spirit are surely one powerful values guide to the future.

Among those values: courage – both physical and moral; endurance, devotion, independence, loyalty, honesty, love of others and never forgetting from where you come, who gave you what you have and made you who you are.

And that is why these museums are vital to our common future.

The responsibility we all share in this common endeavour is to make these stories live. They need to be engaging to and engaged by a new generation.

To our political class, lead us to where in our best selves we need to go.

Our nation craves a vision that is human and social as much as it is economic.

If all economic and scientific problems were ever solved, all important questions would remain unanswered.

The most powerful yet fragile of human emotions is – hope.

We all have to believe that tomorrow will be better than today, next year better than this. Not only or so much for ourselves but those whom we love and our country.

Israel is not a perfect country, none is. But in my opinion it is the repository of that most fragile yet powerful of human emotions – hopeful belief in the freedom of man and a better future.

Israel is a nation built on the belief in political, religious and economic freedoms; the equal treatment of Jews, Muslims, Christians, Baha'is, Arabs and all peoples.

And yet every single day, Israel has to justify its very existence and fight for it – politically, diplomatically and militarily.

It seems we live in a world of fundamentalist intolerance and moral relativism.

My grandparents fought and defeated fascism in the 1930s and 40s, my parents' generation stared down communism.

We now face a resurgent totalitarianism, principally but not only in the form Islamic extremism. Disparate groups have hijacked the good name of Islam to build a violent political utopia, opposed to the equal treatment of women and the liberating power of education.

We live in vast ignorance of the decisions we make and that are made for us, facing extraordinary global uncertainty and immense technological change.

What we need most is one another.

No human being, no Australian who believes in the dignity of man, of freedom and democratic principles, should ever allow through neglectful indifference these events, these people, their lives and stories, to become a distant stranger.

These heinous events and those who survived them teach us many things.

It the importance of commitment to one another and belief in what is right; of conscience and knowing the right thing to do and when to do it; feeling the pain of others and seeing the world through their eyes.

Most importantly they inspire us to have the moral courage irrespective of personal consequences, to act on what in our hearts we know to be right.

In the words of the great 18th century Prussian philosopher, Immanuel Kant:

> *Every human being is an end unto to himself and not a means to be used by others. Respect for one's own humanity will be found in respect for the humanity of others – and morality is freedom.*

That is, doing what you know to be right on the basis of respect for the humanity in others will make you truly free.

Failure in this will render us blind to injustice, deaf to despair and indifferent to the future.

History Informs Us (David Kemp Book Launch), 29 April 2021

> Dr Nelson describes how our history shapes our values and the future of our country, arguing that we should remember and honour those "who gave us what we have and made us who we are".

One of the paradoxes of our human condition is a tendency to take for granted those things that are most important to us in our lives. Whether it's the magic and vitality of our youth, which we certainly don't fully appreciate it until it's gone forever, our physical health and emotional resilience, our Australian citizenship, whether conferred by birth or by choice, affording, as it does political, economic and religious freedoms …

It is tempting to settle for the popular mythology and imagery of our history while neglecting the vision; the sacrifices and the hard-won policy debates that shaped the country, the men and women who gave us what we have and made us who we are …

The most important year in this country's history, after 1788, is 1942. It was also the year in which T. S. Elliot wrote, "A people without history is not redeemed from time, for history is a pattern of endless moments." When little else in the world makes sense, history is the defining discipline. It carries extraordinarily important lessons for us and the future that we seek to shape. It can demolish prejudice. It is a reminder, as David has documented so magnificently in his towering work, that there are hard decisions that have to be made, and the importance of making them and not shying away from them. And it can also inspire and point us to new horizons.

Character, whether of individuals or of nations, is informed by worthwhile intrinsic values or virtues. Those values that define us as Australians have come to us through our triumphs as a people and our failures, the men and women whom we choose to honour and revere and also villains. And the way as a people we have been shaped and defined by adversities and how we will be shaped by those that are coming.

Our values are not the subject of a social media posting. They're not a statement of what we're doing today, or what we think we're going to be doing over the next week, or even what we think we're going to be about for the next one or two decades. They are enduring and are deeply rooted in the history and as I said, the men and women who made us and gave us what we have.

When the late Senator John McCain, whom I regard as a true and great champion of the Republican Party in the United States, came to the Australian War Memorial for a one-hour visit, which went for two and a half hours in May, 2017, I said to him of the Memorial, "This is where we reveal our character. It's hard to understand us until you come here. And indeed, why we're allies of the United States and not just good friends. Here, we reveal our values." I said to him, "And our interests are our values." And he said, "Our values are our interests," something which he subsequently raised publicly with President Trump.

We cannot, in facing our future, in the most consequential geopolitical realignment in our lifetimes abandon what Arthur Schlesinger described as "historic purpose". We have to be informed by a sense of not only who we are, but from where we have come.

David's book is a towering masterpiece. David, I wish that it had been written 30 years ago and that I had read it before I had the privilege to serve the Liberal Party and the people of Bradfield in the Australian Parliament. It is informative, it's easy to read, it brings understanding and enlightenment to who we are and where we are today. There is much in this in particular volume that should be read by our contemporary Liberal Party leaders.

David sets the framework for all in the introduction:

> *This is the story of how Australians fought a bitter political battle over how they were to be governed, and how they came to decide, despite the urgent demands of special interests for privilege*

> *and, notwithstanding the passion of those who promised salvation through the wisdom of government, that they believed the good society was one in which they could control their own lives and express their individuality. Government's role, they still believed, was to empower them to achieve their dreams.*

And then,

> *... the liberal democratic state was one in which power was checked, balanced and devolved, in the interests of preventing its arbitrary exercise against citizens, eroding their liberty to control their own lives. The battle of ideas between utopian socialism and liberalism was therefore a battle over the nature of the Australian state. Hence the title of the book.*

And then David speaks with some eloquence and power about what I think has driven you all of your life David, and that is ideas. You say:

> *Ideas although intangible and invisible, are in fact the principal directors of political life, because without ideas there is no motivation. People cannot act, movements cannot be formed, institutions cannot be constructed, policies cannot be devised, and human betterment will not occur. As the English liberal economist John Maynard Keynes once said, "The world is indeed moved by little else.*

Then speaking of liberals he says:

> *Australian liberals continue to grapple with issues arising from the nation's foundation and the meaning of those ideas for the state interventions that had already occurred: the state enforcement of morality, industry protection, compulsory arbitration of workplace disputes, government service monopolies, organised marketing and industry licensing, and Aboriginal 'protection'.*

And then of the *Forgotten People* talks, the foundation series of addresses again in 1942 which is our true north.

> *The Forgotten People talks show Menzies at his most intellectually distinguished, dealing simply and clearly with weighty matters for the successful conduct of the war and for post-war policies, his vigorous opposition to the rhetoric of class hatred, to the use of racial hatred as an instrument of war, the proper purpose of wartime censorship, the financing of the war, the principles for rationalising industry to provision of the war effort, the role of women during and after the war, education during the war and the need for a massive expansion when the war had ended, and the need to give appropriate attention to planning for the post-war world.*
>
> *He reiterated his strongly held view that the Labor Party's decision not to suspend party politics for the duration of the war was a grave misfortune for Australia and reminded listeners that it was a decision that he had done his very best to avoid, even to the extent of being prepared to serve under a prime minister drawn from the Labor Party.*

Then of values, the underlying disease of selfishness and irresponsibility that David writes:

> *Menzies argued that after the war Australia should establish a contributary insurance scheme to discourage the entitlement mentality, emphasising the importance of wealth creation by private enterprise for a successful system of social security. He warned against the false expectation that the end of the war would inevitably bring with it a better life, in the absence of sound human values.*

His main emphasis was on the culture and values that underlay a liberal and decent society and needed to be rebuilt. As Menzies said: "Men will not necessarily be better because they are better off." And that is one of the key challenges that, of course we all want economic growth, we need it, but the fundamental question is toward what are we striving to grow? It is to build a better society, not only of prosperity and economic security and individual freedoms, but also so the inherent value and dignity of human life and social cohesion [is elevated], which is something which Menzies himself identified:

> *The disease of selfishness and irresponsibility, if the new material order or an improved material order is to serve the biggest needs of mankind, it must be accompanied by a moral revolution, which will make every citizen feel that the wellbeing of his country is his own responsibility, that he is his brother's keeper, and that his stature as a citizen will depend far more upon what he gives than what he gets.*

He said this a long time before John Kennedy's inauguration speech.

David's accounts of the political opponents of the Liberal Party speak not only to David's immense intellect, but also his character as a man. Of John Curtin he says:

> *Curtin embodied within his tormented self the irreconcilable forces at war within his party. He was the very symbol of its divided soul, identification with a version of the utopian mission of Australian unionism on the one hand, and with his country Australia, as a patriot, on the other, warred in his mind. His final decision that Australia was preeminent put him at odds with bitter foes in his own party for whom national unity was a goal of subordinate value and whose primary identifications were with the labour movement, not with the nation.*
>
> *John Curtin's selflessness and decency in his treatment of others attracted wide praise and his desire to put Australia's interests first was recognised.*

Of Ben Chifley, David writes:

> *A decent and patriotic man, and a Catholic, was now in the front line in the battle for Labor's soul. He did not forget those who had attacked him in the NSW party. Nor did Lang – biding his time for revenge – forgive Chifley, nor could the new prime minister pardon those who had imposed such burdens on the vulnerable John Curtin from within Labor's ranks.*

> *Of all Labor's federal parliamentary leaders – as his church mobilised to join the battle against atheistic communism – Chifley would be the one who would at last summon the courage to take the fight to the revolutionary extremists in the Lang tradition that had done so much damage to the party and to the country ...*

So to the 1946 election campaign. Menzies' election campaign address is something if you have not read it, that I strongly recommend to you. History informs the choices, the decisions we have to make now. David writes:

> *His appeal to women was not simply to women in traditional social roles, but also for a transformation in the role of women in Australian life. Menzies said this in 1946: "Tonight, I speak to the women of Australia with profound respect and gratitude. They have established an unanswerable claim to economic, legal, industrial, and political equality. I hope that the time will speedily come when we can say truthfully that there is no sex discrimination in public or private office, in political or industrial opportunity. We are all, men and women, citizens with a common interest and a common task."*

Another aspect which comes through in David's very well-researched and detailed writing is how Menzies, in the early 1960s, worked very carefully to erode support within the Liberal Party for the White Australia policy, to bring Aboriginal Australians into mainstream Australian life in every sense of the word, and create those conditions which would come in the middle of that decade for the referendum, which of course he initiated, for 1967, and of course the abolition of the White Australia policy.

In April 1965, Menzies addressed the Federal Council of the Liberal Party at the Hotel Canberra, where he'd stayed during the meetings of the Unity conference in 1944, when they were establishing the Liberal Party. And he said this:

> *We are twenty-one today and we have the key to the door. That's something we ought to remember politically. We have indeed*

> *been either fortunate or wise or a mixture of both, because one of the outstanding things about this party, twenty-one years old, is that it has secured the support in Australia, I am quite convinced, of the young and ardent who are ambitious and self-reliant … Australia would not have made the enormous advances that it has made if it had been a community of people of dependent minds. The fact that Australia has grown as it has demonstrates that we are a people of independent minds who aim to be contributors as well as beneficiaries.*

He said, as David writes, "that the Liberal Party won their support because it had not been conservative, but innovative." And Menzies said, "Over the whole of this period of fifteen, sixteen years, since 1949, we have won because we have been the party of innovations. Not the party of the past, not the conservative party dying on the last barricade, but the party of innovations … these were evidences of a lively mind and a forward-looking heart. This is the whole thing that we must continue to remember and act upon in the years ahead."

Finally, "In his defence of liberalism during the 1940s, Menzies had reached out for the 'impossible'". The political correctness of the day was that capitalism was finished, that socialism was taking over, the British were going down that road. Menzies resisted all of that, convinced in the liberty and the freedoms and the creativity of the individual.

Therein, as David so powerfully reminds us in the book, liberalism is not about having power for its own sake. It's about how power can be used to shape the future of the country that we need for the next generation. As John Howard said to us so many times, David, that, "Once the mob," as Howard would say, "think that you've run out of ideas, that is when they will look to the other side." We, as Liberals, must be led by men and women who are prepared to fight for the things in which we believe that are essential for the future of the country and not simply to regard keeping and sustaining power as an end in itself …

3. Health, Education and Social Security

Address at the National Press Club as AMA President, 29 September 1993

Dr Nelson's address to the National Press Club in his first year as president of the Australian Medical Association proposes a number of constructive reforms to improve Australia's health system. He also highlights the unacceptable nature of Indigenous health and advocates for a variety of social causes from environmentalism to reproductive rights.

It's not easy being the president of the AMA.

On the one hand, I've got the responsibility of representing to you the consensus view of doctors to express the popular view of most doctors to the community. But on the other I have to lead them and in doing so challenge our members and challenge the society which we serve.

Doctors are intensely individualistic people, they usually hold their views quite strongly and on social issues are as divided as the rest of the community. Today I'm going to speak both about health insurance and some of the issues which some of my critics think that I'm not able to articulate for them, and also some of the social and health issues which undoubtedly affect all of us.

The health minister, Senator Graham Richardson, who is not quite a doctor, has said that the relationship between the AMA and the government over the last 10 years has been pretty bad.

And yes, at times it has. And in the period leading up to the last federal election, it probably reached an all-time low as we believe that the government was allowing the health system in Australia to go down a nationalised path where perhaps the government may allow a single government insurer to effectively control all healthcare and give us the sort of entrenched rationing that would go with that and leave patients without choices to which they are surely entitled.

Since the election there has been a change. Graham Richardson recognises, as I do, that the majority of middle Australians out there, they want their doctors to be working with the elected government – it doesn't matter the political colour of that government – on the solutions to our fairly substantial problems.

In many ways in health, the country doesn't really know where it's going. We have Medicare. All Australians contribute to Medicare according to their income, and are entitled to a minimum level of health insurance and free access, apparently to our public hospitals. Now the AMA accepts that. I accept that. The government accepts that. So now let's get on with the job of honestly recognising the problems we have with the system and the development of solutions that serve the interests of the nation's sick. Not its government, nor its doctors.

Health isn't a popularity contest. It doesn't matter if the public have voted for Medicare five times or 50 times. It has some fundamental problems. It can't survive in its present form without some reform, and those problems can't be ignored.

To those in the Labor movement who feel that health is a class struggle, and doctors perhaps should be seen as class enemies, I say to you that I am not intent on destroying Medicare. The AMA is not intent on destroying Medicare. Medicare's integrity is not threatened by initiatives that seek to reduce the demands placed upon it.

In the same way that our public education system survives because thousands of Australians with a $1.3 billion subsidy from the federal government send their kids to private schools. That, in fact, means that there are affordable, accessible choices in private education to see that we have some chance of giving our children a decent public education. The same kind of thinking needs now to be applied to health. And Australians, whether they voted Liberal or Labor, Democrat or National, they want affordable, accessible choices.

I'm on the ground floor in health, in general practice, and I can tell you that's what my patients say to me. Health policies have to be presented honestly. The rhetoric and conflict, politics of confrontation between us and politicians has to be put to one side now in the interest especially of the sick and the poor. I think we're all tired of ideological knee-jerk responses from people on both sides of politics to solutions that any sensible person can see are needed.

Our fundamental problem at the moment is one of demand and supply. The expectations of Medicare have been raised way beyond the capacity of the community to deliver. We've promised essentially free doctor visits. At least the government's promised them on our behalf. We've also been promised free hospital care, and the facts are that there are around 100,000 Australians on public hospital waiting lists.

We haven't got a national uniform reporting standard. It might be as low as 80. It might be as high as 120. There's a degree of urgency to about one third of those people. Over 60 people died last year on cardiac surgery waiting lists. The percentage of Australians with private health insurance, if you leave the initial flood when Medicare came in, from the June quarter of '87 was 48.3%, it's now down to 39.4%, with 45,000 people leaving private health insurance in the June quarter this year alone.

Now whatever your politics, what that means is extra demand on a public system. A public hospital system which is barely coping as it is. The Medicare levy has never funded more than 9 percent of our national health spending. The $2.8 billion that will be raised by the Medicare levy this year, in fact, will fund some 17 percent of what the Commonwealth's commitments to Medicare will be. And if you contrast that with what's raised by private health insurance, it will raise $3.4 billion dollars. It'll finance the hospital care of over one quarter of those Australians who go into hospitals, employ around 26,000 Australians in private hospitals, and save the government, in the private sector at least, something like $5.5 million a day. There are 600,000 Australians earning less than $250 a week, many of whom I'm sure vote Labor, who continue to have private health insurance. They believe that they need it. They believe that they want it. On the other hand, there are 100,000 people in Australia, earning more than 1,000 a week, who don't have private health insurance.

If you look at Medicare outlays for doctor visits, 9.5 percent growth again last year. An average of 10 percent growth over the last decade. From a diminishing tax base, you have to ask yourself, whether or not that can be sustained. Sure, some of it's the states pushing their outpatient services off to a bulk billing arrangement which shifts the cost to the Commonwealth. But there is still an unsustainability about a system which gives us all a credit card, supported by a political solution which tells us that we should then go and use it. But having said that, I accept that the government has the political fence that it has around bulkbilling.

Health should not be a political football. And when I say this, I'm not talking for the AMA, I'm talking for my patients. I think people are sick and tired of governments, oppositions and maybe even doctors using health as a political football when elections come along. Our frustration at not being able to get our message across in the last, three years certainly, has perhaps provoked our move into the electoral process.

What we really should be looking at, as we look to the year 2000, if I had a dream, it would be that we had a bipartisan health policy in Australia. We had a policy where perhaps the government moved a bit to the right, and perhaps the opposition moved a little bit to the left. And what we should have in Australia is a uniquely Australian healthcare system that's free of the rationing that characterises the national health system in Britain and obviously avoids the excesses of the United States.

A reasonable course of action would be for us to accept that Medicare and the health system basically continue to be based on the principles of Medicare. Universal minimum health insurance, a basically Commonwealth program to support the funding of public hospitals, and a contribution that's made according to your means.

The government should formally recognise then the need to encourage and support private health insurance for hospital services to ensure the viability of Medicare if for no other reason. There should be a higher Medicare levy paid by those Australians in higher income brackets who do not have private health insurance.

Those people who say, 'It's not equitable, we'll have a two-class system,' we already have a two-class system. The people that are getting the raw end of the pineapple are the very people that all of us, Labor, Liberal and AMA are trying to help. The system is desperately underfunded. Some people, tragically, are paying for it with their lives. And more money must come into the system from those people most able to afford to pay it and at the same time have the added effect of cross subsidising premiums for low-income earners and reducing the potential demand in some way on the public hospital system.

The Medicare Benefit Schedule needs a complete revision. And I'm pleased to see that the Health Minister has announced that such a revision is going to be undertaken. What's important though is what is the policy context in which that will be done? Will we have a limited Medicare pie for our Medicare benefits for our patients? So that, in fact, we will simply see doctors and sections of the profession squabbling amongst itself?

We've all heard politicians say that doctors have overcharged, have charged too much money when a patient's been billed above the government schedule fee. But in the five years from 1987, the government schedule fee increased 22%. The consumer price index increased 29.2%. The average weekly earnings of Australians, 33.4%, and the AMA schedule, 34%. The government is overseeing a system that has given itself a legislative monopoly upon it, is arbitrarily setting the fees, and then accusing the profession of overcharging when people are billed above that schedule. That's not keeping anywhere near the cost of providing services.

Now I'm not bagging the government at this stage. I think what we ought to be doing is, I think Graham Richardson is proposing that we actually sit down and work out a better way. And one of the things that I notice he's proposed is that people be offered gap insurance. And of course, the only reason there is a gap is because the government is not allowing us to adequately insure. In fact, at the moment, we're in a disgraceful situation with our Medicare Benefit Schedule, whereas if a doctor gets out of bed in the middle of the night to go and see a sick person, the government value for that less tax and running cost is about $40.

Similarly, for our consultant obstetricians, to look after pregnant women, the fee for that is $615. It costs $400 to provide the service. I mean, you can barely buy a pedigree dog for that price. The $100 million that's been earmarked by the government to buy private hospital beds for public patients in no way is a solution.

Imagine sending the kids from public schools to private schools to try and cope with their educational problems. People would surely say, 'Well, why should I bother to pay school fees?' Similarly, we think that the $100 million that's put aside should be spent on a dynamic evaluation in two or three hospitals.

Let's have a look at what the real problems are. Let's put aside the rhetoric and the fighting about the problems. Let's in fact look at the time from a patient going from their GP to the hospital, to the outpatients department, seeing the specialist, getting on a waiting list, being cancelled a couple of times after one or two years.

Let's look at the way we doctors work. Are we doing the wrong thing? What about our nurses and our unions? Can we get our GPs to look after people more quickly when they leave the hospitals? I mean, they're the kind of things that are really going to give some solutions. Providing that overall we look at the big picture. The big picture of supply and demand. Overall the government, and I think Graham Richardson recognises this, that we must have a balance between the demand on our public system and the supply that's available to look after our sick.

I'd like now to turn to perhaps some of our pressing health and social issues.

The health of Australia's 250,000 Aboriginal and Torres Strait Islanders is nothing less than a disgrace. When I look at the health status of our Indigenous people, and I see that their life expectancies equate to countries like Haiti, Ghana, India, Papua New Guinea, I feel ashamed, not only to be an Australian, but to be president of its peak national body. A medical body, that is. It doesn't matter whose fault it is, nor is there anything to be gained by assigning blame, nor is it relevant whether you live in Perth, whether you live in Launceston, Wilcannia or the North Shore of Sydney. We've all got a responsibility for this. We've got a responsibility to make this, I believe, our number one goal in improving the health of our Aboriginal people.

It will be a great tragedy if the Mabo debate distracts us from the real issues of preventable disease and death in Aborigines. Equally, it's fundamental that we recognise the importance to Aborigines of the land, and that dispossession has, in no small way, contributed to their despair, poverty, ill health, and frequently self-destructive behaviour.

Just to consider the following, that one in five Aboriginal infants has a low birth weight of less than two and a half kilograms. That's four times the rate for the rest of Australia. An Aboriginal mother is eight times more likely to die in childbirth than a non-Aborigine. For every one thousand Aboriginal children born, some 20 to 35 will be dead within a year.

That's three times higher than for the rest of us. A recent Northern Territory study found that 20 percent of Aboriginal children satisfied the World Health Organisation definition of malnutrition. Life expectancies for Aborigines in the Northern Territory are 20 years less than for non-Aborigines.

In the Torres Strait Islands, the life expectancy for Aboriginal women has actually gone down in the last decade. In the '70s it was 53 years, last decade it went down to 48.1. As many as 50 percent of the premature deaths in Aboriginal adults are due directly or indirectly to alcohol abuse, which should be seen as a symptom of their cultural disruption and their social alienation.

The death rate for young middle-aged Aborigines is 10 times higher than for non-Aborigines. The effectiveness of our health services for Aborigines has been limited by divided responsibility and buckpassing, by limited expertise in policy development, the disillusionment of health care, inadequate consultation with Aboriginal people and their subsequently low health expectations and limited compliance.

And we, the AMA, bear as much responsibility for that as anybody. I think that we should be taking as much responsibility for things as anybody else, including the government. The AMA, although having its members and its branches doing what they can to help Aboriginal people, at a national level, I don't think that we have used our national, political influence and lobbying and coordinating capabilities to do enough to advance the cause of Aboriginal health.

Apart from our curative and our preventative roles in Aboriginal communities, we can play a fundamental role in changing the way people think in Australia. And I can play a role, along with my Federal Council, in challenging the way doctors think about Aboriginal health issues. I think if we use our national coordinating role, we can assist in providing the impetus to the development of Aboriginal expertise.

This week, for the first time in its history, the AMA will advertise for a person to work full time on Aboriginal health issues in our Canberra headquarters. The position has the support of the Federal Government and the appointment will be made jointly with ATSIC and with representatives of Aboriginal health services.

I want someone in our office who goes in there in the morning and doesn't go home until perhaps not too late at night, who does nothing but think about Aboriginal health. Who is coordinating the activities of our doctors across the country. Working on initiatives with our educational colleges and our branches of the AMA. Who has the confidence of Aboriginal people, both urban and remote. That also can liaise effectively with government. But most importantly, keeps my eye on the ball, as the head of the AMA, to make sure that we are up to speed with what's happening in Aboriginal health, that we are playing a contributory role and we're taking some responsibility for it.

The AMA believes also that Senator Graham Richardson as the health minister should take ministerial responsibility for Aboriginal health. The AMA genuinely wants to help Aborigines, and we would be assisted to do so if responsibility for their health was shared by the Minister, his department, ATSIC, and the AMA, as representing the medical profession.

I don't think any of us involved in healthcare would sleep so soundly if we were required to consider our national health priorities for, say, chandeliers and plush carpet in Sydney's bulkbilling belt, alongside preventable infant Aboriginal deaths in Western Australia. Those things need to be considered in the same portfolio. And having taken responsibility for Aboriginal health, the Minister should establish a small taskforce, non-bureaucratic, comprising Aboriginal medical and sociological expertise that could consult with Aboriginal representatives and health professionals, review all the sources of government and non-government information that's relevant to Aborigines, assess Aboriginal health needs not being met by available services and recommend initiatives that are going to improve the compliance and uptake of health services by Aborigines.

That small taskforce should have access to an advisory panel. And in the end, there should be one agency finally responsible for improving the quality of healthcare of Aboriginal people. I reflect on the Department of Health at the moment, and there are over 60 people over there working, beavering away on general practice, and wouldn't it be great if we had 60 people over there beavering away on Aboriginal health?

Imagine if we had the same enthusiasm for addressing some of these deplorable health statistics for Aborigines as we have for the

Olympic Games and having them here in the year 2000. I'll tell you, my patients, I speak for them as much as anything, they can't understand why our politicians are having an argument about who's going to open the Olympic Games. They just think that this is crazy. The country has enormous problems, and our politicians seem to be off the beam. If you ask me, I think they should give some thought to having an Aboriginal person do it.

The second major public health concern for the AMA is what we see as the health epidemic that's unemployment. We define ourselves through our employment. Without it, many unemployed people feel that their lives have neither structure nor purpose. Our status, our income, our social contact, our structure in our days, all those things that perhaps all of us in this room take for granted, they are things that for many Australians simply don't exist.

And if you think of some of the statistics in this issue, there's a 17 percent excess death rate for unemployed men in Australia. It's 20 to 30 percent from the United Kingdom research done over 10 years. A 20 percent excess death rate for the wives of unemployed men. Fifty percent more doctor visits a year for unemployed people, 35 percent more admissions to hospital, a suicide rate which is nine times higher in the first year of unemployment, a 14 percent rate of depressive illness in recently unemployed men, and, not surprisingly a much higher rate of domestic violence, and death in children under the age of four.

I noticed that a group of academics from Sydney University ventured to write to the *Sydney Morning Herald* yesterday, criticising the AMA, which I presume was me, about our apparent failure to examine this issue scientifically. Apparently, they feel there's some question as to whether unemployment causes ill health.

Undoubtedly, ill health leads to unemployment. If you're crook, you're more likely to have difficulty keeping a job. But arguably the world's most scientific medical publication, the British Medical Journal, having reviewed all the evidence on this, said in 1991 that the evidence that unemployment kills is now so strong as to be considered irrefutable.

The pervasive problem, and again, I come back to my own patients, is a loss of self-esteem, a loss of hope. And what's out there in Australia at the moment is a loss of confidence in our government. It doesn't matter whether it be the Labor Party or the Liberal Party, the entire process is seriously being questioned. And many of the unemployed people that I look after feel that nobody up here genuinely cares for them or genuinely understands the predicament in which they find themselves. Now I'm quite happy to criticise politicians when they deserve it. But the caucus committee which the Prime Minister has established to develop this white paper on employment is enthusiastic, I think they're focused, they certainly seem to be genuinely listening to some of the proposals that are being put up, and I have some confidence that they will make some announcements which perhaps will go some way to appeasing our concerns.

We think that there should be a volunteer work program for unemployed people who want to maintain structure in their lives. Not digging holes out on roads, but to help us, for example, to look after an ageing population that's at home. We think there should be life skills education in schools. We should use some of our older unemployed people to help our teachers teach one-third of our kids, who will become unemployed, about coping with their unemployment. About maintaining structure in their lives.

We also think that in Australia a national taskforce established to oversee these kinds of programs needs to look at changing the values of Australians in relation to work and unpaid work. In the same way we've tried to change the way people think about AIDS, we should be changing the way we think about unpaid work. The reason why it's devastating to lose your job is not just because it's an economic and a social disaster, it's also because we define ourselves through our work. Why should women in Australia continue to feel demeaned to say, 'I'm just a housewife'? Why is it so important for so many people to have a job that pays them something rather than say, 'I'm unemployed'? We've got to stop this process in Australia where we allow people in positions of privilege to continue to promote the view that people on the dole are bludging.

I think equally important, there's a whole lot of things here we're worried about. Equally important to doctors has to be our concern for the environment. What kind of jobs are people going to have in a world that doesn't have any resources, with poisoned water, foul air, in a world where ozone depletion and greenhouse warming make it difficult for people to even survive? And I think it would be futile for us and certainly in my time leading the AMA for us to focus simply on Medicare, private insurance and the odd social injustice without looking at the big picture. Not only in Australia, but in the world in relation to our environment. I think it's time for us to put it on our agenda to see that our concern for air quality, water quality and deforestation and population growth is no less important to the nation's doctors than any of the other issues we're concerned about. Not only do we have a duty to educate our patients about simple changes to their domestic behaviour, which can have an effect on our environment, I think we've got to be prepared to stand up and be counted on important environmental issues for which there's a scientific basis.

I think that where people are fighting for environmental issues where there is a sound scientific argument, that we have an obligation to support them. Not all people concerned for the environment are ratbag obstructionists. And I've asked our Ethics Social Issues Committee to develop a formal policy for us on this and to consult with industry, government, environmental groups in the process.

If you look at the current issue of lead exposure, for example, there's 400 tonnes of lead going to the Melbourne air every year. The AMA stands willing to work with the government, to help the government, educate the community about the problems of lead exposure, to support initiatives to reduce lead contamination in our environment in Australia. And to be involved also in screening those children who need to be screened. And we would also support initiatives to reduce emissions in lead. But maybe we ought to be thinking innovatively also, and not just fiddle with the price of petrol. Because those of you who are doctors would certainly know that the battlers out there have a lot of trouble getting in their cars, and transport is as important to health as a Medicare card.

Perhaps at an international level, the biggest threat to our environment is our population. There are 5.4 billion people in the world at the moment, we double our number every 38 years. We've got enough food to feed five billion, but one billion of these suffer from hunger and malnutrition because of poverty and lack of water and natural resources.

We're told by demographers and economists that fertility rates will decline apparently when we're fully urbanised and our population will stabilise at between nine and 10 million. At the moment, though, we're at the risk of breeding humanity beyond its ability, or the ability of its finite physical resources unless we simultaneously develop improved food output.

Makes you wonder, as my Vice-President said, whether in fact the world might become a big feeding lot. A group of scientists in the United States, the Earth Group, said in 1988 that arresting global population growth should be second only in importance to avoiding nuclear war on humanity's agenda. And in this context, I'm concerned to see that in his next encyclical, Pope John Paul reaffirms the Catholic Church's ban on artificial birth control on the basis that it apparently blocks the transmission of life.

I have great respect for the Pope. I am a Catholic, but I must point out that an environment that's not able to sustain human life of value and integrity must be taken into consideration. The Australian Medical Association, I believe, must work within the World Medical Association to see that contraceptive choices are available to all the world's people, not only for their sake, but for the sake of the world that may barely be able to sustain life.

While dealing with social issues, I want to briefly allude to something that's important in Tasmania. You wouldn't expect a Tasmanian to come to the National Press Club and not come up with some parochialism, but it affects us all. It's relevant to us all. It remains in Tasmania a criminal offence to engage in a homosexual act. Homosexuality is not something that I understand, nor is it something about which most Australians feel comfortable in discussion. However, I ask all of you, and the Tasmanian government in particular, to understand what it must be like to have your sexuality contravene the law.

What's the purpose of such a law? Other than to reaffirm the comfort of those of us who are not homosexual and alienate a group of people who potentially do harm only to themselves. What should be illegal now, and always illegal, is to force another human being against his or her wishes, to submit to a sexual act and similarly to exploit the sexual development of young people before they've reached adulthood. This law over which the Tasmanian government presides is an indictment of the humanity and understanding that should be in all caring human beings. It is long past time to repeal that criminal code.

And turning now to illicit drugs, I make no apology for focusing on these real issues. At the moment we've got much more emphasis on law enforcement than health. We spend over $300 million a year on illicit drug law enforcement, while the National Campaign Against Drug Abuse cost us $240 million over six years.

I'm told that in the best year, we stop about 15 percent of the illegal drugs which are available in Australian society. And as we pursue our policies of supplier control, there's very good evidence of increasing crime rates. Increasing prison rates and drug-driven crime and violence against innocent people. As the President of the AMA, I now find myself in the position of having to argue for a needle exchange program, but against the availability of known dosage and purity of drugs which go through those needles. It's time we asked ourselves as a nation whether our approach to this problem is the correct one.

Perhaps it is. Perhaps we are doing the right thing. And my friend Bruce Shepherd, several years ago, convened a meeting to try and examine this issue in some scientific and social detail. And coming back to the real issues in Australian life, I think it's time that we did this again. I think it's time that the government, supported by the opposition, and certainly with my support, started a national debate of this. And it's more important to my patients, the parents of children, that this issue be debated than the colour of our flag, or who's going to open the Olympic Games, or what kind of constitution we're going to have.

Somewhere in Australia now, and I say to the parents of Australia and those who think they may become parents, someone's child is injecting an unknown quantity of an unknown substance into their arms. Having committed a crime to pay for a few life-threatening moments of misplaced pleasure to avoid the hardships which our society has given them. I think it's time that we faced up to some difficult issues.

Another issue of social and health concern to the AMA is the deinstitutionalisation of patients who have a mental illness. According to the National Health Strategy, there are about 800,000 people in Australia who suffer from schizophrenia, manic depressive illness or anxiety. And we've been right as a nation, we've been quite right to shift our emphasis from institutional or hospital care to community care. And that insists that we take into account the societal or the human context in which mental health occurs. It's had the positive effect of heightening our awareness of the humanity and needs of mentally ill people.

However, are we in danger of going too far? Mental illness is really at risk of being pushed out of the health arena and into the social and community arena. We're in danger of having our centres of excellence in psychiatry under-resourced as we shift from hospital and institution into community. And when governments are sitting down there with a razor, if they're on the left of the political spectrum, they tend to support this because it's civil liberty, it's the rights, the freedoms of individuals and so on. Those sentiments which I think we'd all share. And on the right side of politics, it can at times be an easy way of saving some money and recovering some very attractive land that was dedicated originally for psychiatric institutions.

How many of our deinstitutionalised mentally ill people now occupy the agencies such as Salvation Army? I'm told it's something like 30 percent of the people in the Salvation Army in Sydney tonight will be people with mental illness. Or how many are being exploited by unscrupulous individuals, as recently exposed on some national television reports. Hospital closures that follow deinstitutionalisation programs have not always been matched by community support programs. And if it's going to be done properly, it's just as expensive as running a hospital. In New South Wales in the last 10 years, 1,500 beds for mentally ill people have disappeared. And that may be right. But have we really stopped to think about it? That's the equivalent to three large hospitals. And patients who would previously have spent time in hospital have ended up in boarding houses, or living with their elderly parents, or in some cases on the streets.

There are a number of other issues confronting my profession that impinge on our ability to care that I can talk to you about, but I really don't have enough time. They include the despondency, the loss of morale, and the fear of government control that permeates the nation's 23,000 general practitioners.

The maldistribution of the medical workforce that sees 420 country towns without a doctor. The crisis in obstetrics, and don't let anybody tell you it's not a crisis, that finds one third of the specialty giving up doing obstetrics, that finds a third in training saying that they will not practice obstetrics when they finish their training, that finds malpractice costs forcing many practices to close. We've had a 68 percent increase in malpractice premiums this year alone for obstetrics. You won't find that catered for in the Medicare Benefit Schedule. And finally, a fee, that of $615 dollars, which I can only describe as an insult to some of the nation's leading obstetricians.

The increasing trend for ethical, moral, and professional issues to be determined as points of law. As evidenced recently we had a doctor removed from a medical register by a medical board for sexual impropriety with a patient. He then successfully appealed this in a court of law. The basis for this appeal apparently being that medical boards have an obligation to protect the public, not to penalise doctors.

It's very important to us, we are desperately concerned that the ethical, moral and professional behaviour by which doctors should live and work is being usurped by the role of courts. I wonder whether in fact some of the feminists in that particular case decided that they disliked us more than the judiciary.

The internal challenges for the AMA are to make this association relevant to all doctors, irrespective of their gender, their personal politics, or their geographic location. To put the AMA on the cutting edge of social and health policy. To have it respected as a body prepared not only to address difficult social issues, but also as one that is prepared to, if necessary, stand and fight for its principles.

Medicare, private insurance, medical fees, Aborigines, smoking, car crashes, it doesn't matter what the issue is. This AMA is working for all Australians, for all doctors, and I want every doctor in this country to feel that the people running the organisation are listening to them.

And finally, I want to instill in our young graduates the value of commitment, to an ethic of service upon which the profession is based. And to challenge the still predominantly male framework within which the association works. Being a doctor is tough enough. Trying to be a mother, a doctor, and a wife must be the hardest job on earth.

It's time for Australia's doctors to lead the way in showing that national progress can be made by placing the welfare and consideration of other human beings ahead of our own. Doctors who join the AMA do so to give much more than they will ever receive.

Drugs: The Doctor's Dilemma, 27 April 1999

In this speech, Dr Nelson reflects on the history of drugs in Australia and shares his own experiences with drug users in his medical life. He heralds the resources the Howard Government was putting into policing, enforcement and education, making the case for a trial of safe injecting rooms and methadone treatment.

... The drug debate is rarely a sane pursuit. All too often it is little more than dialogue with the deaf, who, at either extremes of the debate see little other than simple solutions to what are the most complex issues to face humankind. To the issues are brought conviction, experience, expertise, ignorance, prejudice and fundamentalist intolerance deeply rooted in a desire to apply a code of morality to the lives of others. Less often do we see discussion of drug policy in the light of reflected wisdom informed by reasoned argument.

As Robert Kennedy reminded us shortly before his death in 1968 of the words of the Greek dramatist, Aeschylus: "In our sleep, pain which cannot forget falls drop by drop upon the heart and in our despair, against our will, comes wisdom through the awful grace of God."

"Wisdom" was not a word which sprang to mind when former Liberal Party President and Elders IXL boss, John Elliott said in early March 1999 that drugs are an overstated issue. "It's bloody important that they (the government) won't be sidetracked by it." He went on to tell his luncheon audience from The Institute of Chartered Accountants that, "Economic policies are the only reason you have government. I say that very strongly."

I spent a decade of my medical life servicing some of the poorest suburbs in the country. I am now privileged to represent one of the most affluent in the federal parliament. The one thing they have in common is that each harbour a deep concern for the legacy left for their children. The destiny of this country will be determined not by the economic indices with which we seem so understandably obsessed, but by our values and beliefs, the way we relate to one another and see our place in the world. If all the economic problems of life were solved, all important questions would remain unanswered. Few are more important than drugs.

Drugs are defined by the World Health Organisation (WHO) as "any chemical entity or mixture of entities used for treatment or alleviation of disease, or for non-therapeutic purposes. Psychoactive drugs are those that alter mood, cognition or behaviour." Drug policies are not a recent invention. Around the tenth century Persian writers were warning of dangers in the consumption of opium. China promulgated its first edict against opium in 1729. Western societies first became concerned about the abuses of alcohol in the beginning of the seventeenth century, when public drunkenness was made a criminal offence.

Australia has a history of drug use and addiction from the time of early European settlement as a penal colony. The first currency was alcohol. The use of proprietary medicines containing opiates, cannabis extract and cocaine was daily ritual for many Australians last century continuing well into this one. Bayer gave birth to heroin as a mainstream pharmaceutical in 1898 for babies' catarrh of which doctors were enthusiastic prescribers. By 1936 Australia had the highest rate of cocaine and heroin dependence in the Western world.

How much has changed? Heroin and cocaine are ubiquitous, more potent and cheaper than ever before. These and other drugs have been embraced by a significant and growing minority of disillusioned, disaffected and demoralised young Australians, more of whom will die from drugs this year than were killed for the entire Vietnam War. In 1996, the conservative US journal *The National Review*, led with an article by the very conservative William F Buckley Jnr, entitled "The War on Drugs is Lost". In support of his conclusion he cited the fact that 1.2 million Americans were then imprisoned for drug offences and that a quarter of Afro-Americans are either in prison or on parole for drug use and related crime. The critical question should be whether we want drug policy to reflect the world as we want it to be, or the reality with which we are faced. No less important is the principle. Do we wish to continue policies we know will not succeed but in the belief it is the right thing to do?

If this is a "war" there are few winners but many casualties, the first of which are pitiable users who lose self-esteem, personal integrity, financial security, health and, in some cases — life itself …

In response to escalating drug use and related crime, the National Campaign Against Drug Abuse (NCADA) emerged from the April 1985 special Premiers' conference on drugs. It also gave birth to what would become known as "harm minimisation".

Like multiculturalism, "harm minimisation" has been distorted by its proponents and critics alike. It is neither a gateway to liberalisation of drug attitudes and laws, nor is it a policy that marginalises the importance of policing and enforcement. Harm minimisation represents a three-pronged approach to illicit drugs:

- Supply-reduction strategies designed to disrupt the production and supply of drugs.
- Demand reduction including education, prevention and abstinence.
- Initiatives to reduce harm to individuals who will inevitably use drug and the communities within which they live.

Two components of Australia's approach, which find themselves regularly under attack, are needle exchange and methadone maintenance programs.

Needle exchange programs in Australia operate under the National Drug Strategy and the bilateral Public Health Outcomes Funding Agreements (PHOFAs). In 1997-98 some 9.24 million needles and syringes were distributed in NSW at a cost of $9 million. In 1997, 50 percent of users in needle exchange were hepatitis C positive, a decline from 66 percent in 1996. In Australia, HIV infection among injecting drug users is less than 2 per cent. In contrast, the World Health Organization attributes to unsafe injecting practices 43 percent of all cases of HIV in Europe; 40 percent in Edinburgh and Bangkok and 75 percent in Malaysia, Vietnam, South West China, North East India and Burma.

A 1997 Australian study of the effectiveness of needle-exchange programs, internationally, in preventing HIV infection found that HIV prevalence had decreased by 5.8 percent in the 29 cities with needle exchange programs, and had increased by 5.9 percent in the 52 cities without such programs. When Windham, Connecticut, recently closed its needle exchange program, the percentage of users obtaining needles and syringes from unsafe sources increased from 14 to 51 per cent. Worse still, the re-use rates increased from an average 3.5 times to 7.68 times.

The risks of HIV in injecting drug users are not limited only to themselves but also to their sexual partners, and especially their children. New York City has a population approximating that of NSW but it does not have, until recently, a needle exchange program. HIV is a much more common legacy of intravenous drug use in New York City than it is in Australia. By 1997, more than 17,000 cases of HIV had been reported in children living in New York City. In NSW there had only been 42. As the founder of the first US needle-exchange program, David Purchase said, "We can't stop them being silly but we can stop them being dead."

Methadone was first used as an orally administered drug-substitution treatment for heroin addiction in the 1960s. Despite national guidelines for its use, patterns of prescribing and provision vary both within and across jurisdictions. In 1998, the Australian National Council on drugs endorsed methadone as a "valuable and legitimate drug substitution therapy and confirmed its support for the National Policy on methadone". The 1995 national Review of Methadone Treatment in Australia argued that: "Methadone treatment is without competitor as the best researched of all treatments for opioid dependence which has been clearly demonstrated to reduce illicit opiate use more than either no-treatment, drug-free treatment, and detoxification in randomised controlled trials."

The reality is that methadone treatment may have a variety of goals. Abstinence is clearly one but so too is stabilising an addict's life, reducing the use of illicit drugs and eliminating participation in criminal activity. In treatment, tolerance is deliberately induced to a stable dose of methadone sufficiently high to block the narcotic and euphoric action of methadone and other opiates. In proper doses it does not create euphoria, sedation or analgesia and should not have adverse effects on motor skills, mental capacity or employability …

Prime Minister John Howard is to be congratulated. His government, largely through his own commitment, has put more resources into combating drug use than any other government in this nation's history. Tough on Drugs may not be everyone's preferred title, but in spreading resources across policing, enforcement, education, prevention, treatment, rehabilitation and research, Australia now has a more comprehensive and better funded drug strategy …

The Council of Australian Governments has now also committed to a diversional strategy for drug offenders enabling the courts to direct eligible drug users into treatment rather than jail. At last we are moving drug use more to a medical, rather than criminal model. For some it will mean much better outcomes. Similarly, the trial in NSW of drug courts enabling drug users who plead guilty to certain crimes to choose prison or 12 months of treatment and rehabilitation provides new hope. It is here in particular that oral naltrexone may have a real place.

And so what of the others? What do we do with those who use heroin once and have an overpowering compulsion to do so until they die? Faced with what is a chronic, relapsing and, in all probability, fatal condition, do we have everything available to us that we need?

I am privileged to represent the electorate of Bradfield on the Upper North Shore. I am aware of some 30 families in my electorate who have either lost children to heroin or as one woman put it to me, "are currently living the nightmare". Two have teenaged daughters working as Kings Cross prostitutes to maintain their addiction. Another had his own son arrange a break-in to the family home …

I was President of the Australian Medical Association when, in 1994 the Ethics, Science and Social Issues Committee brought a recommendation to the federal council that it endorse a trial of the controlled injection of heroin in the ACT. My instincts told me that this was nonsense. I well recall Professor Priscilla Kincaid-Smith, then Chairman of Council and an internationally eminent physician remarking that "it seems an odd thing to give people heroin in order to get them off it". I am ashamed to say that I used my position to kill it. Several weeks later the researchers came to see me, explaining why and how the trial would be conducted. It was subsequently brought back to the AMA and endorsed. A heroin trial seeks to answer the following question.

If you take a person who is already addicted to heroin, whose only obsession is one thing and one thing only – their next fix; someone who has failed repeatedly in treatment programs and is prepared to prostitute his/her own body, commit crimes against innocent people including their own families to maintain their addiction; if you take such a person and require them to inject under supervision – no takeaways, in a drab but safe and supervised environment – is that person less likely to die?

Are they less likely to contract a serious disease from which they will eventually die and in the meantime cost the taxpayer an enormous amount of money? Are they less likely to be homeless? Are they less likely to be unemployed? Are they less likely to be committing crime against innocent people and are they more likely to have some semblance of relationship with their families and those who still continue to love them? Until we do such a trial we do not know.

The trial itself is not by any means the solution to the "drug problem". There is no single solution and the goal of a drug-free society, as noble as it may be, is a utopian dream. In the context of the leadership shown and initiatives now undertaken by the prime minister, a trial should be revisited. The trial is not about a permissive attitude to heroin, nor is it about legalisation. It is instead about taking a subset of heroin addicts for whom all other options have been exhausted, for whom death is a day to day expectation, and asking ourselves whether they, their families and society are likely to derive some benefit from heroin administered in this way.

I am personally nauseated by the prospect, as I am of injecting rooms. But one of the most difficult and critically important responsibilities of medicine and politics, is to put aside your personal feelings, to ask yourself whether what you seek to do serves the interests of those individuals and the society which you purport to lead. As a doctor, I find it difficult, notwithstanding the self-inflicted dimension of drug use, to stand aside and allow policies that kill people.

From the Jesuits, I learned four principles – courage, commitment, conscience and compassion – compassion that requires you to share another person's pain, to place yourself in the shoes of another human being. I challenge anyone here tonight to place themselves in the shoes of a parent of a 20 year-old son or daughter hopelessly addicted to heroin. What options might you want to be available?

One constituent said to me last year: "Dr Nelson, my husband and I are very conservative. There is no way we would have ever voted for someone like you – and we did not. A year ago we would have been appalled at the thought of a heroin trial, giving heroin to addicts in this way. But for nine months we have been living the nightmare of heroin addiction with our 18 year-old daughter. All I can say is that I am proud to have you as my member and we will give you every possible support in what you are trying to do. A heroin trial won't do anything for us and our family crisis, but it will give hope that someone else might find it easier to get through this than we."

I don't support the legalisation of currently illicit drugs. We made that mistake with tobacco. But to build on the Government's diversional program there is a legitimate and growing place for a trial similar to, but more scientifically disciplined than that conducted by the Swiss …

The most intellectually bankrupt of the arguments put forward is scepticism about success. Or is it a fear of success in terms of improved health, social and economic outcomes? Nothing is ever achieved in science without experimenting to prove or disprove a hypothesis. Would penicillin have been discovered had Florey taken the view that success was not likely? Nothing of importance is achieved in life, medicine or in public policy without taking a risk – without having a "brave heart" …

If we are to give the next generation the confidence to believe that the future is as much theirs as ours to shape, to give them the sense of belonging and meaningful purpose coined by Richard Eckersley so critical to resisting drugs, then what we need is an attractive, inspiring and achievable vision for our country – a vision which "embraces human, economic and social objectives". Something obvious is eluding us – our legislators, leaders and certainly the John Elliott's of this world, but which is quietly understood though not articulated by everyday Australians, and that is that the emerging political battles are not one of Labor and Liberal, nor are they of the left and right.

The political divide is rapidly becoming one fought between those who have an ethics, values-based approach to life's problems on the one hand, and materialists who see little other than the primacy of markets as an end unto themselves on the other. The German philosopher and physicist, Bemhard Philberth, in his book entitled *Revelation*, said of change:

> *Progress leads to chaos if not anchored in tradition: Tradition becomes rigid if it does not lead to progress. But a perverted traditionalism and a misguided progressivism, propel each other toward a deadly excess – hardly leaving any ground between them.*

In reflecting on this telling observation, we may find some answers to what is an all-consuming problem.

The Vision for Education, Address to the Sydney Institute, 10 April 2002

> Speaking as Minister for Education, Dr Nelson discusses the importance of continual improvements and reform in the education sector, to fulfil "our responsibilities to the next generation".

… When I was asked if I would be prepared to be the Minister for Education, Science and Training and to serve in the Cabinet, I was naturally pleased, and in fact I was overwhelmed. I consider it a great privilege to be Australia's Minister for Education, Science and Training in the first government of the twenty-first century. But I came into the job without any predetermined agenda. I didn't carry any educational baggage into it. For those who read *The Australian*, you'll know that I'm still learning how to spell. The Prime Minister gave me no agenda in relation to higher education other than to respect it, and to enunciate to society the value of it, and of course to continue to implement workplace relations reform in the sector. But within three weeks of being in the portfolio, it became obvious to me that a number of things are true …

The failure to undertake reform in higher education today, in preparation for the future, will be an abrogation of our responsibilities to the next generation. It is time that we as a country had the maturity to recognise that we should be discussing, in a dispassionate but informed way, in the public arena the policy options that we have before us in relation to Australian Universities. And that debate ought to be informed and it ought to be free of some of the emotion and highly politicised language which has characterised it in the past. There are some things that should transcend what comprises public division in this country. The future of education, and higher education in particular should be one of them …

When I spoke to the Vice-Chancellors, I said they needed to understand that there are three things in any approach to reform. The first, which is the easiest, is to do absolutely nothing. The second would be to simply have a look at things. There has been an enormous amount of work done in the sector – in a sense it has been reviewed to death. There are many quite informed and well researched views in terms of what should happen, and a lot of material already exists in the public arena. At present we have a review in progress to bring as many Australians along with us as we possibly can. But review alone is not the best way to go. The third alternative is what I'm proposing to do. To see that everybody has a say, everybody has an input. As I said to the President of the National Tertiary Education Union when I met with her and her colleagues, you will know what finally comes of this because you will contribute to it. I will be consulting with you and you will understand the direction in which we are going, and what that means for a union. There will be some things, perhaps ultimately, with which they will agree and agree quite strongly and of course other things to which they remain quite opposed.

There are a number of issues that need to be looked at. Some of them are philosophical as much as they are practical. One of our problems in public policy in our country is that we don't often think so much about the philosophy as what we are doing. The first question for me is, what defines a university? At the moment, in Australia, we see universities as undertaking three things – research, scholarship and teaching. A Vice-Chancellor said to me recently, in a kind of a critical tone of another institution, that a particular institution was not so good because there was far too much emphasis on teaching and not enough emphasis on research. But when you think about what Australians want, and what they expect from their universities, and especially for students who attend them, it is teaching which is a very high priority. We need to be asking ourselves – 13 years after John Dawkins' reforms in amalgamating colleges of advanced education with existing universities – what defines a university in the beginning of the twenty-first century?

There's a debate at present over Melbourne University Private and it has been suggested by some, including the Victorian Education Minister, that Melbourne University Private perhaps should not be described as a university because the research that it undertakes is essentially commercially driven. It's a legitimate argument for people to say well, it shouldn't be a university. But it's equally legitimate for others to say – yes it should, and perhaps our definition of universities should not be so narrow as to exclude one that undertakes research which is driven predominantly, but not entirely, by industry. But the one thing we certainly don't want is that to be the only model of an Australian university.

The second question I ask myself is, who goes to university and why do they go there? For example, of the 1992 cohort, 40 percent who commenced a university education did not complete it and of those, 10 percent came back at some later point while the rest did not complete and it's still at that level. And of those who don't complete – half of them drop out or leave in the first year. In a climate where we've got 52,000 people who try to get a place at university this year (half of what it was ten years ago, but still a significant amount of unmet demand) at a time when we've got people who are going to university who perhaps are not likely to complete. So one of the questions I've been putting to the Australian public is, should everybody be going to university?

Having spent much of my earlier life dealing with young people who feel disengaged and feel that perhaps there's no place for them in modern society, when you scratch away the surface when you're working with kids who are on the edge, you find that many of them feel that they are being pressured to be what they are not. As a parent myself, I think one of the easy mistakes we can make is that we often project onto our children our own unfulfilled ambitions. I've dealt with too many young people who are pursuing a particular field of study or a career, not because in their hearts that's what they want to do but because a parent has throughout their lives, said "this is what we want you to be" and "this is what we want you to do".

A further problem we have is the one-size-fits-all model of funding for our publicly funded institutions. There are a number of Australian universities, not all sandstones, who do and should aspire to compete with the rest of the world. It's rather interesting that Ian Macfarlane, the Governor of the Reserve Bank, commented recently on having an Australian university rank in the top 100. If twenty years from now we are to have a university that is considered to be in the top 50 or top 100 throughout the world, what policy reforms do we need to undertake now to achieve it? Or, indeed, is it desirable? Is it something that we should strive for? And then at the same time, is it possible to have a set of funding arrangements that includes regional universities but in no way threatens the viability or continued growth of those institutions. Currently regional universities are increasingly meeting quite complex and onerous community service obligations, and facing quite different challenges from a lot of the larger institutions. I can assure you nothing will be done to undermine the role of regional universities, whatever happens in reform in higher education. In fact, we need to do everything we can to strengthen those particular institutions.

Another issue we need to be looking at is the way in which our universities are governed for this century. We need to look at the structures that underwrite universities, notwithstanding some of the reforms that have already been undertaken, particularly in some of the institutions. We have to ask ourselves are these the best models for accountability – reporting, restrictions on commercialisation and so on. There are many issues here for the institutions themselves when you think that we're running $400 million institutions. A number of Vice-Chancellors have put particular views to me in relation to this. It is an issue that needs to be discussed in the public arena. There is the matter of intellectual property, and the extent to which it's been commercialised or not commercialised in a number of institutions. Why are there barriers, cultural and regulatory, which make it difficult for universities to commercialise their IP?

Private sector investment in university infrastructure; why is it that it is not as prominent a part of university life here as it is in some other countries? I asked the chairman of a very large company why, for example, it was not possible to build the XYZ Department of Information, Communication and Technology at a particular university and then go into a long-term intellectual property share arrangement with the institution and researchers. He said, well we'd actually love to do that sort of thing, but there is a culture within Australia that rejects that sort of investment, and also there are some tax laws which would make it difficult to do so. I've also said to the Secretary of my Department that I want every aspect of the regulation that the Commonwealth Government imposes on universities to be reviewed from the point of view of asking to what extent are we making it harder for universities to undertake research and to teach students? In other words are universities doing a lot of things which are required to meet administering requirements which are set by my Department which go beyond the reasonable realms of public accountability for a significant amount of public funds? And when I talk about review, I'm talking about review from our point of view, the Commonwealth government's point of view, as much as I am about the Higher Education point of view.

With the issue of research resources and the way we distribute them, obviously much competitive research funding goes to institutions, but there is a lot of other research funding which is distributed to institutions as well. We ought to have a public and a transparent discussion about how we distribute those resources. Are we doing the best we can with them at the moment? Then there's specialisation and differentiation, arguably one of the most important things. One university I visited, for example, offers 167 courses but 96 of the courses have fewer than five students enrolled. I go to universities and I travel from one university to another. It takes about 30 minutes. They are marvellous institutions, but the everyday person would go along and say well everything that I'm looking at here is being provided by the institution I was just at. Do we have a funding system which, instead of encouraging differentiation and collaboration between institutions, is instead encouraging institutions to offer all things to all people and at the same time perhaps not making the quality of what institutions want to provide as high as those who run them aspire them to be?

Last on my list, though certainly not least in priority, is my concern that if we continue further into a future, as we should, with a commercialisation of intellectual property predominantly in the areas of applied science, where does that leave the humanities? Fine arts, literature, language and philosophy are what give meaning to us as a society. In a sense, universities are passing the soul of one generation to the next. And, as important as science and applied science is, it's how we use science that is much more difficult. We've been through this recently with human cloning and stem cell research. One thing I'm determined to do, if there is any reform, is to make sure that we're able to put humanities, literature and fine arts and the like on a sound footing, areas of study where it is much more difficult to seek private sector support.

Higher education is an area of concern to electors. In that, I can see that priority setting in science has the potential to change our country in ways that most of us wouldn't begin to imagine. There are people who are arguing that as a small country, with a relatively, by global terms, small amount of money to spend on research that we should focus it into specific areas, highly technical, special areas. There are others who say we should be looking at broader thematic priorities. And it's to this that I am attracted, as one Australian, and one member of the government. I see the opportunity to set some goals, some economic, social and human objectives for our country that might see us 5, 10 and 15 years from now having a clear idea about where we want to be. What we want to be good at and how we want to be seen by the rest of the world. Then the priorities that we set in science become a logical, strategic outcome, a logical way of achieving what we want. You could be looking at Australia's carrying capacity, which will be examined in applied science, ecological, environmental science, social sciences and start thinking about where we want to be in a whole variety of ways, as I say, in a decade from now.

On my wall I have, if you like, my vision of Australia. What I'd like to see us become. I see this portfolio as a great way of trying to achieve it. We should strive to become a people that values the health and integrity of human life, as much as we value our economic objectives. We should see barriers to the creation of wealth as being the enemy of an equitable social policy of which education is probably the foremost. We should also strive to be an outward looking and compassionate country, reconciled with our indigenous history, and the values of hard work, self-sacrifice, tolerance and courage. That's what this portfolio is all about. It's about building a better Australia and building resilience in young people and seeing that education is a process that begins in early life and ends only when you leave this earth.

Voluntary Student Unionism, 16 March 2005

Introducing the Higher Education Support Amendment (Abolition of Compulsory Up-front Student Union Fees) Bill, Dr Nelson makes the case for Voluntary Student Unionism. Nine months later, the numbers were finally secured to pass this legislation in the Senate.

In its first term of office this government extended the principle of freedom of association to the Australian workplace. Freedom of association is a basic right that should be available to each and every Australian.

At present that is not the case, Mr Speaker, with students at Australia's higher education institutions still denied the right to freedom of association. Students have fewer freedoms than other Australians, because almost all of them must join a student organisation when they enrol at university. They also must pay for amenities, facilities and services that they do not use and in many cases do not want.

Mr Speaker, this bill will give students the right to freedom of association, allowing students the right to join student organisations but, equally, the right not to.

From 2006, no student will be compelled to join a student organisation, union or guild, unless they choose to. In addition, no student will be compelled to pay a fee to an institution for non-academic amenities, facilities or services unless they choose to pay a fee to make use of those services.

This bill now before us will amend the *Higher Education Support Act 2003* to insert additional 'fairness' provisions into the quality and accountability requirements that apply to all higher education providers. These fairness requirements will ensure that institutions cannot require a student to be a member of a student association, union or guild. They will also ensure that students are not required by their provider to pay any fees to it or any other entity for the provision of an amenity, facility or service that is not of an academic nature.

These fairness requirements are a condition of the grants that are made to higher education providers and a condition of continued approval as a higher education provider under the act.

Mr Speaker, the government's intentions are clearly articulated in this bill. Higher education providers are not to require their students to join a student association, and they are not to require a student to pay for amenities, facilities and services unless a student has chosen to use them or join them.

The bill provides that institutions that receive grants under the Commonwealth Grant Scheme may have their grant reduced if they are found in breach of these conditions.

The bill does not intend to disrupt normal university operations. This bill will not impact on institutions' ability to collect fines and penalties for breach of the institutions' statutes, by-laws and regulations. It will also not impact on institutions' ability to collect fees for goods or services essential to a course of study but that are available for purchase through other providers, for example musical instruments, stethoscopes and artwork.

What this bill will do is put non-academic services onto a basis that allows them to operate without forcing students who do not use them to subsidise them.

Students will purchase or organise in support of the services that they want. Commercial enterprises, as in the rest of the Australian community, will be effective providers of services for which there is demand. Many voluntary organisations and cooperatives thrive based simply on mutual support for agreed objectives. Sporting clubs operate on this basis throughout the country.

Australian students currently pay between $100 and $590 a year in union fees as a condition of enrolment. This is a significant sum. These fees are unconnected to students' academic courses and are charged with little regard for their ability to pay. Ironically, it is those that regularly and vigorously oppose changes to the Higher Education Contribution Scheme who argue so passionately for the right to compulsorily require up-front fees from their fellow students for services they may not need nor want.

Student services are an essential part of university life, but why can't these things be funded by choice?

For example, why is a single mother who is training to be a nurse paying for the canoeing club or the mountaineers? Every year – indeed, every month – I receive letters from students and their parents rightly angry that they have no choice in paying union fees. Even angrier is the growing army of fully online students who don't even set foot on campus but who also have to cough up for student 'services'.

Many students believe, as the government does, that no student should be forced to become a member of a student union. Nor should they be forced to financially contribute to a student or service organisation when they are either opposed to its activities or indifferent to its services.

The government is committed to the principle of freedom of association. Australian higher education students should enjoy the same rights on campus as they enjoy off campus. This bill will give them those rights.

There will obviously be a debate ensuing on this bill. I expect that in parts it will be emotional and uninformed in some quarters. I will read into *Hansard* an excerpt from a letter sent to the member for Cook by a constituent. It says:

> *I also write as a concerned parent of a daughter who is doing her nursing degree at University of Western Sydney. As a single parent pensioner with two children and a mortgage left to her by an adulterous husband she is finding the going very tough. However, always wanting to be a nurse from way back she took the opportunity.*
>
> *When enrolling this year she was asked for $300 Student Union fees. When she objected due to lack of money she was told*

> *she wouldn't get her exam results or be able to do her clinical training. Reluctantly she paid although the benefits seemed very minimal ...*

It turned out that of the six universities in Sydney 3,000 students couldn't or wouldn't pay. They received notification that if they didn't pay their $300 PLUS a $100 fine they would be dis-enrolled from the university.

This seems monstrous and I would like to know how a Student Union can dictate to the university. I was under the impression that this government encouraged voluntary union membership. What has gone wrong?

Another correspondent to the Prime Minister said in part:

> *Some of the things that my money has been spent on in the past year include a bus to Woomera for a protest, a sausage sizzle and balloons to protest the Tampa incident and bail for those arrested for the aforementioned Woomera protest. How is this furthering my education?*

Indeed, how does any of that further the education of those students? This is the 21st century. Those of us who live on planet commonsense fail to understand why it is that, in this century, in a climate where services are made available in a free, open and competitive society, students wanting an education are compulsorily required to join a union, to be represented in a way or to receive services that they may neither want, expect or use. The government is extremely committed to making sure that the choice in Australian universities is no less than applies in the rest of Australian society.

The good news for the National Union of Students and for the Australian Labor Party is that all of those students who are clamouring so loudly, supported by the members opposite, to see that student union contributions continue will be able to continue to pay their fees. There is no law banning any Australian student from making a contribution to a student union, but it is long past time that those students had a choice. I commend the bill to the House and present the explanatory memorandum.

The facts eventually added up, *North Shore Times*, November 2005

> Dr Nelson recounts personal experience to highlight the need for plain language report cards, so parents can have clear information about their child's educational progress.

I managed a paltry 25 percent for my trial Year 10 maths exam. My mother was not impressed when my report turned up at home and that's putting it politely.

She then swung into action, finding a tutor from her limited resources to help me. Six weeks later I finished at the top end of the top quartile.

In those ensuing 30 years something has taken drip of the education sector.

As Australia's Minister for Education I have placed conditions on the $33 billion of school funding. These range from a common starting age, education values, to publication of school performance and plain language report cards.

Not only are all schools in receipt of Commonwealth funding to tell parents results in an A to E format or equivalent, they will also rank students into quartiles.

Obviously someone has to be in the bottom quartile. But if my son's there I want to know about it. It doesn't mean he has a problem, but he's more likely to have one if he's there.

It is the notion of telling parents how their children perform in relation to others in the class that has sent the educational class into orbit.

I am told that it will destroy the self esteem of children if they know they are underperforming in relation to classmates. I am further told that a child in the top 25 percent of the class could still be well below a state or national average.

Of course they could. Surely it is not beyond the wit of intelligent educators to explain that on the report or, more importantly, during the parent/teacher interview.

The problem is that many school reports have assumed a language neutered jargonistic tone over the past 20 years. In a well-meaning but misguided attempt to protect the sensibilities of children and their parents, eduspeak has replaced commonsense.

When time-poor parents, who themselves may be educationally limited read a report that describes as "working towards, consolidating, sometimes", it is easy to think things are okay.

For some parents, the only thing that rings the alarm bell is knowing their child has fallen behind everyone else.

I am told it is "educationally unsound" to rank students against one another.

As a caller to ABC radio observed last week, "Why is it all right for the teachers to tell my Year 2 son he finished 11th out of 20 in the cross country, but give me no idea where he's coming in reading?"

Parents can exclude their children from plain language reporting if they wish. Schools don't have to place quartiles on the report, but they do have to tell parents it will be provided on request.

Had my mother been told in 1975 that "Brendan is working hard, moving toward mathematical concepts and consolidating his understanding of calculus", my life would have been quite different.

Whatever the impact of truth on parents, what's the long term effect of hiding it from them?

Valuing Vocational Education/Plain Language Report Cards, Liberal Party Federal Council, 25 June 2005

> Addressing the Liberal Party Federal Council in 2005, Dr Nelson expresses his vision of education to enable all Australians to "find and achieve their own potential". He discusses the measures that his government has taken, including implementing conditions on school funding to drive national consistency and lift standards, and expanding the availability of apprenticeships and vocational training for young people.

Our vision of education is that every human being and every young person in this country should be able to both find and achieve their own potential whatever that is, and to recognise that they are all different. And what informs it are many things, but two of them in particular.

Firstly, Winston Churchill in September 1943 went to Harvard University to receive an honorary doctorate in a world which is quite different from the one in which we are now living. And the Americans asked him to speak specifically about the British Empire. And essentially that day, Churchill had said to them, "look you can forget about all of that, when the war ends, as it will, the empires of the future will be 'empires of the mind'".

And it was of course, a year later here in Canberra in Australia, that Robert Menzies in addressing the representatives of the eighteen organisations who had come to Canberra to found what would become, of course, the Liberal Party of Australia. In setting out his vision for not only our party but, more importantly, the country, he said in part, that to every good citizen, the state would owe not only a chance in life but a self-respecting life. And we who are privileged to govern in this, the early part of the 21st century, every single thing we do in education and science and training is informed essentially by the statesman that made those comments just over 60 years ago …

We earned more last year from exporting education and training than we did wheat and wool and so everything that we are endeavouring to do is to make sure that Australia is internationally competitive on standards and to drive national consistency whether it's across training, universities, schools or science and research. And the Menzian vision is equally if not more important, because of all of the things we have achieved as a country of which we can be extremely proud. One of our failings is that over the last two generations, we have created a country in which young people feel that their lives are valued by the educational choices that they make …

But no matter how hard I try, I cannot see Australia through their eyes. But if I did, I could be forgiven for thinking that if I don't get an outstanding year 12 result, and a university education, a BMW and a mobile phone and fashionable clothes, then maybe perhaps, my life is of lesser value to my country than those who do. Every single thing that we are endeavouring to do in policy is about challenging and changing that cultural orthodoxy.

For many young people, apprenticeships and training and moving into TAFE is as equally valued as a university education. And for some young people, just getting from school to a job emotionally intact is a far more significant achievement than anything that any of us here have ever been able to do. So what we're endeavouring to do right across the education system is to challenge and change a cultural orthodoxy for which we pay a very high human price and economic price. We have a 40 percent dropout rate from University, for example, significantly because many young people are not there because they want to be there, they are there because someone else wants them to be there. Frequently parents are supported by a school and a broader media culture that promotes university programmes, essentially to the exclusion of all else in terms of value. We also have eleven key industries with significant shortages and we have a significant minority of young people who are disengaging in early secondary school because they mistakenly think that, without going to university, perhaps there may not be a place for them.

Right across the portfolio, firstly in schools, I would just say to you that our approach to school education is many things, but the first is that we believe that every Australian should support well-resourced public schools through their hard-earned taxes, but having done that, if Australians, whether they be through their own hard work and sacrifice, well-off, or whether they be not, that they will receive both political and financial support, should they choose to send their child to a Catholic or an independent school.

It is extremely important that we never lose sight of the ideal that every child should be able to be sent by their parents to the school which they believe best meets the educational aspirations they have for their children. You should also know, and not that this audience would need reminding, that there are 1.1 million children in this country in Catholic and independent schools and every single one of them receives less money for their education, less public money than if they attended a government state school. For every dollar that's invested in a child, a public dollar invested in a child in a government state school, there is somewhere between 13c and 70c invested in a child that attends a Catholic or Independent school. They all get less, but they all get something.

Now one of the other problems that we continually face year after year, is that we, the Federal government, are minority funders of public state schools. We provide about fifteen percent of their funding, increasing our funding according to the cost of running a state school and educating a child. And this year we increased our funding by 8 percent across the board. The states and territories between them increased the funding to their state schools by less than 4 per cent. Had they increased their funds at the same rate as did the commonwealth there would have been another $882 million dollars available to fund government state schools in this one year alone.

What we have done for the first time as a government is put conditions on school funding. Instead of handing over $33 billion to the states and the non-government sector, and essentially saying "In

God we trust" you go and do what you think is appropriate. We have said we will drive national consistency and we will lift standards. So there will be a national common starting age in schooling in 2010. All states and territories will be required to test our children in years 3, 5, 7 and 9 in literacy and numeracy against national benchmarks and report to parents.

They will also be required to ensure that principals have a say over who actually teaches in the school. Imagine running a business where some government bureau sends ten staff and says "take them, they're all terrific". That unfortunately is how school education is delivered in most parts of the country, with the exception of Victoria and SA, thanks to previous Liberal state governments.

They will also be required to publish the median year 10 and 12 results for qualifications of teachers. The participation by teachers in their ongoing professional learning and how much money is spent on it at the school level. They will also be required to publish teacher attendance, not one but two state ministers, said to me seriously, what has a teacher attending school got to do with the education of children. They will also have to publish the student attendance rates and one of the other things we are also requiring, apart from flying the Australian flag, for which I make no apology is that they will have to deliver plain language report cards to parents.

The average parent in Australia is sick and tired of getting school report cards at home which describe progress of their children as being almost achieving, achieving, competent sometimes, not yet, needs attention. I mean what on earth does that mean? And do you know that the parents who have been strongest on this to me, who in some cases, particularly at Brewarrina in Western NSW, in tears, said to me, I do not understand at the age of twelve my son cannot read, but the reports have been fine. So now as a condition of funding, schools will be required to report plain language [grades] A, B, C, D or E.

In addition to that, how does my child compare to the other children in the class. So in other words, which quartile of the class, does my child fall in? Someone needs to be in the bottom 25 percent, but if my son is in the bottom 25 percent I want to know about it. He is more likely to be there because he's got a problem, so we are requiring that the schools for the first time will be required to meet those things and a number of others as conditions of funding.

In training, in a practical sense, apart from the Prime Minister and the rest of us using the privilege of leadership to challenge Australian attitudes to apprenticeships and training. I've got two kids that are doing them by the way, so I am working on the home front. What we are doing in a practical sense, is firstly, we are establishing 24 technical colleges throughout the country. This is not to replace or to duplicate TAFE at all, but we made a mistake a generation ago when the technical schools were closed down and we've paid a heavy price for it.

Belatedly we've introduced vocational training into school programmes and we have got about 40 percent of our secondary kids doing them. But we want an unashamed centre of excellence only for years 11 and 12 students that is presented to them as a model of excellence, that is presented to them as a choice that is of no lesser value than the university or the TAFE route. And there will be about 7 500 school-based apprentices in these technical colleges at any one time.

But the agenda isn't just about dealing with the skills shortage, it is also about demonstrating to public education that it's future is going to rely increasingly on devolving money and autonomy from centralised bureaucracies to the school level, so that technical colleges will be run, if you like, like non-government schools, where they hire and fire their own principal. The chair will in most cases be a local industry person and teachers will be recruited and retained on a performance basis. We cannot in this century expect a culture of excellence so long as the most mediocre, disengaged, disillusioned teacher in the country is paid exactly the same as the one that is in early, home late, on the phone to parents and constantly doing and updating courses. And so there are four objectives for the technical colleges.

And in addition to that, we are offering toolboxes and scholarships to apprentices. I have distributed a lot of your money to our most outstanding students going to university and it occurred to me 18 months ago, if you can give scholarships to kids going to uni, why can't we give them to kids doing apprenticeships? And for the first time, we are, at the cost of $400 million, giving apprentices access to welfare payments, youth allowance, Austudy and other things which they would be eligible for if they attended university. We are driving industry-led training, which is one of the reasons we are folding up the Australian National Training Authority and we are bringing it into our Department because there are three things we have to do.

We have got to make sure training is industry-led, it doesn't matter how good a TAFE or private provider is, if the young person leaves with skills that are inappropriate to the needs of industry, we have set them and our country up for failure. The second thing that we are demanding is that there be user-choice, and I am not talking about drugs here, I am talking about employers being able to choose to use the TAFE, or alternatively, a private provider that meets the needs they have and requiring the states to use their money and ours to make it available to private providers as much as to TAFEs.

And the other thing is national consistency. Why on earth is it, you can train to be a hairdresser in the State of Victoria and the following the week, be cutting hair in Milan or London, but you cannot cut it in NSW. Why is it that a carpenter can come to the Hyatt and repair damage that might be done, but if the same person goes to Queanbeyan, they have to go through two more occupational licensing programmes before they can cut a piece of wood. Those things and industrial relations reform which in no small way militates against us getting more apprentices into traditional trades are the things that we are trying to address …

Suffice to say with universities, we are putting $11billion more of your money into the universities over the next ten years. We have moved them to a performance-based funding basis, with some resistance as you can imagine. We have increased the government-supported HECS places by 39 000 over the next four years. We have made HECS-style loans available for the first time for students who pay their own way through public and private universities, and now the key reforms we are driving are to make sure that there is good industrial relations reform in the University sector.

We believe that every person is entitled to join a Union and be represented by it, but especially in the university sector, they should be free to negotiate their own working arrangements, to not have the Union involved unless they request it, and most importantly, I have got to say it is the 21st century. It is time that students who want to get an education will not be forced to pay for something else on the way through the university gate. We are determined to drive voluntary membership of student unions, guilds and associations. I am happy to answer questions from any of you that may have concerns in that regard.

And the other point that has got to be made, is we have put a lot of effort, diplomatic and financial effort into internationalising education. As I mentioned, we earn more from it than wheat and wool, but it not just about economic development. The entire basis of our political, cultural and economic relationship with the rest of the world is going to be built in education. The most important struggles in this world are fundamentalist intolerance, ignorance, and all the things that drive it, and prejudicial attitudes that are founded in it. The most effective weapon we have against all of that is education.

Suspension of Standing and Sessional Orders (Aged Pension), 15 September 2008

> Speaking in the Parliament, Dr Nelson notes the difficulties facing Australian pensioners. He contrasts the "enormous amount of reforms" to assist pensioners in the Howard government with the Labor government's inaction and "complete disregard" for these Australians. He calls for an immediate increase in the base rate of the age pension.

Under the previous Coalition government, Australian pensioners received on average, for each of the 11 years, a two percent real increase in the pension above and beyond inflation. The indexation of the pension was matched to a minimum of male average total weekly earnings or the consumer price index. A 30 percent private health insurance rebate was introduced. There were changes to the tapering rate to allow and encourage pensioners to earn a little bit more income. A utilities allowance was introduced. A lump sum payment annually was introduced. An enormous amount of reforms were introduced to assist the plight of Australian pensioners.

A report which we know that the Prime Minister received prior to the budget this year confirmed, amongst other things, that in the 10 years to 2007, under the previous government, there was an increase in the financial position for people surviving on the age pension of 19 percent for singles and 19.4 percent for couples. In other words, through a long period of economic growth and economic certainty, when this country was governed by a government that actually made decisions, a Coalition government, Australian pensioners and Australians generally had certainty in relation to their position and their economic future.

In 2007 the then Leader of the Opposition, now the Prime Minister, went around Australia and said a lot of things to Australians. He led them to believe that he would do something about petrol. He led them to believe that he would do something about cost-of-living pressures. He led the pensioners of this country to believe that he would do something about groceries. He led all Australians to believe that in some way he would make things better. Well, less than a year since he came to office, Australians are worse off today than they were under the Coalition. And there is no group that is worse off in this country than those living on fixed incomes and, in particular, single age pensioners surviving on $273 a week. In the past week the Prime Minister and six of his frontbench ministers have said that they could not live on $273 a week. They have said they could not do it, and yet they demand that close to 900,000 Australians – full and part pensioners, trying to survive on $273 a week – do exactly that …

So the Australian pensioners sat down to their processed sausages and jam sandwiches for dinner and watched the budget to find out what was going to happen to pensioners in the budget. They watched the budget speech from the Treasurer – that nervous bloke that is in charge of our $1.1 trillion economy – and waited to find out what was going to be delivered for them. In a 30-minute speech on the budget, the word 'pensioner' appeared once. Once in 30 minutes, the Treasurer mentioned the word 'pensioner'. But thanks to *The Hollowmen*, that ABC documentary about the Prime Minister's office, the term 'working families' appeared, in contrast, 12 times – 12 times for 'working families', once for 'pensioners'.

It is important that the Prime Minister appreciates just how desperate the situation is for Australian pensioners. This is a Prime Minister who next week is not going to be in Australia. He is not going to be in the Australian parliament. He is going to visit his 16th country since he has been the Prime Minister. So at the same time that this parliament will be debating the issues of Australian pensioners trying to live on $273 a week – not $273 an hour – the Prime Minister of the country is going to go to the United Nations. He has got a plan for the world, he has got a plan for Asia, but he has got no plan for Australia and no plan to do anything other than wait for a committee to tell him what he has got to do for Australian pensioners.

The Prime Minister needs to understand something, and that is: to live on $273 a week under a Rudd Labor government is the most distressing and hardest thing that close to 900,000 Australians are doing. I have received, for example, an email today from a lady in Woodcroft, South Australia, who says:

> *I am appalled at Kevin Rudd and Wayne Swan's response to suggestions for an immediate increase for single pensioners. Does this not indicate a complete disregard and lack of understanding for the plight of pensioners or is it simply a contempt for a section of the Australian community that are unable to give Kevin Rudd the global kudos he appears to crave? I have to go to the supermarket to buy packets of toilet rolls, bread and a can of Homebrand baked beans plus any visits I might have to make to my local GP.*

Prime Minister, that is the reality for Australia's pensioners – baked beans and jam sandwiches. That is what they are living on when you are at the United Nations General Assembly and the parliament sits at the cost of $1 million a day.

It is time that the government made a decision, instead of having a committee to organise a committee to tell you what to do. Prime Minister, these are the men and women who have made this country what it is. It is their sacrifices that gave our generation what we have. They did not buy something until they had saved up for it. They thought their responsibilities to one another and their country were more important than their rights. They thought that values were more important than the value of things. Thanks to the previous Coalition government, the Labor government sit on a $22 billion surplus while Australian pensioners live on baked beans and jam sandwiches.

Prime Minister, the whole idea of being the Prime Minister is to make decisions in the interests of Australia. The pensioners of this country are diminished. You are diminished. Your government is diminished. You have demeaned our country by not delivering an immediate increase in the single base rate of age pension. It is disgraceful.

Science Diplomacy: *The Curious Country*, Canberra: ANU Press, 2013

Dr Nelson discusses the importance of "science diplomacy" to allow scientific collaborations between nations in order to plan and address common challenges.

The Jesuits taught me that four virtues are essential to a 'successful' life. Unsurprisingly perhaps, the first was compassion.

Beyond the spiritual and humane, it's held me in good stead. In a practical sense it has meant to try and understand how others think, to always ask myself how the person with whom I am dealing thinks and formulates his or her world view. Knowing what others think is one thing, understanding how they think is quite another.

Graeme Davison, in *The Use and Abuse of History*, similarly observed that ethical and responsible citizenship relies on each of us being imbued with the imaginative capacity to see the world through the eyes of others.

As a non-professional diplomat arriving in Brussels early in 2010, it also seemed a sound basis for diplomacy. The European Union, to which I was accredited, had just published its EU2020 vision. Its stated ambition was for a "Smart, Sustainable and Inclusive Europe". One of the seven ways of achieving this was to lift EU investment in research and development to 3 percent of GDP.

I have found in life that when fronting for a meeting, it's helpful to have something on the agenda that is also on the other party's agenda. As I thought about the fifteen minutes I would have firstly with the President of the European Commission and then the President of the European Council, I asked myself how Australia might advance its own interests by also helping the Europeans meet theirs.

Research co-operation seemed an obvious area for discussion.

At the time, we were also contemplating our bid for the next-generation radio telescope, the Square Kilometre Array (SKA). As Australia's relationship with the EU had historically been framed by us narrowly around conflict in agriculture and market access, I was anxious to broaden the engagement into different areas. Simply saying to the bloc's leaders that Australia should be awarded the SKA on the basis of its scientific research quality, seemed likely to have negligible impact.

We needed to position ourselves as being helpful to Europe in the field of science and in doing so demonstrate the strength of Australia's research output.

So, when meeting President Barroso to present credentials to the European Commission, I went with four issues. He listened carefully to the first three with the polite, interested air of a seasoned politician with a busy day ahead.

Then I got to science.

I told him I had noted the ambition set out in the EU2020 agenda. Whilst agreeing that was one of the key levers the European nation states could pull in order to lift themselves from the economic crisis engulfing them, it was unlikely to be achieved. A number of finance ministers were already publicly stating they could not – and would not – invest more money in research.

I went on to explain that Australia produced 3 percent of the world's intellectual output. In some disciplines it's much higher. I reminded him of our Nobel Prize winners, members of the Royal Society and citation rates amongst other things. I told him we realised, however, that to go further we needed to substantially lift our levels of international collaboration. Further to this, if the EU was to get anywhere near its 3 percent target, one key device for doing so would also be collaboration.

I had his attention.

I proposed that what Australia and the EU could do would be to pool some of our research money in support of joint projects. This could be at both the researcher and institutional level. The specific projects to be funded would be selected on a peer reviewed basis by our respective scientific communities. But what we could do jointly would be to nominate areas for joint research collaboration. I proposed water resource management, agricultural productivity, energy efficiency, renewable energy and human adaptation to new and emerging technologies by way of examples.

I pointed out to President Barroso that if such a model was developed and implemented it would not only deepen co-operation between my country and the EU, it would leverage up our respective research spend. I told him that whilst Australia's research budget was small in comparison, such a model applied to similar 'like-minded' countries, had the potential to be a 'win-win'.

He got it, telling me with some enthusiasm that he saw considerable potential in this idea.

He said I must see the EU commissioner for research, Marie Geoghagan-Quinn.

Given the EU nations produce 38 percent of the world's scientific papers and the European Commission has a budget for research and innovation exceeding 120 billion euros, the potential for Australia was, and remains, significant. Collaborations between Australian and EU scientists exceed those with the US.

When I de-briefed staff at the Australian embassy on my meeting and discussion, Dr Martin Gallagher, our then indefatigable science counsellor said, "Brendan, excellent science diplomacy". I presumed this was an expression thrown around in the science community as part of the jargon used in his world. It was not something I had heard before, even though as science minister in the last decade I had discussed scientific co-operation with my counterparts in a number of countries.

I have since discovered that is far from the case.

Prime Minister Gillard came to Brussels only several months later and similarly raised and discussed research co-operation with her two key EU interlocutors. The conversation continued when Barroso visited Australia the following year. It was certainly a change from the traditional confrontational nature of dialogue we had experienced in the past, lambasting the Europeans for agriculture and trade policies.

From this early, positive engagement we were able to build a relationship with the EU that was much more constructive. The multiplier effect for increased co-operation in education was an early, positive impact. So too, as the EU established its own diplomatic service with the European External Action Service, Australia's relationship reached further into foreign affairs and security.

Similarly, in overseas development assistance, environment, climate change, economic issues and the G20 agenda, I endeavoured to shape our overarching engagement around areas where we might advance a common interest. That interest, wherever possible, would be evidence and research based.

I've since learned that science diplomacy is basically the use of scientific collaborations between and among nations that seeks to meet common challenges. If skilfully applied it becomes the foundation for constructive international partnerships.

The Obama administration has been particularly enamoured with Joseph Nye's "Soft Power" as described in his 1990 book *Bound to Lead: The Changing Nature of American Power*. Greater investments by the US in areas such as science diplomacy are regarded as essential to complement its economic and military power.

President Obama's 2009 "New Beginning" speech in Cairo, in which he sought to reach out to the Muslim world, argued for a greater engagement by the United States through science, technology and innovation. He saw the linking of scientists as a basis for common understanding.

The world has undergone a major transformation in less than a decade, the scale of which is not well appreciated by most Australians. The political and economic power shifting from North America and Europe to the Asia-Pacific over the past twenty years was rapidly accelerated by the Global Financial Crisis and the world's response to it.

China's re-emergence and the critical shape of the template for its relationship with the US are critical to our future. As Henry Kissinger observed, the template for that relationship is being forged now in our region. It is into this global and regional environment that science diplomacy can and should, play a pivotal role.

As China rapidly accelerates its investment in research and relentlessly drives the transformation of a handful of its leading universities, the scientists within them will largely shape the direction in which the nation goes. Its challenges – economic, environmental, agricultural, health, social and diplomatic – will all require guidance from science. Researchers in humanities and social sciences will be no less important in this regard. Australia has skilfully managed its relationship with China, balancing our economic needs with concern for human rights and rule of law. We have a programme for research cooperation, but there is much more we could do to deepen the ties between men and women whose passion is knowledge. Similarly, those Australian companies that join our political leaders in their visits to countries such as China are themselves, to varying degrees, conduits for science diplomacy where new knowledge is the basis for wealth creation. Whilst the East Asia Summit, now including the US and Russia, traverses security issues, its agenda is largely in areas where Australian scientists, working with their counterparts, can collaboratively inform reasoned decision-making in key areas ranging from climate change to food production.

Neither the Australia nor the US has fulfilled their respective, considerable potential in science diplomacy. We should. Our future depends on it; whether it's the West reaching out to the Islamic world or it's deepening stable multilateral integration in the Asia Pacific.

The other three Jesuit values for success – commitment, conscience and courage – will all need to be applied to this task. It also requires sustained, whole of government political will and resources.

4. Indigenous Affairs

Neville Bonner Tribute, 31 May 2000

Speaking in 2000, Dr Nelson acknowledges the courage and compassion that Neville Bonner embodied throughout his life, despite being subject to "extraordinary adversity".

A few special Australians have burrowed into our hearts over the course of the twentieth century. Foremost amongst them is Neville Bonner. His life is a study of not only courage, conscience and compassion in the face of extraordinary adversity, it is also one of personal and national reconciliation … Neville attracted at times the hurtful criticism of those whom he sought to represent and a society that yielded so slowly to a vision we might now describe as reconciliation. But he never lost sight of his goal – the fair and just treatment of his fellow human beings irrespective of race, geographic location, socio-economic background or political affiliation.

His mother, Julia Rebecca Bell, was a Jagera woman. Neville's non-indigenous father absconded shortly after his birth under a palm tree on Ukerebagh Island in the mouth of the Tweed River, south of the Queensland border. Although his parents were married, his birth certificate was marked 'illegitimate'.

He grew up in a humpy and under a hollow carved by his Aboriginal grandfather on the banks of the Richmond River. Destitute, his mother took alcohol fuelled beatings from her partner in the presence of Neville, other children and his grandfather. His mother made clothes for him from rags to attend the school in Lismore. He lasted only days when the parents of non-indigenous children boycotted in protest of the Aboriginal boy.

After his mother's death when he was nine, his Aboriginal grandparents, Ida and Roger Bell assumed responsibility for raising him and his brother.

"I owe a lot to my grandmother", Neville would say toward the end of his life. It was she who insisted he go to school when he was fourteen. In response to the young boy protesting this, she said

"Neville, if you learned to read and write, express yourself well and treat people with decency and courtesy, it would take you a long way". It did. In Queensland, he spent one year at the Beaudesert State School completing two grades in a year.

He worked as a ringer and a stockman, cleared scrub and tried unsuccessfully to enlist for World War Two, rejected for having had a broken wrist. He met and married his first wife, Mona at Palm Island where he surrendered his own freedom to the Superintendent. Here he nurtured his leadership skills, rising to Assistant Settlement Overseer responsible for a workforce of 250 men. The Bonner family returned to the mainland after 16 years in 1960. He worked on a dairy farm, meat works and then as a bridge carpenter … Mona and Neville separated and several years later she died.

His interest in politics was piqued by the 1967 referendum which sought to give the Commonwealth the power to pass laws in relation to indigenous Australians and to count them in the census … He nominated for Liberal Party selection to fill a casual Senate vacancy in 1971. To the members of the Liberal Party, he said in part, "In my experience of this world, there are two qualities of which we are always in greater need – human compassion and understanding." He turned and wept when candidates returned to the room and were told he had won on the first ballot.

Only two Aborigines sat in the gallery when he delivered his maiden speech. He summarised then what would drive him: "I have graduated through the University of Hard Knocks. My teacher was experience. However, I shall play the role, which my state of Queensland, my race, my background, my political beliefs, my knowledge of men and circumstances dictate. This I shall do through the grace of God, to the benefit of all Australians."

In 1972 he married Heather, his personal secretary, an event he would describe as "One of the greatest blessings God has ever given me in bringing us together".

Neville was an advocate in the Liberal Party for Aboriginal land rights but also criticised some non-indigenous people for "encouraging' the impatience of young, militant Aborigines. Throughout his tenure in the Senate, he was patronised, enduring racism and condescension … but whether it was such incidents or losing the coveted winnable position on his party's ticket for the 1983 election, he was never consumed by bitterness. Instead, his was a life of grace, humility and gentility acknowledged in part by appointment in 1979 as Australian of the Year.

Asked by his biographer, Angela Burger in 1979 whether he was a "Senator for blacks or whites?", he replied: "My responsibilities are first to God Almighty, secondly to my nation, thirdly to my State, fourthly to my party, and entwined through it all, my love for my race."

In 1992, Robyn Hughes asked him to nominate his greatest achievement in Canberra, to which he said: "It is that I was there. They no longer spoke of boongs and blacks, they spoke instead of Aboriginal people."

When this country is finally reconciled with its indigenous people, a special place will be accorded to an early pioneer, Neville Bonner, his party and the democratic institutions that enabled him to serve in the Australian senate.

Apology to Australia's Indigenous People, 13 February 2008

> Speaking to the Australian Parliament in 2008, Dr Nelson offers a formal apology to the Aboriginal people, to those who were forcibly removed from their families and communities, and asks Australian to pause and reflect on this past. He honours those who in the past have suffered, and who have made sacrifices, and expresses his hope for a future "as one people".

Mr Speaker, members of this the 42nd Parliament of Australia, visitors and all Australians, in rising to speak strongly in support of this motion I recognise the Ngunnawal, first peoples of this Canberra land.

Today our nation crosses a threshold. We formally offer an apology. We say sorry to those Aboriginal people forcibly removed from their families through the first seven decades of the 20th century. In doing so, we reach from within ourselves to our past, those whose lives connect us to it, and in deep understanding of its importance to our future. We will be at our best today and every day if we pause to place ourselves in the shoes of others, imbued with the imaginative capacity to see this issue through their eyes with decency and respect.

This chapter in our nation's history is emblematic of much of the relationship between Indigenous and non-Indigenous Australians from the arrival of the First Fleet in 1788. It is one of two cultures: one ancient, proud and celebrating its deep bond with this land for some 60,000 years; the other, no less proud, arrived here with little more than visionary hope, deeply rooted in gritty determination to build an Australian nation for not only its early settlers and Indigenous peoples but also those who would increasingly come from all parts of the world.

Whether Australian by birth or immigration, each one of us as Australians has a duty to understand and respect what has been done in our name. In most cases we do so with great pride, but in others it is with shame. In brutally harsh conditions, from the small number of early British settlers, our non-Indigenous ancestors have given us a nation the envy of any in the world. But Aboriginal Australians made involuntary sacrifices, different but no less important, to make possible the economic and social development of our country today. None of this was easy. We cannot, from the comfort of the 21st century, begin to imagine what they overcame – Indigenous and non-Indigenous – to give us what we have and make us who we are. We do know, though, that language, disease, ignorance, good intentions, basic human prejudices and a cultural and technological chasm combined to deliver a harshness exceeded only by the land over which each sought to prevail.

And as our young nation celebrated its Federation, formality emerged in arrangements and laws that would govern the lives of Aboriginal and Torres Strait Islander people. The new nation's Constitution, though, would not allow for the counting of 'natives' or for the Commonwealth to pass laws in relation to Aborigines. Protection boards and reserves were established. Aborigines in some jurisdictions were excluded from public schools, episodic violence in race relations continued, assimilation underwrote emerging policies and churches heeded their Christian doctrine to reach out to people whom they saw in desperate need. Though disputed in motive and detail and with varying recollections of events by others, the removal of Aboriginal children began. In some cases, government policies evolved from the belief that the Aboriginal race would not survive and should be assimilated; in others, the conviction was that 'half-caste' children in particular should, for their own protection, be removed to government and church run institutions where conditions reflected the standards of the day. Others were placed with white families whose kindness motivated them to the belief that rescued children deserved a better life.

Our responsibility, every one of us, is to understand what happened here, why it happened and the impact it had on not only those who were removed but also those who did the removing and supported it. Our generation does not own these actions, nor should it feel guilt for what was done in many, but certainly not all, cases with the best of intentions. But in saying we are sorry, and deeply so, we remind ourselves that each generation lives in ignorance of the long-term consequences of its decisions and actions. Even when motivated by inherent humanity and decency to reach out to the dispossessed in extreme adversity, our actions can have unintended outcomes. As such, many decent Australians are hurt by accusations of theft in relation to their good intentions.

The stories are well documented, and I thank the Prime Minister for reminding us of Nanna Nungala Fejo's experience. I will repeat two stories. The first is from a submission given to the Human Rights and Equal Opportunity Commission inquiry, and I quote:

> *I was at the post office with my Mum and Auntie [and cousin]. They put us in the police ute and said they were taking us to Broome. They put the mums in there as well. But when we'd gone [about ten miles] they stopped, and threw the mothers out of the car. We jumped on our mothers' backs, crying, trying not to be left behind. But the policemen pulled us off and threw us back in the car. They pushed the mothers away and drove off, while our mothers were chasing the car, running and crying after us. We were screaming in the back of that car. When we got to Broome they put me and my cousin in the Broome lockup. We were only ten years old. We were in the lockup for two days waiting for the boat to Perth.*

In his black oral history, *The Wailing*, which I commend to every Australian, Stuart Rintoul recalls the thin pain of an Aboriginal woman from Walgett:

> *Something else that never left my mind, my memory, was of a family of children being taken away and this little girl, she must have been about the same age as myself, I suppose she might have been about six. But I can still see that little person on the*

back of the mission truck with a little rag hat on, and she went away and we never seen her any more. She was crying. Everyone was crying. Things like that never leave your memory.

It is reasonably argued that removal from squalor led to better lives: children fed, housed and educated for an adult world which they could not have imagined. However, from my life as a family doctor and knowing the impact of my own father's removal from his unmarried, teenage mother, I know that not knowing who you are is the source of deep, scarring sorrows, the real meaning of which can be known only to those who have endured it.

No-one should bring a sense of moral superiority to this debate in seeking to diminish the view that good in many cases was sought to be done. This is a complex issue. Faye Lyman's life is one of the *Many Voices* oral history at the National Library of Australia. Faye left her father when she was eight. She said this:

Personally, I don't want people to say, "I'm sorry Faye", I just want them to understand.

It was very hurtful to leave Dad. Oh, it broke my heart. Dad said to me, "It's hard for Daddy and the authorities won't let you stay with me in a tent on the river bank. You're a little girl and you need someone to look after you." I remember him telling us that, and I cried. I said 'No, but Dad, you look after us.' … But they kept telling us it wasn't the right thing.

She went on:

I don't want people to say sorry. I just want them to understand the hurt, what happened when we were initially separated, and just understand the society, what they have done … You don't belong in either world. I can't explain it. It hurts so much.

There is no compensation fund for this – nor should there be. How can any sum of money replace a life deprived of knowing your family? Separation was then, and remains today, a painful but necessary part of public policy in the protection of children. Our restitution for this lies in our determination to address today's injustices, learning from what was done and doing everything we can to heal those who suffered. The period within which these events occurred was one that defined and shaped Australia. The governments that oversaw this and those who elected them emerged from federating the nation to a century characterised for Australia as triumph in the face of extraordinary adversities unknown to our generation.

In offering this apology, let us not in our language and actions create one injustice in our attempt to address another. Let no-one forget that they sent their sons to war, shaping our identity and place in the world. One hundred thousand Australians in two wars alone gave their lives in our name and our uniform, lying forever in distant lands, silent witnesses to the future that they have given us. Aboriginal and non-Aboriginal Australians lie alongside one another. These generations considered their responsibilities to their country and one another more important than their rights. They did not buy something until they had saved up for it, and values were far more important than value. Living in considerably more difficult times, they had dreams for our nation but little money. Theirs was a mesh of values enshrined in God, King and country and the belief in something greater than yourself. Neglectful indifference to all that they have achieved while seeing their actions in the separations only, through the values of our comfortable, modern Australia, will be to diminish ourselves.

Today our nation pauses to reflect on this chapter of relations between Aboriginal and non-Aboriginal Australia. In doing so, however, given that there are so many Australians who, perhaps unusually today, are focused on Aboriginal issues, spare a thought for the real, immediate, seemingly intractable and disgraceful circumstances in which many Indigenous Australians find themselves today. As we meet and speak in this parliament, Aboriginal Australians continue to die long before the rest of us. Alcohol, welfare without responsibilities, isolation from the economic mainstream, corrupt management of resources, nepotism, political buck passing between governments with divided responsibilities, lack of home ownership, underpolicing, intolerance by authorities and neglect and abuse of children that violates all for which we stand all combine to see too many Aboriginal and Torres Strait Islander people living lives of existential aimlessness.

Indigenous life expectancy is still stubbornly 17 years less than for non-Indigenous Australians. An Aboriginal baby born while we speak still has only a one in three chance of seeing the age of 65. Diabetes, kidney disease, hospitalisation of women from assault, imprisonment, overcrowding in housing, educational underperformance and unemployment remain appallingly high, despite gains in some areas over the past decade. Annual Indigenous-specific spending by the Commonwealth has reached $3.5 billion a year, plus half a billion dollars this year on the Northern Territory intervention.

The sexual abuse of Aboriginal children was found in every one of the 45 Northern Territory communities surveyed for the *Little children are sacred* report. It was the straw that broke the camel's back, driving the Howard government's decision to intervene with a suite of dramatically radical welfare, health and policing initiatives. I cannot imagine the strength upon which she drew, but the Alice Springs Crown Prosecutor, Nanette Rogers, with great courage, revealed to the nation in 2006 the case of a four-year-old girl drowned while being raped by a teenager who had been sniffing petrol. She told us of the two children, one a baby, sexually assaulted by two men while their mothers were drinking alcohol. Another baby was stabbed by a man trying to kill her mother. So too a 10-year-old girl was gang-raped in Aurukun, the offenders going free, barely punished. A boy was raped in another community by other children. Is this not an emergency, the most disturbing part of it being its endemic nature and Australia's apparent desensitisation to it? Yet governments responsible for delivering services and security have resisted elements of a Northern Territory style intervention.

I ask the Prime Minister to report to this parliament regularly on what his government is doing to save this generation of Aboriginal Australians from these appalling conditions. I also offer on behalf of the opposition my unconditional support to participate in the commission for policy which he proposes. This is far, far more important than any of the things that would normally divide us as a nation in philosophy and politics.

Our generation has over 35 years overseen a system of welfare, alcohol delivery, administration of programs, episodic preoccupation with symbolism and, at times, even excusing the inexcusable in the name of cultural sensitivity, to create what we now see in remote Aboriginal Australia. With good intentions, perhaps like earlier generations, we have under successive governments created lives, in many cases, of misery for which we might apologise. I certainly do. The best way we can show it is to act, and to act now. I challenge anyone who thinks Aboriginal people get a good deal to come to any of these communities and tell me you wish you had been born there.

The first Aboriginal Australian who came to this parliament was Neville Bonner. A Yagara man abandoned by his non-Aboriginal father before his birth on Ukerebagh Island in the mouth of the Tweed River, Neville was born into a life of hardship known only to some who are here today as visitors. He grew up in a hollow that had been carved by his grandfather under lantana bushes. The year before his mother's death when he was nine, she sent him to a school near Lismore. He lasted two days before the non-Aboriginal people forced his exclusion.

It was to his grandmother Ida he attributed his final success. Arguing that at 14 the boy must go to school, she had said to him: "Neville, if you learn to read and write, express yourself well and treat people with decency and courtesy, it will take you a long way", and it did. Through a life as a scrub clearer, a ringer, a stockman, a bridge carpenter and 11 years on Palm Island, it brought him to this parliament in 1971, as the events of this motion were nearing an end. He said in prophetic words to the Liberal Party members who selected him: "In my experience of this world, two qualities are always in greater need – human understanding and compassion."

When he was asked by Robin Hughes in 1992 to reflect on his life, Neville observed that the unjust hardships he had endured "can only be changed when people of non-Aboriginal extraction are prepared to listen, to hear what Aboriginal people are saying, and then work with us to achieve those ends". Asked to nominate his greatest achievement, he replied: "It is that I was there. They no longer spoke of boongs or blacks. They spoke instead of Aboriginal people."

Today is about "being there" as a nation and as individual Australians. It is about Neville Bonner's understanding of one another and the compassion that shaped his life in literally reaching out to those whom he considered had suffered more than him. We honour those in our past who have suffered – many of whom are here today – and all who have made sacrifices for us by the way we live our lives and shape our nation. Today we recommit to do so – as one people. We are sorry.

For our Country Dedication, 28 March 2019

> Speaking at this Memorial, Dr Nelson shares his vision that there "should be a special place afforded to the first Australians".

Before I begin, I firstly want to say that just over three years ago we conceived the idea of this Memorial, this tribute to Aboriginal and Torres Strait Islander service to our nation Australia over 120 years.

As is always the case, the idea is a lot easier than the money. With all of the sculptures that we conceive and are able to place on these grounds we have to raise the money. The Australian War Memorial of course committed initial funds for it, but what you see before you has been delivered as a result of the generosity of Mr Kerry Stokes AC, the Drummond Foundation and the Bruce Rivers Ellis bequest. The Department of Defence and the Department of Veterans Affairs both agreed to my request that we contribute $265 000 from money that we had saved from the Spirit of the Anzacs centenary exhibition.

But I also want to say, that having just conceived the idea of the Memorial, I was explaining it to the Indigenous Affairs Minister, Senator the Honourable Nigel Scullion. He asked me how much it was likely to cost. Having listened, he said, "okay, we'll give you $225 000". He said we'll shake hands on that, and that's exactly what he and the Department of Prime Minister and Cabinet have done.

So to those that have contributed, and that's all Australians through our government and the individuals, I say thank you.

The most important year in this continent, this nation's history, is by any standard 1788.

The British first fleet arrived. Captain Arthur Phillip, eleven small ships on 26 January 1788. George III's instructions to Phillip were to apply "maximum beneficence to the natives", as they were then described. That event devastated – simply devastated, millennia of rich Aboriginal history, culture and custodianship.

But from that event and everything that would follow, the origins of the Australia we now are, and the people we have now become. Inevitably and tragically, over more than a century, in the process of dispossession, violence and brutality was perpetrated against the first peoples, by pastoralists, police, and at times mounted Aboriginal militia.

Yet only four or five generations after that, with all that they had endured, they then denied their Aboriginality, denied their kinship and families to enlist, serve, fight, suffer and die for the young nation that had taken so much from them. They were often enlisting alongside the sons of those who had perpetrated violence against their own families.

They then gave their all, and in many cases – their lives for us, for Australia.

Enlisting from a society and an Australia of desperate inequality, they found for the very first time ever, equal treatment in the Australian Imperial Force.

Charles Mene was born on Mabuiag Island in the Torres Strait. On 1 June 1944 serving in the 2/33 Battalion, he was reported in the *Tribune* newspaper here in Australia, speaking from New Guinea.

He said,

> *I know that I am fighting for a new world in which my people will get a better deal. I want to come back to an Australia where my people will have full rights as citizens; to an Australia where Aboriginal children will have the right to education, to work, and to a healthy, happy life.*

That man served and fought in Syria, the Kokoda Trail, Shaggy Ridge, Gona, Balikpapan, then the British Commonwealth and Occupational Forces. He fought with 1RAR in Korea, was awarded the Military Medal, and then served in the Malayan Emergency.

And over the 22 years of his service, not a thing changed, not a damned thing.

This Australian War Memorial was conceived in the bloodbath of Pozieres in July and August 1916. Charles Bean, the First World War official historian, witnessed 23,000 Australian casualties over 6 weeks.

One of them was Harry Thorpe MM (Military Medal) from the Lake Tyers Mission in Lakes Entrance Western Victoria. Thanks to the Commonwealth War Graves Commission, his headstone is displayed in the galleries here at the Australian War Memorial.

A mortally wounded Australian asked of Bean, "Will they remember me in Australia?" Bean subsequently conceived and resolved that at war's end he would build this, the finest museum and memorial to these men of the AIF and to the nurses.

This is a unifying institution in a nation that at times – including today, one would be forgiven for thinking is not so unified. But here there is no party politics, there's no religion, everyone is equal in death, no rank, no military honours, no race.

But we say to Australians, and to our political leadership, from this unifying institution, within that framework of equality, we can demonstrate to Australians that there is, can and should be a special place afforded to the first Australians, of which For Our Country is but one of practical demonstration to the nation.

Graeme Davison in the *Use and Abuse of Australian History* wrote that,

> *... ethical and responsible citizenship requires each one of us to be imbued with the imaginative capacity to see the world through the eyes of others.*

And through Daniel Boyd's magnificent work, when you sit behind that mirrored glass and look through those rings towards the dome of the Australian War Memorial, you will see through the eyes of Aboriginal and Torres Strait Islander Australians – the service that they have given to this country – and continue to give, wearing the uniform of the Royal Australian Navy, the Australian Army and the Royal Australian Air Force.

And in doing so, be imbued with respect for all Australians that served and especially this remarkable group of Australians.

Welcome.

The John Howard Lecture, 16 December 2021
Our National Character and Outlook – Values matter

> Presenting the John Howard Lecture in 2021, Dr Nelson expresses the importance of all Australians uniting around shared, timeless values and reconciling their differences. He also shares his practical proposal to bring together two conflicting narratives about Australian settlement, and to end the controversy surrounding Australia Day.

The John Howard lecture, the privilege bestowed on me in delivering it, is in the end about leadership.

Although there is an entire industry dedicated to it, I don't think leadership can be taught.

But it can be learned.

You don't realise what you are learning when you are learning it.

The qualities that inform leadership can be revealed through observation of, reflection upon and absorption of the leadership qualities we see in others.

The power is in the story.

At the groundbreaking for the Robert Frost Library at Amherst College in October 1963, President John F. Kennedy observed that a nation reveals itself not only by those whom it chooses to lead, but those whom it chooses to honour.

So too for a political movement.

Honouring John Howard

We gather here to honour John Howard, Australia's second longest serving Prime Minister, chosen to lead our party on three occasions. His conservative convictions lifted the Menzian vision, encompassing and respecting the philosophical legacies of both Edmund Burke and John Stuart Mill, passing them to the next generation of Liberals.

The principal motivation for John Howard's political life was reform – ideas to challenge orthodoxy, to inspire and create the future worthy of and needed by the next generation.

Some lead from position. Leader of the Party, Chairman of the board, captain of the team.

Others eschew position to pursue principle, William Wilberforce's crusade against slavery offering perhaps history's most compelling illustration.

Exceptional leaders do both.

John Howard led from both position and principle. He used the position given him by the Liberal Party and our nation to turn conviction into policy for the advancement of Australia.

Politics with purpose.

He changed the Liberal Party. Remarkably, in the 1980s, he also changed the Labor Party …

The signs of our times

The pace and scale of change is immense.

It is possible that as occurred over four decades through the late 15th century, humankind is moving to a new age as described by Yale's Professor Paul Kennedy. Though free of the world changing cataclysms of Napoleonic wars or World War Two, the transformation we are undergoing is profound.

We are living through the most consequential geopolitical realignment in our lifetime.

The institutions built after World War Two that have underwritten the global order through our lifetime are being severely tested. Some key instruments are failing the world that is, let alone the one that is coming.

Democracies of the anglosphere are increasing fractious and polarised, significant minorities, cynical and disillusioned driving a re-emergent counter-culture.

Humankind faces the existential environmental challenge of a changing climate.

A once in a century global pandemic, far from over and in which power has concentrated in the hands of health officials and medical science.

We face immense global economic uncertainty with pandemic induced disruption to global output, consumption, liquidity and supply chains. With necessarily growing debt and the need for foreign investment, Australia will rely even more on its most important economic partner, the United States and its capital markets.

So too, vast technological change along with exponentially expanding space exploration and its militarisation.

Sino-American rivalry is taking us into a world we have not lived in since the Franco-Prussian war or the Qing dynasty.

In all this, what is most important is that we be clear about who we are, in what we believe and the truths by which we live.

What is it that we believe worth fighting for – politically, diplomatically and perhaps even militarily? …

A comprehensive sense of who we are, where we want to go, why and what we will need to do to get there. Neither Robert Menzies nor John Howard ever allowed members of the Liberal Party to forget what it is in which we believe, what binds us and the constant need to look to the future …

We are Australians. We revere the idealism and heroism of the everyday Australian upon whose shoulders ultimately rests the defence of all we hold dear.

Indigenous Australia

There is a confluence of three issues.

The long overdue repatriation of Aboriginal remains to Australia from mainly British museums and what to do with them.

Calls for the recognition of violence perpetrated against Aboriginal people in dispossession and the colonisation of Australia.

A growing controversy around Australia Day being 26 January.

Aboriginal people recognised they needed a presence here. Almost 50 years ago in 1972 the Aboriginal Tent Embassy was established on the grounds in front of the first parliament. It seeks to visibly focus the nation's leadership on injustices endured by Indigenous Australians.

It is now time for Indigenous presence here to be formalised in a way that advances understanding of and respect for, the first Australians.

Decades of hard work seeking to repatriate the remains of Aboriginal people from mainly British institutions, has finally come to fruition. Taken as trophies or objects of scientific and cultural curiosity, Aboriginal remains stored in the vaults of mainly British museums are slowly being returned.

Where the origin of those remains is known, they are returned to their traditional lands. But in many cases ancestral origin is unknown. Remains already returned are stored in multiple places void of the dignity they deserve.

They are owed better than this.

The area just up from Lake Burley Griffin is known as Reconciliation Place. It lacks a presence commanding the respect its purpose deserves, obscured in the vista from both Parliament House and the War Memorial. It could be redeveloped as a dignified precinct, honouring Aboriginal custodianship, culture and history.

At its centre would be an Ossuary of major proportions. Into it would be solemnly interred the remains of Aboriginal people repatriated to Australia, centuries after they were taken.

The symbolism would be powerful.

At one end of Anzac Parade is the Unknown Australian Soldier.

At the other end before our parliament would effectively be the Tomb of the Unknown Custodians, a *Resting Place*. That is a matter for Indigenous people. Whatever the name, it must be on the centre axis with visible presence.

The precinct around the Tomb would be inlaid with granite, marble and stonework from regions right across Australia. It would tell the story of Aboriginal life, history and culture. It could list the tribes, nations and languages and feature curation in some common Indigenous languages. All of it would need English curation.

It would tell the story of Aboriginal presence from its known origins, history, culture and customs.

It would mark European arrival, what occurred with contact and what followed. It would tell dispassionately of the devastating impact of European colonisation on the first peoples and key milestones in this journey. From the beneficent, awkward relationship to dispossession and violence perpetrated. It might also present Indigenous war service for Australia. Significant Indigenous Australians might be profiled. The 1967 referendum, the 1992 Mabo High Court decision, 2008 Apology and other major milestones could be documented in our journey of Aboriginal Reconciliation.

The Ossuary, or Tomb would periodically see the ceremonial interment of repatriated remains. It would have a presence above the ground and visibility in the vista.

The entire area should have a spiritual ambience of reflection and sanctity, being the destination for pilgrims in search of knowing more of Aboriginal history and paying respect to it. A visitor welcome and interpretive centre could be established from which groups could be taken to the Tomb and precinct.

It would not impinge upon the Tent Embassy in any way, being distant from it, close to or emerging from the lake's edge.

The construction of an Ossuary, Tomb or Resting Place in such a Memorial precinct would complete the 'picture' in our nation's capital. From the Australian War Memorial or the Parliament, we would look upon and be reminded of the first peoples, their culture, sacrifices and contributions to the nation.

It would also provide a practical yet spiritual solution to the destination for repatriated remains. Having such a place would help leverage negotiations with British Institutions reluctant to return Aboriginal remains.

In the journey of Reconciliation, this would be a major step, likely to be supported by the overwhelming majority of Australians. Whatever the debate of constitutional recognition, we are a fair-minded practical 'mob'. Our reluctance to change the constitution is exceeded only by our reluctance to read it. This proposal is one I believe most Australians would 'get'.

When completed, the Commissioning event would likely be one of the most significant practical and symbolic acts of reconciliation this nation has seen.

If such a significant site were to be so developed and curated, it would also provide a national focal point and basis for a new structure for Australia Day …

A major national event could be conducted at the 'Tomb' early on 26 January.

It would reflect upon millennia of rich Indigenous history on the threshold of the arrival of the First Fleet. It would mark the last hours of undisturbed Aboriginal isolation on the cusp of upheaval beyond our modern comprehension. The ceremony would evoke a commemorative event that celebrates all this continent was, those who cared for it to sustain life and a unique culture.

It would also reflect on Indigenous endurance in the face of existential adversities.

It should be a major, nationally televised event attended by the nation's leaders, Indigenous and non-Indigenous. Its centre piece could be the ceremonial interment of remains repatriated over the preceding year.

Those events would precede a day of common celebration of who we now are; the people we have become and restate our aspirations for a common future. A celebration of Australia and Australians, Indigenous, non-Indigenous and immigrants.

The Indigenous precinct and such restructuring of Australia Day would do a great deal for the cohesion of our country around our national day.

What we have all achieved is simply remarkable, something of which we can and should be immensely proud …

Liberal philosophy and ideals

Guarded by the Menzies Research Centre, ours is a philosophy born of familiarity with the idealism, hard work and self-sacrifice of the everyday Australian. Those men and women identified by Menzies in his 1942 'Forgotten People' broadcasts whom he described as "the backbone of the nation".

Our heroes are often people who work at the most humble of occupations.

To the 18 organisations who went to Canberra in October 1944 to form the Liberal Party of Australia, Sir Robert Menzies furthered the vision to which we must remain true:

> *What we must look for is a true revival of Liberal thought, one which will work for social justice and security. True Liberals have great and imperative obligations to the weak, sick and the unfortunate … to every good citizen, the state owes not only a chance in life, but a self-respecting life.*

That other towering giant of our movement, Sir John Carrick in his 1967 *Australian Quarterly* essay wrote:

> *The true Liberal is always concerned for the welfare of the individual, for the creation of the opportunities for the preservation of human dignity, and the development of human personality.*

To young people, gratuitous advice.

Never stop believing you can make a difference. One person believing he or she can, is the only thing that ever has.

As Neville Bonner and John Howard – different men and vastly different lives, have both shown, turn setbacks, failure and pain into new goals and determination to achieve them.

Keep an open mind. Be open to new ideas and people that are different. We all have our own inherent biases and prejudices. We tend to think we are right about everything, but we aren't. The age of social media and algorithms reinforces your own prejudices in everything from politics to culture, threatening you fulfilling your own potential.

Those who close their mind set themselves up for failure.

Foremost of threats to our Liberal values is intolerance.

To listen to and respect the legitimacy of another person's point of view is but one hallmark of a true Liberal. Finding solutions to seemingly intractable problems is far more difficult and noble a task than ideological posturing and personal invective…

Nurture and protect the inner integrity of your intellect. Your ability to think, articulate ideas, to challenge and change the attitudes of others, is critically important. Make time to reflect and read. Be interested in the world and make yourself interesting to others.

Build and develop your character. Derived from the Greek word meaning the impression left in wax by a stone seal ring, the Greeks called it the stamp of personality. Informed by worthwhile intrinsic virtues or values, character transcends everything – position, rank, influence, wealth, intellect, talent and looks.

Embrace values for the world you want, not the one you think you are going to get.

You need look for them no further than the end of the Kokoda Trail. Values endure, that is why they are in granite.

Imbue yourself with the imaginative capacity to see the world through the eyes of others. Understanding how people think is more important than knowing what they think. Wise people penetrate the character of people and the circumstances in which they find themselves.

In the end, we are all remembered not for what we are, but who we are and the humanity shown to others.

In our parliamentary ranks we need those skilled in the science of politics.

But the overwhelming, aching need of the nation is for men and women of conviction, shaped by and bearing layers of life experience. When a preponderance of those representing us regard their profession as little more than a game of snakes and ladders, respect for our precious democracy is diminished as are we all …

5. Foreign Affairs, Defence and Trade

The Role of Government and Parliament in the Decision to go to War, July 2015

> Dr Nelson discusses the complexity of governments choosing to engage in war, and remarks that in his view, past Australian governments have made "the right decision" regarding "Australia's geopolitical circumstances and best interests".

Private Jake Kovco – age 33
Captain Mark Bingley – age 35
SAS Trooper Josh Porter – age 28
Trooper David 'Poppy' Pearce – age 41
SAS Sergeant Matthew Locke – age 33
Private Luke Worsley – age 26
SAS Signaller Sean McCarthy – age 25
Lance Corporal Jason Marks – age 27

These eight men died as a direct result of decisions I made, supported or administered during my tenure as Australia's Minister for Defence.

For me, those at a ministerial level with whom I served, those ministers who came before me and for those that have followed, the issues we are about to explore are anything but academic hypotheticals.

They are real. They are very real.

Those decisions, carried most heavily by prime ministers, are also ones from which enemy combatants will be killed. They, like Australia's own defence personnel, have families who love them and give meaning to their lives, whatever the misguided, distorted and perverse nature of their cause.

When Her Majesty, Queen Elizabeth II visited Australia in October 2011, I was watching the news broadcast of her visit to Canberra in my Brussels office on BBC World News.

The British journalist concluded his 'package' on the front steps of Parliament House. Looking down ANZAC Parade he said, "There is something the Australians have right. Looking from the seat of government here, in the direct line of sight is the Australian War Memorial. It reminds Australia's politicians that some of their decisions come at a very high price."

The Australian War Memorial was the vision of Charles Bean, Australia's official First World War historian. Bean landed with the Australian Imperial Force (AIF) at Gallipoli on 25 April and stayed with them – at the front, right through until the war's end …

Bean resolved that at the war's end, he would build the finest memorial and museum to the men of the AIF and nurses. He returned to Australia to convince the government to pass an Act to give effect to his idea. The men fighting and dying in France, Belgium and Sinai-Palestine would know that at war's end, they would be remembered.

The political capital of our nation resides within this, our national parliament. But the War Memorial is custodian of its soul …

Every nation has its own story. This is ours.

Much of it is embedded in the service and sacrifice of two million men and women who have worn – and who now wear – the uniform of the Royal Australian Navy, Army and Royal Australian Air Force. So too, the decisions our governments have made to deploy those uniformed Australians are integral to that story.

A history of Australian Government decisions for war

Perhaps the two most significant powers vested in government are to deny freedom of its citizens and to deploy its defence forces for war.

Since federation, neither the Australian Constitution nor defence legislation has required the government to gain parliamentary approval to deploy forces overseas. Nor in the rare cases that it has occurred, has the government *had* to consult parliament in its decision to declare war.

It would be reasonable to expect this to be explicitly stated in Australia's Constitution. Section 51 of the Australian Constitution empowers the Australian Parliament to pass laws in relation to "naval and military defence". Section 68 entrusts the Governor-General, as representative of the monarch, with commander-in-chief of Australian forces, although in practice this is purely titular.

There is no explicit statement in the Constitution setting out specifically who should commit Australia to war.

Paradoxically perhaps, the answer does lie in the Constitution.

Finding it requires the context of understanding that our Constitution is a document framed in the nineteenth century according to British conventions and practices.

For centuries in Britain, the power to declare war was one of the royal prerogatives, entirely a matter for the Crown. Under the Australian Constitution, former royal prerogatives – including the power to make war, deploy troops and declare peace – are part of the executive power of the Commonwealth.

Executive power is recognised in section 61 of the Constitution. It vests executive power in the Queen and permits its exercise by the Governor-General on the Queen's behalf.

The Governor-General acts on advice of ministers in accordance with the principle of responsible government. That principle is at the very heart of British and Australian constitutional arrangements. It is one which requires the 'Crown' to act on the advice of ministers who are in turn members of, and responsible to, the parliament.

Contemporary practice is that decisions to go to war are ultimately matters for the prime minister and cabinet, involving directly neither the Governor-General nor Federal Executive Council.

Although the government is not legally required to consult parliament when declaring war or deploying forces overseas, on most occasions the prime minister or defence minister has informed parliament of cabinet's decision through a ministerial statement or tabled papers. This invariably is followed by debate and vote on a motion.

The newly elected Howard Government established the National Security Committee (NSC) of cabinet in 1996. This body has since assumed pre-eminence in the decision-making process.

It is the NSC that considers, debates and resolves to commit Australian defence personnel to domestic or overseas deployments. The full cabinet then considers the advice and recommendation of the NSC. Once a position is adopted, the Opposition leader, members of the full government executive and its back bench are briefed.

Since 1985 the Australian Democrats, firstly, and more recently the Australian Greens, have attempted to remove the exclusive power of the government to commit Australia to war.

Attempts have been made to repeal section 50C of the *Defence Act 1903*, which allows the deployment of Australian troops overseas, replacing it with a requirement for both houses of parliament to approve a declaration of war and commitment of troops.

While the power to make war, deploy troops and declare peace are essential elements of the executive power of the Commonwealth, it is open to any government to put such matters to the parliament for debate. The Hawke Government did just this in January 1991.

Both Canada and New Zealand have similar constitutional arrangements in place to Australia.

The Clark Labour Government offered to supply New Zealand SAS troops to the United States within days of the attacks on 11 September 2001.

The decision was not referred to parliament until 3 October 2001. Prime Minister Clark emphasised that although the government did not need the approval of parliament, she brought the matter to a vote because she 'wanted the troops to know … they had the full support of MPs'.

Although the legal position in the United Kingdom remains unchanged from that of royal prerogative exercisable by ministers, it is standard practice for governments to keep parliament well informed of decisions to use force and the progress of campaigns.

Since 2003, and Britain joining the coalition that would forcibly topple Saddam Hussein, there have been calls for the royal prerogative, including the monarch's war powers, to be codified and subject to parliamentary scrutiny.

A precedent for military action being subject to parliamentary approval was set in 2013. The Cameron Government sought in-principle support from the House of Commons for United Kingdom military action against the Syrian government of Bashar al-Assad. The government motion was defeated.

Prime Minister Cameron, speaking in the House, subsequently ruled out any involvement by the United Kingdom in military action against Syria. When Opposition leader Edward Miliband asked by point of order for the prime minister to rule out use of the royal prerogative for the UK to enjoin any military action before another vote in the House of Commons, the prime minister responded:

> *I can give that assurance. Let me say that the House has not voted for either motion tonight. I strongly believe in the need for a tough response to the use of chemical weapons, but I also believe in respecting the will of this House of Commons. It is very clear tonight that, while the House has not passed a motion, the British Parliament, reflecting the views of the British people, does not want to see British military action. I get that, and the Government will act accordingly.*

The Constitution of the United States grants to Congress the power to declare war, to raise and support armies, and to provide and maintain a navy (Article 1, section 8, clause 11). The president is made the Commander in Chief of the armed forces (Article 2, section 2, clause 1).

The *War Powers Resolution 1973* (also known as the *War Powers*

Act) provides for the president to consult, report and terminate deployment of armed forces with the approval of Congress.

Presidents have not always followed this Act. Courts have failed to uphold its legality, the US Supreme Court especially has been reluctant to take on cases which deal with it, regarding it as a political rather than judicial issue.

In 2003 the district court's Judge Tauro rejected the contention that the president *must* have congressional authority to order American forces into combat. He concluded, "Case law makes clear that the Congress does not have the exclusive right to determine whether or not the United States engages in war.." This decision was upheld in an appeal later that year to the First US Circuit Court of Appeals.

The North Atlantic Treaty Organisation (NATO) arising from the Washington Declaration of 1949 has two essential articles which govern its founding principle of mutual defence.

On 12 September 2001, NATO invoked Article 5 for the first and only time in its history in response to the attacks on the United States the day before. Article 5 provides for individual and mutual self-defence and is consistent with Article 51 of the Charter of the United Nations …

Personal reflections and observations

I have reached the conclusion that peace is not a natural state of affairs.

It is something towards which we must constantly work, making sacrifices and compromises in the pursuit of a peaceful regional and world order.

A visitor to the Australian War Memorial asked me last year why we do not tell Australians what the nation does to avoid war. Good question.

A museum for both democracy and Australian diplomacy could serve such a purpose.

The R.G. Casey building houses the Department of Foreign Affairs and Trade (DFAT). Its corridors, theatres and meeting rooms are adorned with photographs of Australian prime ministers, foreign ministers and diplomats at key moments in our nation's history, prosecuting Australia's interests. These are often the stories of a nation working to avoid war and shaping peace. They need to be told.

Giving Australians an insight into and understanding of what the nation's leaders and diplomats have done to maintain peace and prevent conflict is no less worthy than that of telling our experience of war.

I am also reminded each day at the Australian War Memorial that in the end there are some truths by which we live that are worth fighting to defend.

Proponents of the parliament making the decision for the nation going to war assume and frequently assert that a parliamentary decision is more likely to reflect public opinion. It is assumed that the executive is removed from public opinion and as such, the momentous decision to go to war should be one made "closer to the people" who elect their representatives. It also assumes that the popular view is correct and should prevail – informed or not.

One of the most difficult and important tasks before a member of parliament is to know the difference between what is popular and what is right. Some parliamentarians regard themselves not as representatives in the mould of Edmund Burke, but as delegates.

I well recall in debate of the bill to overturn the Northern Territory's euthanasia legislation, the then Member for Cowan told the House that he found the issue very hard, so he had surveyed his electorate. As the majority supported euthanasia, he would vote in accordance with their opinion.

The parliament, with some notable exceptions, is a reflection of the society from which its members come. Men and women come from all walks of life, bringing with them the experiences that have layered their lives, differing intellect, prejudices, interests and capacity to understand.

Some wars enjoy broad popular support – at least at first. Others do not.

These decisions are never taken lightly by those who make them. But they are informed with the best intelligence, military, strategic and diplomatic advice that can be offered.

Would the House of Representatives make the decision where the government has a majority? Would the Senate also vote, and what then of it having a different view from the House?

By definition a divided parliament means the Opposition opposing involvement in a particular war.

If the key instruments of authority were vested in the parliament and one deeply divided, the impact on deploying defence personnel, enemy propaganda and sustaining morale for the operation would be dramatic.

The truth of it is that when these decisions are made, very careful consideration is given to every aspect of the proposed operation by those in the executive of government. The prime minister, defence and foreign ministers are integral, carefully weighing up the many issues.

Where lies Australia's national interest? What are the likely consequences of involvement in this conflict? What are the geopolitical and geostrategic risks? What is the attitude to this proposed deployment of the international community and of Australia's key allies? What will be the human and economic costs? What is our objective and how likely is that to be achieved and at what cost? What are the precedents and experiences of history upon which we can draw? What will be the disposition of members of the outer ministry and back bench? Will the Opposition leader support this? Where will the Australian public line up on this and how much information can we safely make available to them?

The prime minister and key ministers know, along with their

back bench, that they will have to explain and defend their decisions extensively once made. They know that parliamentary question time is likely to be dominated with probing into what will become increasingly difficult questions. They know that the media will relentlessly scrutinise, probe and question.

And of course, they also know that at some point there will be parents, widows, widowers and children whose questions will be hardest to answer. If you are not clear in your own mind why lives were lost in a particular cause, it will never be clear in theirs.

In the end, from my own experience, after all the advice from the Australian Security Intelligence Organisation, DFAT, Defence Intelligence Organisation, Office of National Assessments, Australian Secret Intelligence Service, Defence Chiefs and other agencies, it comes down to this – "what is the right thing to do?"

Afghanistan was the right thing to do.

Three thousand civilians had been murdered on 11 September 2001 in an attack on the US mainland. Australia activated the provisions of the ANZUS Alliance to do what would be needed. A little over a year later 88 Australians were among those murdered in Bali by three men who had trained with Al-Qa'ida under the protection of the Taliban.

Beyond that though, it is clear that our generation is facing a resurgent totalitarianism in the form of Islamic extremism, having hijacked the good name of Islam to build a violent political utopia.

But the other reason is that it is the 'right thing to do'. It would be delusional and irresponsible to think we should leave this to a handful of other countries. To do so would violate all this nation has stood for in its short history …

The decision to go to war is the most important any nation will make. It cannot be one that could be held hostage to populism in any form.

Looking back over our history, in my view all our governments have made the right decision. It was right at the time based on all the information available to them, having regard for Australia's geopolitical circumstances and best interests.

It is equally clear that when regarded as being in the national interests, our governments have gone to considerable lengths to involve the parliament.

In hindsight, it is easy to contest a number of those decisions. Hindsight is a wonderful thing of course – my kids have it.

But I am also confident that if the parliament had been fully responsible for making these decisions over more than a century, we would be a different nation today with a different view of itself and its place in the world.

In the end, someone has to be held responsible for decisions. That should be the government and its prime minister of the day.

Whatever the view any one of us adopts for the decisions made to go to war, to Bean's 'man lying out there at Pozières and the low scrub of Gallipoli' who in his last moments has thought, 'Well ... well, it's over. But in Australia – they will be proud of this', I say – we all say – 'Yes we are' ...

60th Anniversary of Israel, 12 March 2008

> Speaking in 2008, Dr Nelson speaks of the shared values between Israel and Australia, including democratic values and the "hopeful belief in the freedom of man, freedom of speech, freedom of religion and freedom of assembly".

I rise on behalf of the alternative government to provide our very strong support for this motion and to support the remarks on the historical circumstances of the development of the state of Israel, the role that Australia played in that, the relationship between our two countries, the initiatives that are being taken by the current Australian government and indeed those taken by the most recent government to further the peace process between Israel and the Palestinians.

Jewish identity over the last 100 years has been shaped by three things. The first is anti-Semitism, which remains a virulent and repugnant force still in far too many parts of the world and in the dark recesses of some people's hearts. The second is the holocaust, which saw the systematic extermination of more than six million Jews through the course of the Second World War. The third is the continued threats to the very existence of the state of Israel, which is constantly embattled and, every single day, every week and every year, needs to struggle to defend its very existence.

In a region of the world that is characterised more by theocracies and autocracies, the state of Israel is the custodian of the most fragile yet powerful of human emotions, and that is hopeful belief in the freedom of man, freedom of speech, freedom of religion and freedom of assembly. There are many things for which Israel stands and which characterise the modern state of Israel, but included amongst them is the celebration of knowledge for its own sake and knowledge as the driver of economic development and emancipation from human poverty. Israel also stands for personal independence, a free parliament and an independent judiciary. It is a nation where Christians, Baha'is, Muslims and Arabs enjoy equal rights. Israel, like all democracies, is far from perfect, but it is, in every sense of the word, on the front line of the struggle for the things that we hold dear, not only as Australians and free people but as human beings. And it is far too frequently on the front line of the struggle against all the things that are repugnant to universal human ideals.

On 14 May 1948, the day that the British mandate expired, the Jewish People's Council gathered at Tel Aviv Museum and approved the Declaration of Independence of the State of Israel. It read, in part:

> *The state of Israel will be open for Jewish immigration and for the ingathering of the Exiles; it will foster the development of the country for the benefit of all its inhabitants; it will be based on freedom, justice and peace as envisaged by the prophets of Israel; it will ensure complete equality of social and political rights to all its inhabitants irrespective of religion, race or sex; it will guarantee freedom of religion, conscience, language, education and culture; it will safeguard the Holy Places of all religions; and it will be faithful to the principles of the Charter of the United Nations.*

Israel is home to many things that are spiritual, but it is home in the end to the human spirit of resilience, of confidence, of determination and of respect for one another irrespective of political, religious or other affiliations. It is a land that boasts many ancient buildings, but its people are firmly focused on building the future. That it is difficult to achieve a peaceful resolution to the tensions surrounding Israel's existence should only strengthen our resolve to reach out not only to Israel but also to Palestinians of good heart who genuinely seek and should achieve a two-state solution. No Australian who believes in the dignity of man, in freedom and in democratic principles should ever, through neglectful indifference, allow Israel to be a stranger. To do so would be to diminish ourselves and our own true security.

To any Australian who has not done so already and who has the privilege and the opportunity to visit Washington: I urge you to visit the Holocaust Memorial Museum. There is a very large sign out the front of the museum that says: "Never forget what you have seen here." There are piles of shoes that were worn by Jews exterminated, photographs of men and women and children looking out into lives that were never lived, and many other things to remind us of why our relationship with Israel and our respect for the Israeli cause and the two-state solution is so important to our own beliefs, our own values and ultimately our own freedoms and security. Shabbat shalom forever.

Europe and the Asia Pacific, 31 October 2012

> Speaking in 2012, Dr Nelson discusses the emerging challenges facing the world including technological advancement, economic uncertainty and fundamentalist intolerance. He iterates the importance of nations around the world which value "political, democratic and religious freedom, free academic inquiry and the co-existence of faith and reason" to work together to respond to these global challenges.

The world has changed. It has changed in ways we possibly may not yet fully comprehend. It won't be changed back.

Last year, Yale's Professor of History and head of its International Security Studies Centre, Paul Kennedy, wrote that not only has the world changed, but we are moving from one age to another. At times in history he said, it is obvious after cataclysmic events that a new age has arrived. The end of the Napoleonic wars and of World War two, were such occasions.

But at other times humankind moves from one age to another, failing to appreciate the momentous scale and nature of what is happening. As one example he cited the world of 1530 as being unrecognisable to a person who had lived only fifty years earlier – new nation states, the splintering of Christendom, European expansion to the Asias and North America, along with the Guttenberg communications revolution.

Kennedy asserts that now is also such a time.

As evidence he offers the shrinking role of the US dollar as the global reserve currency; Europe's existential economic crisis and consequent, necessarily inward-looking posture; and his view that the United Nations Security Council is ill-suited to the world that is, let alone the one that is coming. But the other compelling reason he says, is the Asia Pacific's move to centre stage.

Europe is only beginning to fully understand the scale and pace of the transformation in the Asia Pacific. Australia is looking at an Asian century and has just published a white paper on the subject (asiancentury.dpmc.gov.au). As Kennedy observes, after five hundred years the world of 1500 is at an end.

After world war two we had two superpowers. Then we had one.

Although the capacity of the United States to reinvent itself is extraordinary and not to be underestimated (as it is now in energy), within a decade the US may not be the dominant global economic power. Not since the Qing dynasty and the Franco Prussian war will this have been the case.

While appreciating the increasing importance of Asia and the need for Europe to coherently focus on it, a number of European officials have intimated to me that it will take time given other priorities. If that is the attitude Europe adopts, Asia may find Europe sooner than it thinks and in ways it might least expect.

Consider some facts.

The Asia Pacific is already home to more than half the world's population.

In 1992 it was 22 percent of global economic output.

By 2030 it will be 40 percent. In 1982 China's economy was 9 percent that of the US. It is now half and Chinese purchasing power parity, on current trends, will exceed that of the US within five years.

China's net foreign assets exceeded those of the US in 2003. Today China's net foreign reserves approximate that of US net foreign debt.

Chinese exports exceeded those of the US in 2007, fixed capital investment in 2009 and manufacturing and energy consumption in 2010.

On present trends, expect Chinese retail sales and imports to exceed that of the US in 2014 and by 2016, China will have more companies in the global Fortune 500 than the US. Its companies' market capitalisation will pass that of the US in value around 2020.

Finally, Chinese defence expenditure is doubling every five years and is likely to be that of the US around 2030.

Five of the world's economic powerhouses are in the Asia Pacific – US, China, India, Japan and the Republic of Korea.

Five of the world's biggest militaries are also there – US, China, Russia, India and North Korea.

As economies grow, so too does expenditure on defence. India has increased defence expenditure 17 percent this year, Vietnam 34 percent and Indonesia 300 percent since 2006. Singapore is now a major importer of defence material.

Asia this year (not including Australia) will spend more on defence than Europe.

Concurrently, economic and trade interdependence is growing, including the ambition for a comprehensive regional economic agreement.

The Region is stable, but potentially very unstable, replete with deep geostrategic uncertainties. These include maritime and territorial disputes and unresolved historical enmities.

Anyone in Europe thinking this is of little relevance should think again.

The Korean peninsula.

The Taiwan Strait.

Kashmir.

The South China Sea through which passes half of the world's maritime merchant traffic and almost all of Europe's EUR700 billion trade with north Asia. It is also the subject of heated dispute amongst a number of member states in the region.

The Sea of Japan and its disputed islands. The East China Sea in which Japan and China are in dispute over the Senkaku or Diaoyu islands.

The Straits of Malacca through which passes 40 percent of the world's trade, a quarter of global sea borne oil, half the world's energy and 90 percent of Japan's crude oil.

Add to these border disputes, transnational crime, terrorism and 80 percent of the world's natural disasters and the challenges are as apparent as the global consequences of their mismanagement.

Should any conflagration emerge, the consequences for Europe and the global economy will be significant and sudden. This is not an abstract consideration.

There are similarities between the Asia Pacific and late 19th century Europe after the unification of Germany. At that time, as Henry Kissinger observed in his book on China, diplomacy became a zero sum game in a model of bi-polar relationships. Whilst we cannot be captive to history, we must learn from it.

Today a large, economically and politically powerful China is re-emerging with all the consequences that has for changing the regional and world order. The rules by which it and the nation states in the region engage one another is uncertain and the outcomes, even less so.

The most important relationship in the Asia Pacific – as globally, is that of the US and China. The template for it in this century is being forged now and it is being done in the Region.

Australia is optimistic about China's re-emergence and deeply convinced of the need for a range of stable, rules based multilateral structures for the discussion and advancement of common goals. It is also essential for the consideration of disagreement.

China's priorities are to maintain economic growth to lift 150 million of its people still living in poverty to a higher standard of living. It must create 24 million jobs every year for those entering the workforce. The imperative is social stability. The second priority is to modernise its military. In this context though, it should be remembered that China has no history of territorial acquisition, its borders being essentially those of the Han dynasty.

Its challenges are immense.

They include corruption, urban pollution, rapidly collapsing age dependency ratios, internal cohesion, protection of energy and raw material supply lines, the divide between rich and poor, a growing and desperate need to increase domestic consumption and a political system considerably less flexible than that of my own country.

From Beijing's perspective, the last 160 years have been an aberration. It now behoves all of us to help China re-emerge into the rules-based world order which serves its interests as much as our own.

Attempts to base foreign policy on the export of Western ideology to China and other nation states in Asia are not credible. But steadfastly believing in your own values is. The region respects strength.

The United States presence in the western Pacific since World War Two and its guarantee of maritime security of the world's waterways has been the bedrock for stability, growth and prosperity in East Asia for more than sixty years.

Now the US has nominated its highest foreign policy priority for the 21st century as the Asia Pacific. This should be welcomed by anyone with an understanding of the transformational nature of global events.

This is not about the containment of China nor any other country in the region. Such an ambition would be as irresponsible as it is unachievable. It is instead about ensuring that the US presence in the region, so indispensable to peace and prosperity, is strengthened in support of harmonious co-operation and dialogue. As such it is welcomed by a number of nations in the region, including Australia.

Some Europeans have expressed surprise; bewilderment and disappointment in response to the US rebalance to the Asia Pacific. The best response will be to firstly understand why and then to substantially escalate Asian engagement. A number of EU member states have clearly begun to do so.

The currents of political and economic power shifting from Europe and North America over the past twenty years have been rapidly accelerated by a confluence of events culminating in the global financial crisis.

What we need, what the world needs, is a coherent European engagement with and understanding of – the Asia Pacific.

Not only do European nations need consistent, strong bilateral ties with the nations of the region and its multilateral fora such as ASEAN, we need coherence.

One of the most important priorities is to turn up and do so regularly. Like marriage, making it work can be tough, but turning up is an essential pre-requisite.

The ASEAN Regional Forum (ARF) is a key and pivotal part of the multilateral architecture, bringing together the nations of the region for dialogue with others including the EU. High Representative Ashton's attendance this year was as welcome as it is important. The nations of the region need not only the US, but also the liberal democracies of Europe engaged with and supportive of, the structures they themselves have created for regional harmony.

Australia worked closely with its neighbours to get the US and Russia into the East Asia summit at leader's level. In addition to economic, environmental, educational, energy and agricultural challenges, Chinese and the US leaders can discuss security issues with nations most directly affected by the outcomes.

Asia Pacific dialogue in relation to disagreement must be a habit in multilateral fora.

So where is Australia coming from?

Australia built its foreign policy after World War Two on a number of key foundations.

The first was our alliance with the United States, formalised in 1951. Not a day goes by in Australia where we do not privately or publicly reflect on American sacrifice in the Pacific from 1942 until the end of the war.

Second was Australia's foundation membership of the United

Nations. This commitment to multilateralism has been sustained with Australia taking a seat on the United Nations Security Council in 2013.

Third was a then understandably ambivalent relationship with Asia given the events of World War Two, but knowing nonetheless our destiny would lie to our immediate north.

Fourth was Europe. For Australia it was principally the United Kingdom and to varying and lesser degrees, the other capitals of Europe.

Having invested heavily in a peaceful Europe with the loss of 70,000 troops in two wars, Australia readily 'signed on' for Robert Schumann's 1951 vision. Who would not support a means to ending centuries of European conflict?

When Britain joined the 'common market' in the early seventies it was Australia's major trading partner. Suddenly we found the ready market we had enjoyed for agricultural products especially, all but dried up. Australia's political class was deeply scarred and readily embraced the posture of a deeply Eurosceptic nation. Paradoxically though, those tumultuous events forced us to open up to the rest of the world – opening markets, reducing tariffs, undertaking painful domestic economic reforms and accelerating our engagement with Asia. All this and more laid the foundation for us now being the 12th largest economy in the world.

But we defined our relationship with the EU and its antecedents very narrowly around conflict in agriculture and market access. That is, until only a few years ago. The world had changed, demanding a deeper, broader relationship with the EU.

The global financial crisis; emergence of the G20 at leader's level for global economic governance of which both we and the EU are members; passage of the Lisbon Treaty with its redistribution of patterns of authority in Brussels, including new powers in the parliament; birth of the European External Action Service; a decade of deep economic challenges for Europe and the US all demanded a meaningful Australian engagement with the EU.

The world – and indeed the Asia Pacific – needs a Europe representing the values that it does, looking outwards and engaged as coherently as it is able.

Australia is a country unashamedly imbued with Western values, a middle power that sees a way forward in this new uncertainty. It is one that is neither appeasement at one extreme nor an apocalyptic clash of cultures at the other. But we have to work at it.

We need to prepare for the unknown in a globalised world where the speed and impact of events in one part of the globe have major consequences for another.

We live in a world of extraordinary technological change, global economic uncertainty and in much of it, fundamentalist intolerance.

We live in vast ignorance of the decisions we make and that are made for us. But we do know the future will be shaped most not by what we know, but what we do not.

What we need most is – one another.

Europe's influence, if it is to be maintained – let alone grow, will be determined by the capacity of its member states to work together as much as is possible. A new world order is rapidly approaching.

Those nations founded on the principles of political, democratic and religious freedom, free academic inquiry and the co-existence of faith and reason need to work with one another more than at any other time.

The future we want and need depends on it.

National Press Club Address, 18 September 2013

> Addressing the National Press Club, Dr Nelson describes how the global order has evolved in recent decades in key areas of trade, research and security, among others. Dr Nelson suggests that these changes are occurring in a way that "we don't yet fully appreciate, nor indeed understand", and shares his perspective on how Australia should respond.

Today I'm going to speak largely about three areas with which I have had and now have significant engagement, and each of them relates to the other. But it's essentially the importance of values to our nation in a changing world. The world has changed. It's changed in ways that in returning to Australia I think that we don't yet fully appreciate, nor indeed understand. But most importantly, it's not going to be changed back. Paul Kennedy is the Yale Professor of History and head of its Security International study centre, and just under two years ago published what I thought was a quite provoking essay on changes and changes in history. And he made the observation that at the end of the Napoleonic Wars, and the end of the Second World War, it was obvious that the world had changed. It was not going to ever be the same again.

But, equally there are other times in history when there is change and it's very difficult for people who are living through this period of change to fully appreciate the scale and pace of it. As an example, a person who lived in 1480 would not possibly recognise the world of 1530, the formation of nation states, the splintering of Christendom, the expansion of Europe into the Asias and North America, and the Gutenberg communications revolution amongst many others.

The argument that he prosecuted is that we are now living through such a period, and as evidence of which it's not the revolution in telecommunications which has swept this world certainly through my generation, but amongst other things the US dollar which was once 80 percent of global reserve currency is now barely 60 per cent.

The United Nations Security Council and the key instruments of the Second World War world are barely serving the world we have, let alone the one that's coming. The Eurozone crisis has necessarily meant that the Europeans are even more focussed on themselves in this existential challenge than they would normally be, and that has consequences for the rest of us, Europe as it does representing more than half a billion people who live on this planet, but most importantly, that the world of 1500 is about to come to an end. That Asia and Asia-Pacific is moving to centre stage.

When I was in Europe and I had the privilege to be Australia's ambassador to the European Union and also to NATO, I remember when I was frequently meeting, as you would expect, in some cases, leaders of nation states and certainly commissioners from the European Commission and senior officials, and those from the European Council, I'd always talk about the issue of the day, so to speak, and on this particular occasion I'd been talking about economic issues. And as was always the case, I then raised the importance of the Asia-Pacific, and the person to whom I was speaking and meeting, a very senior individual, said to me, "Ambassador, it will be years before Europe will be able to turn its attention to Asia in any serious way," and I said oh, really? I said, "Because if that is the attitude that Europe does take, Asia is going to find you sooner than you think in ways that you might least expect, because the region is replete with very deep geostrategic uncertainty."

As Henry Kissinger observed in his book on China, there are similarities between our region, the Asia-Pacific, and late 19th century Europe that after two cataclysmic wars of the 20th century, divergence of opinion in Europe does not result in anyone talking about war. Kissinger made the observation that in the Asia-Pacific region with nations recently emerged from colonialism and, understandably, with a deep sense of independence and commitment to it, and the re-emergence of China which he regarded as being analogous to formation and the unification of Germany in 1871, that in our region no one, of course, is looking for a war, but Kissinger makes the observation that no-one's ruling it out. And we are in this decade, in fact before the end of the decade that lies ahead, we will live in a world that we've not lived in since the Franco-Prussian War and the Qing dynasty. We had, after the Second World War, two superpowers for 20 years or so. We are just about to finish the unipolar moment and, before the decade is out, it is likely that we will live in a world where the United States is not the dominant economic power globally. And the most important relationship in the world to Australia is that between the United States and China. In fact, I would argue the most important to the world itself, and the template for that is being forged now in our region.

Amongst the many changes that have been worked into our society, and indeed to our world, is an understanding that China on so many fronts is surpassing the United States, whether – its economy is now about half the size of the United States, having been barely nine percent in the early 1980s. Net foreign reserves, of course, exceed that of the US. Fixed capital investment, exports, manufacturing, energy consumption and within the decade we'll see retail sales and imports in China exceed that of the United States. It's likely to have more companies in the Fortune 500, the capitalisation of its companies is likely to exceed that of the United States by 2020 and, of course, Defence expenditure at the moment is likely to equate to that of the United States toward the end of the next decade. And we are moving into a world which will be unfamiliar territory, certainly for us as Australians.

Australia's history with the European Union has been a mixed one. We invested very heavily in a peaceful Europe, 70,000 Australians lie in Europe from two wars as silent witnesses to the future that they have given us and which we have a responsibility to shape. When Robert Schuman enunciated in 1951 his vision of a way of avoiding war with a common coal and steel community, particularly between France and Germany, Australia signed onto that. But then, of course, in the early '70s, perhaps for the second time in the 20th century, we felt let down by Britain. After the fall of Singapore in

1942, of course, we knew we would have to look across the Pacific to the United States for the protection and security of our nation. And I've said to the Americans in particular in various roles I've had that not a day goes by in this country where we don't give thanks and gratitude for American sacrifice in this part of the world.

But when Britain joined the common market in the early '70s it deeply scarred our political class and indeed our nation. Suddenly markets that we had enjoyed, particularly in agriculture, had all but dried up. And the European Union, the supra-national construct that it is, is an anathema to many of us Australians. The idea of handing over some of your autonomy and your sovereignty to another body, in this case in Brussels, is not something that we in Australia can easily adjust to. And we narrowly defined our relationship with Europe around conflict in market access and agriculture.

But the currents of political and economic power that was shifting from North America and Europe over the last 25 years have been rapidly accelerated by the global financial crisis. And it demands that Australia now have quite a different approach to the European Union and relationship with it. There are a number of reasons for that. As we emerged from the global financial crisis, Kevin Rudd, then as Prime Minister and, I think, to his immense credit, played a significant role in seeing that the existing G20 at Finance Minister's level became a grouping of 20 at leader's level for global economic governance, which would see Australia as the 13th largest economy in the world as being a part of that G20 grouping. The European Union itself has a seat at the G20 table, the President of the European Commission and the President of the European Council.

Late in 2009 after a decade in development, the Lisbon Treaty took effect which would be unknown to most Australians, but what that significantly did is redistributed the patterns of power and authority in Brussels so that there would be a permanent president of the European Council which would chair the meetings of the then 27, now 28, leaders of the member states. And it has met almost monthly through the period of the Eurozone crisis. In addition to that, the European Parliament, 750 members of that Parliament, now have real power in 85 different areas. So all kinds of issues which affect us in terms of treaties, passenger name record agreement for example, which is an essential part of border protection architecture, had to go through the European Parliament. Chemical standards, food labelling, kangaroo meat imports, a whole variety of things that affect us in day-to-day life are now determined in significant part by the European Parliament, and it demands we engage it more effectively.

And the Americans got their wake-up call in February 2010 when the European Parliament exercised its new muscle by knocking over the swift agreement, the terrorist finance tracking agreement which is so essential to US efforts in counter-terrorism, and the US vice-president Biden actually had to go to Brussels and speak to the European Parliament and undertake a flurry of diplomacy to see it be renegotiated in parts. In addition to that, the European External Action Service was formed so that Europe would have its own chief diplomat, currently Baroness Catherine Ashton, and what that will do in my very strong view with the passage of time is give coherence to European diplomacy.

And you see glimpses of it, the way in which the European Union has brought together its member states to deal with Iran, and sanctions on Iran, and having Australia and Canada and other countries working hand in glove with it is a glimpse, in my view, of the future. And I'd often noticed that you'd see foreign ministers from certain countries who are members of the European Union in their own member state criticising the European Union and then arrive at the Justus Lipsius building in Brussels, or the Berlaymont, and say to the world how important the meeting would be in driving consistency of foreign policy and determination of action in relation to Iran and other particularly important issues.

I constantly when I was ambassador there, constantly was saying to the Europeans and to NATO, to the North Atlantic Council, that you need to understand that the scale and pace of the transformation in the Asia-Pacific is something that has already changed the world as Kennedy observed. And I said to the senior interlocutor who said it would be years before we could focus on Asia in any serious way, I said, well look could I just run through a few things for you; the Taiwan Strait, the Korean Peninsula, Kashmir, the Sea of Japan, East China Sea, the South China Sea, the straits of Malacca, terrorism, 80 percent of the world's natural disasters and, as one example, the South China Sea through which travels half of the world's merchant maritime traffic, and $960 billion of European trade almost all of it into North Asia goes through the South China Sea. If it's closed down for a couple of weeks you're going to know about it. And, apart from anything else, the United States presence in the Western Pacific which has guaranteed security and been the bedrock for prosperity in our region since the end of the Second World War. The United States is arguably the key partner in the NATO alliance, apart from anything else, will have particular interest if there were, God forbid, any conflagration emerging from our region.

I said to then Foreign Minister Stephen Smith in early 2010 that I thought we Australians had two threshold questions in relation to the European Union. The first was whether we should seek a tier one relationship. The Europeans were attracted very much to Kevin Rudd's early ratification of Kyoto which was strongly supported by the Opposition led by me at the time. The real head-turner was the parliamentary apology to forcibly remove generations of Indigenous Australians in February 2008, and Kevin Rudd's early visit as Prime Minister to Brussels enunciating a vision for the future of the relationship.

But I said to Stephen Smith the two threshold questions is whether we should seek a tier one relationship, we're the only G20 country that doesn't have it. And the second is whether we should seek a free trade agreement. I said to officials here back in Australia, and I said certainly to the then minister and the Prime Minister that traditionally in Brussels what we had done is just bang them over the back of the head about agriculture and market access. Not unreasonably, but if the only thing you ever do is complain about something and the same issue, and we have every reason to do so, then it's not surprising that we're not going to make a lot of progress.

And after 30 years we finally got a breakthrough in 2010 with high quality grain fed beef quota which was a product of the fact that Catherine Ashton had a very good relationship as Trade Commissioner with Simon Crean and also we were broadening our engagement beyond that which we had traditionally pursued.

So we have negotiated a treaty framework agreement with the European Union. It's the one language that everyone does speak in Brussels. And that sets a shared vision and a legal architecture around the relationship in foreign affairs, security, trade, economic issues, in overseas development of assistance of which the EU is the source of 56 percent globally, of climate change, environment, research, innovation and science, to have a broader and deeper engagement.

And for the Euro-sceptics in our country where we are fed largely on an entire industry which operates not only in Brussels but in member states throughout Europe, I say to you firstly the EU has a seat at the G20. It has speaking rights at the United Nations. Its high representative is actively involved in the Middle East peace process. It also now has real power in its parliament, as I have described.

But most importantly, in our region we need not only the United States to be supporting multilateral architecture as China re-emerges into what should be a rules-based world for us and for it, we also need a coherent European engagement in our region, an understanding of it, and it's important that the nations in this region, the ASEAN nations and those of the rest of us, including China, know that the liberal democracies of this world represented still largely by those countries within Europe, are working with the United States in seeing that we have a broad stable multilateral dialogue in our region. And that is the fundamental reason why this is important.

The other reason, in terms of a free trade agreement, we have to have a treaty framework agreement in place in order to seek a free trade agreement. Fifteen percent of Australia's two-way trade is with the European Union and its member states. We've negotiated pretty much everything, but one thing that the Europeans will not give ground on is what they call essential elements, noncompliance provisions, and my strong view is that the Europeans need to have a very serious look at this. The idea that we would link all of our existing agreements and future agreements to any accusation of noncompliance on human rights and rule of law and other things of which Australia can be very proud is in my view nonsense.

So and then in relation to NATO, very similarly, we went into Afghanistan in 2001, we went back in in 2005 and I remember as Defence Minister midway through 2006 saying to Air Chief Marshal Angus Houston, the Chief of Defence, I said look, I think we'd better go to Brussels and have a talk to these NATO people. Now, at that stage we dealt with Washington, London, Kabul and, of course, The Hague because we were partnered with the Dutch. And Angus said to me, he said, "Oh minister, there's a lot of red tape there," and I said, "Yeah I know, but they're running the war, I think we'd better go and have a look."

So we went to Brussels and we went to the Mons, the Supreme Headquarters Allied Powers Europe, and I came back and recommended to our then government we should become a contact country. In hindsight, NATO didn't understand us and we didn't understand them. We had virtually no relationship with them at all and yet we went into a NATO-led war which has become our longest war and the low point was when Prime Minister Rudd in 2008 was excluded from the discussion on Afghanistan at the NATO summit and his request to me when he asked me if I'd go to Brussels was, in relation to NATO, can you bust down the door and make sure we have a seat at the table and we are heard?

We've now done that. We've negotiated what's called a high-level political declaration with NATO and the Secretary-General of NATO came here last year to specifically sign that with our then Prime Minister Gillard. What that means in plain language is that we will never be in a situation again where we go into a NATO-led war and have no relationship with the alliance that's actually running it. But it also means that we have regular dialogue at the highest level with our Prime Minister and the NATO leadership, with our ministers and their counterparts at NATO, and then with our officials and also, of course, with our military level.

We also have an ambassador now to NATO. We have a two-star military appointment in Brussels. And, of course, apart from anything else, our key ally, the United States, is the key player at NATO itself. But we worked very hard to see that NATO took a global approach to Euro-Atlantic security. For the NATO leadership I kept saying to them you've got to understand that threats to Euro-Atlantic security can come from any part of the world including our region …

6. Lest We Forget: Saluting their Service

Menin Gate: 30,000th Last Post Ceremony, 9 July 2015

In this speech, Dr Nelson emphasises the significance of the ritual sounding of the Last Post at the Menin Gate, commemorating its 30,000th sounding, to honour those who lost their lives, their memory, and their sacrifice for a "better world at peace".

… It is easy from the safe distance of our comfortable 21st century lives to allow the past to be a distant stranger – to forget individual sacrifices made in our name.

In May 1928, the friend of an Australian mother, inconsolably grieving her missing, only son wrote to the Australian War Graves Commission asking for a photograph of the Menin Gate:

> *… his mother is very old and feeble and it would give her great pleasure, or at least comfort, to know her son's name is inscribed among those heroes and is not forgotten as she now thinks. He was all she had and it was a terrible blow to her.*

Such was the meaning to my nation and its families of the Menin Gate, the names inscribed on it and, from 1928 – the nightly sounding of the Last Post.

Husbands, sons, fathers – missing, dead. No remains, no grave.

Of the 18,000 Australians killed in Flanders, more than 6,100 were missing – never to be heard from again.

William and Fanny Seabrook were raising their family in the Sydney suburb of Petersham, when Australia joined the Great War in 1914. Of their seven children, the three sons old enough to enlist in the Australian Imperial Force (AIF) did so late in 1915. George, Theo and William served in France but then saw their first action in Belgium.

On 20 September 1917, the 17th battalion attacked the German position in front of the village of Westhoek, advancing more than a kilometre. Australia sustained 5,013 casualties in that battle of the Menin Road.

Lieutenant William Seabrook was hit by a phosphorous bomb that killed or wounded the full section of the platoon he was leading. He died the next day. In the breast pocket of William's tunic was found a photograph of his mother containing a single bullet hole.

While William was being stretchered from the battlefield in the early hours of that September day, George and Theo were both hit by the same artillery shell – killed instantly. George was 25 and Theo, just a year younger.

George and Theo's bodies were never found. Their names are on the Menin Gate.

William was buried in the Lijssenthoek Military cemetery next to the casualty clearing station where he died. He was 21 years old.

One family, three sons – all dead in a single day.

The devastating impact on the Seabrook family of the loss of their sons is beyond our comprehension.

Mrs Seabrook desperately wrote to the military authorities on 27 November 1917, in the knowledge of William's death but seeking information about Theo and George:

> *… it is all very confusing to our minds and if you could explain to me we would be much obliged and thankful. The blow of losing our three sons in one battle is terrible. We are heartbroken.*

She later wrote to her member of parliament:

> *Having given our three boys as a sacrifice to the country … their loss I will never recover and now my husband is a complete wreck … I have put my property up for sale as it seems there is no other way. Mr Seabrook has been raving about our three boys and has delusions of all kinds. Please pardon me for telling you all these things, but I have no one to confide in.*

She wrote again to the Defence Department in 1925 desperate still for any news:

> *... after all these years, surely something should be known. It is heartbreaking for us.*

A chance encounter in Ypres (Ieper) two years later would inspire a focal point for such raw, inconsolable grief. It would also offer a sense of intimate closeness and meaning to the memory of those so loved and missed.

During an evening walk on 23 July 1927, the Australian War artist Captain Will Longstaff encountered an Englishwoman, Mrs Mary Horsburgh at Hellfire Corner. She had run a British canteen during the war near the entry to the Ypres Salient. When Longstaff asked her if he could be of assistance, she replied:

> *No. I just want to be with my dear boys. I can feel them all around me.*

The following day, Will Longstaff was among the 15,000 who had come for the official dedication of the Menin Gate Memorial. Within that throng of humanity were the forlorn families who had no grave to visit, no personal place to lay tokens of love and memory. The families of the missing from the Dominion countries such as Australia had neither hope of being there nor any reasonable prospect of ever being so.

Lord Plumer famously reached out to them across oceans and across time, "He is not missing, he is here."

The Somerset Light Infantry sounded the Last Post and pipers of the Scots Guards, standing on the ramparts, played a lament.

Longstaff was so profoundly moved, he could not sleep that night. He walked instead to the newly unveiled edifice and, standing under the Menin Gate felt the soldiers with him marching under it. He returned to London and painted Menin Gate at Midnight in a single sitting.

Lord Woolavington purchased the painting in 1928 and presented it to the Australian government as a gift. After its display in London and at Buckingham Palace for King George V, it toured Australia in 1928 and 1929.

Words cannot describe the impact of the battle of 'Passchendaele' nor the meaning of the Menin Gate to our young nation.

When Australia's population was six million, one million people went to see the painting as it toured the continent. A replica model of the Menin Gate, built as a part of the design and construction process of the actual memorial toured with the painting.

This hauntingly beautiful and evocative painting of the Menin Gate was the closest the Seabrooks and families 20,000 kilometres away, would ever get to their lost son, husband or father. Then there were the prints and reproductions sent to town halls, schools and the commemorative halls erected by veterans and their representative associations across the country.

The sounding of the Last Post at the Menin Gate – tonight for the 30,000th time, means more to Australia and Australians than you will ever know. The same can be said of the other dominion nations of the First World War.

This simple gesture, undertaken with such generous dignity by a small number of buglers and overseen by its volunteer association, resonates in the hearts and homes of all families whom you honour in this nightly ritual.

Yours is not a ceremony for the great, the noble and people of position. It is an expression of loss, suffering and love reaching into us all – across class, age, nationality and religion. With awkward humility, pilgrims bound by abiding reverence and a single emotion pause under the Gate as stillness descends. The cloak of remembrance wraps all who gather in mourning as a reminder that we are all equal in death.

The Last Post sounded at the Menin Gate arrests the soul.

The silence that surrounds it is the most powerful sound ever heard.

In that silence, I have always looked up to the names of young men whose lives are silent witnesses to the future they have given us. Those gathered from all parts of the world – including former foes, in their reverential reflection; quietly recommit themselves to one another and the ideals of mankind.

Each name reminds us of what was lost.

But as Reveille sounds, we are stirred to remember that the most fragile yet powerful of human emotions is – hope.

On 30,000 occasions, visitors to the Last Post ceremony have left inspired by twin fundamental ideals.

There are some truths by which we must live that are worth working to defend.

We honour them and their memory best – sustaining precious belief in a better future, by the way we live our lives and shape our world.

At her kitchen table, Mrs Seabrook was forced to find the words to give meaning to why so much that she loved had been given. She penned the epitaph for her son's headstone and the grave she would never see:

A WILLING SACRIFICE

FOR THE WORLD'S PEACE

Every night, The Ode is recited from Laurence Binyon's *For the Fallen*, written in 1914.

Also bequeathed to us in this poem is this:
Solemn the drums thrill
Death august and royal
sings sorrow up into mortal spheres
There is music in the midst of desolation
And a glory that shines upon our tears.

For the music in the desolation of our mournful grieving that speaks directly to the hearts of William and Fanny Seabrook, families and people everywhere – we honour and thank the Last Post Association for this simple, nightly ritual.

For in it, you have given meaning where there was none and enriched each one of us.

In doing so, you have made your willing sacrifice for that better world at peace for which William Seabrook, his brothers and millions of others gave their lives.

70th Anniversary of the End of WWII, 15 August 2015

Commemorating seven decades since the conclusion of World War Two, Dr Nelson recalls the horrors of the "most destructive conflict in human history", and how it changed the world forever. He recalls the one million Australians who mobilised to defend their nation, and to whom we will always owe our freedom.

Life's paradox is that what is most important to us, too often we are tempted to take for granted – families that love us and give meaning to our lives; political, economic and religious freedoms; being an Australian and carrying an Australian passport.

We are free in no small way as a consequence of the events that bring us here today to commemorate the end of the Second World War in the Pacific and all that had preceded it.

Spanning six years, this cataclysm is the most destructive conflict in human history.

The defeat of Nazi Germany, Fascist Italy and Imperial, Militarist Japan – claimed 60 million lives; six million Jews were murdered in the Holocaust.

A life was extinguished every three seconds.

Mankind moved from one age to another.

The world would never be the same again.

Seventy years ago today, Prime Minister Ben Chifley addressed the nation:

> *Fellow citizens, the war is over. The Japanese government has accepted the terms of surrender imposed by the allied nations.*

Hundreds of thousands of jubilant Australians spilled into the streets of the nation's cities, swept up in celebratory pandemonium.

No one that day needed reminding of the value of freedom – or the price that had been paid for it.

But for the men fighting in the jungles of New Guinea, Borneo and Bougainville – their reaction to the declaration was sombre. It was one of conflicting emotions.

There was relief that the war was finally over, but apprehension about the future. They had been witness to events beyond comprehension and seen too many friends wounded, maimed and killed.

Lance Corporal Peter Medcalf was an infantry rifleman serving on Bougainville. He was 19 years old. Reflecting on the day, he said:

> *Strangely, no one laughed or cheered ... All afternoon we sat quietly and speculated. We found it hard to understand fully.*

We were a nation of seven million people on 3 September 1939, when Prime Minister Robert Menzies performed his "melancholy duty" to tell Australians they were at war: "We are therefore, as a great family of nations involved in a struggle we must win at all costs."

Australia's mobilisation for "total war" was unprecedented.

One million Australians mobilised, amongst them almost 70,000 women.

Half a million served across the world: from the deserts of North Africa to the Arctic convoys to the Soviet Union; from the skies over occupied Europe to the jungles of Malaya and New Guinea.

The 'cost' foreshadowed by Menzies six years earlier, included 40,000 dead, more than 100,000 wounded and 30,000 prisoners of war, most of whom endured brutal, inhumane treatment beyond civilised imagination…

The most important year in this nation's history is 1788.

The First Fleet arrived with its devastating impact on millennia of rich indigenous culture and custodianship, but from it and the pioneers who would join them through the 19th century, the origins of the Australia we now have.

The next most important year was 1942. Prime Minister John Curtin described it as "the gravest hour in our history".

Singapore had been Britain's Asian fortress. Immediately after its fall, Prime Minister John Curtin addressed the nation on 16 February:

> *The fall of Singapore can only be described as Australia's Dunkirk … On its issue depends not merely the fate of the Commonwealth, but the frontier of the United States of America, indeed all the Americas, and therefore in large measure the fate of the British speaking world.*

The protection of this country is no longer that of a contribution to a world at war, but the resistance to an enemy threatening to invade our shore.

Bombs fell on Darwin four days later, the first of 63 raids on the northern city and of 100 attacks on the Australian mainland. Battles of epic proportions were fought at Midway, the Coral Sea and Guadalcanal. There was the gripping struggle at Kokoda, extraordinary heroism at Isuarva and the repulsion of the Japanese at Milne Bay. Three Japanese midget submarines launched an attack in Sydney Harbour.

The Second World War was no mere extension of the First World War.

Australia's vital interests were at stake.

A nation reveals itself in certain subtle, yet powerful ways.

The power is in the story.

Private Ray Colenso and his three brothers served in the 2/18th Battalion. He wrote to his mother as he left for overseas service:

> *Weep not my Mother darling*
> *Drive away those tears*
> *You think I'm still a baby*
> *But I'm older than my years.*
>
> *Now that I've joined the colours*
> *I must go away … I must do my duty*
> *As you would wish me to*

Although I know it hurts you
To see your son depart.

Ray Colenso was killed in the defence of Singapore on 9 February 1942. He was 22 years old. His brother Bill was killed two days later. Edward and Frank would survive their captivity, but would never be the same again ...

Sergeant Jack Sim of the 39th Battalion, a former shop assistant from Ballarat, described the conditions along the Kokoda Track:

Oh it was murderous.
It was that hard.
You know what was our worst enemy – the terrain. You perspired all day.
At 4 o'clock in the afternoon it would rain so you were continually wet.
And it was cold at night.
It was so cold at night and boiling hot in the day time.
Some prayed, some swore, with fear – but you couldn't show it in front of your mates.
One of the boys got shot fair between the eyes right alongside of me.
It was a perfect shot.
Buggers.
They used to attack us by screaming out.
Terrible to be afraid.
Yet it's the brave ones that are afraid and still keep going.
That's what they did you know.
Scared bloody stiff and still kept going.
They were so young.
They were so young.
I loved them all.
Nobody went to that war, or any other I suppose, that didn't get wounded mentally if not physically.
It wasn't possible.

On 10 January 1943, Salvation Army Chaplain R. Smith, from the 2nd 9th Australian General Hospital, wrote home from New Guinea:

Although I find this work a great strain I am grateful for the opportunity of serving these men.

I do not believe there has ever been a campaign when men have suffered hardship, privation and incredible difficulties as in this one.

To see these men arrive here wounded and ill from terrible tropical diseases, absolutely exhausted, clothes in tatters and filthy, long matted hair and beards … no description of their incredible suffering could possibly be an exaggeration …

I have seen so much suffering and sorrow here that more than ever I have realised the tragedy of war and the heroism of our men.

This was not about the forging of our nation's 'story' or defining our place in the world. Upon the bedrock of despair and courage, these men gave Japan its first land defeat.

Prisoner of War Stan Arneil, of the 2nd 30th Battalion, described the return to Changi, from toiling on the Burma–Thai Railway:

It was a moonlight night and Changi with the tropical waters round the island was so beautiful. I can still hear the squeal of the brakes as the trucks lined up.

The people from Changi knew we were coming, and they came over to see us, to look for old friends, and see how we were.

We got out of the trucks, a couple were dead and we laid them on the ground, and we lined up on the road. We were not ashamed because we were soldiers, and we wanted to look like soldiers.

The people from Changi stood back and uttered not a word. It was really quite strange.

We lined up on the road as best we could and stood up as straight as we could.

Those who couldn't stand up straight were on sticks. And those who couldn't stop shaking with malaria were held by their friends.

We thought this was what we should do as soldiers to say that we were not beaten.

> *The sergeant major dressed us off and we stood in a straight line as he went over and reported to Major Johnston.*
>
> *Johnston went over to "Black" Jack Galleghan and he said, "Your 2/30th all present and correct sir."*
>
> *And Galleghan said, "Where are the rest?"*
>
> *The major said, "They're all here, sir."*
>
> *And we were.*
>
> *Black Jack Galleghan, the iron man, broke down and cried. It was an incredible scene.*
>
> *We wanted to show them we were soldiers.*

On the Australian War Memorial's Roll of Honour, listed beneath HMAS *Yarra* are the names of 138 Australians. None is identified by rank or military honours. All are equal in death.

On 4 March 1942, HMAS *Yarra* was escorting a small merchant convoy to Fremantle off Singapore in the Indian Ocean. She encountered three Japanese Cruisers and two Destroyers.

Lt Commander Robert Rankin turned the ship to engage the five warships and as the convoy dispersed. She had been hit many times and was sinking fast when Rankin ordered to abandon ship. He was killed minutes later by a salvo to the bridge.

Leading Seaman Taylor kept firing the last remaining gun until he was killed just as the ship went under.

Able Seaman John F, Murphy was witness to it from the Japanese Cruiser, Maier where he was captive:

> *Silently we stood and watched the little sloop, white ensign flying and guns blazing against the hopeless odds … hers was a gallant death and one of which Australia should be proud.*

Bill Newton was posted to No. 22 Squadron in 1942, flying Boston light bombers from Port Moresby.

He flew 52 operational sorties during his career, most were "against difficult targets under intense tropical weather conditions and enemy fire". He was known as a "well-balanced" man with a "cheerful, natural and infectious personality".

He also possessed extraordinary courage.

On at least three occasions he dived through intense anti-aircraft fire to bomb his target.

On 16 March 1943, his Boston bomber was leading an attack on Salamaua through intense shell-fire. Though hit repeatedly by enemy fire with major tears to its fuselage and wings, a holed petrol tank, badly damaged engines and one burst tyre, Newton continued the attack. He then nursed the plane 200 miles back to base, landing it with a flat tyre.

Two days later he attacked the same location.

Hit by flak, the aircraft burst into flames. Newton flew along the shore and brought the plane down on the water. Sergeant Basil Eastwood was killed in the crash, but Newton and Sergeant John Lyon escaped, swimming to shore.

Newton and Lyon were captured by the Japanese and taken to Lae, where Lyon was executed by bayonet. Newton was taken back to Salamaua on 29 March 1943 and beheaded by the Japanese. He was 23 years old.

On his last home leave, he had told his mother that he didn't think she would see him again:

> *If you hear – when you hear – there's a bottle of sherry on the mantelpiece. Have a drink for me … don't make a fuss.*

William Newton's body was later recovered and now lies in the Lae Cemetery.

He was posthumously awarded the Victoria Cross.

The Second World War had major consequences for Australia. We were transformed.

Unconditional victory infused us with confidence, achievement and pride tempered with grief and fear of an unknown future before us.

After the fall of Singapore, we knew we could no longer rely on

Britain for security. Instead we looked across the Pacific to the United States.

Not a day should go by in this country where we do not publicly or privately give thanks for American sacrifice in the Pacific from 1942 to the end of the war – 103,000 dead; half those Americans have no known grave. The Australia-US Alliance would be formalised in 1951 – the bedrock for our security. American presence in the western Pacific would be the basis for stability and prosperity in the Asia-Pacific region.

The era of European colonialism ended. Conditions now lent themselves to an emergent Asia and for Australia to become a respected player in it. We had experienced our first 'mass engagement' with Asia – not all of it bad. Many veterans such as surgeon 'Weary' Dunlop advocated and built deep links into the region.

It would also herald a generational struggle between democracy and communism. The ensuing long and bitter Cold War would shape Australia's view of the world and engagement with it.

Post-war migration from Britain and war-torn Europe, forever diversified Australia's population and society.

Women entered the workforce in large numbers, the war having changed their place in society and attitude to it.

The rapid expansion of Australian industry and science equipped the nation for its productive boom.

Ideals, perspectives, frameworks for belief and accepted norms of attitudes and behaviour – all changed.

Serving in New Guinea, the Official War artist, Eric Thake summed it up:

> *I am seeing so much every day that is new and strange. I am seeing in minutes and hours and days more than I ever expected to see in my lifetime.*

From the safe distance and comfort of this century, it is tempting to settle for the broad brushstrokes of our history. It is easy – human beings that we are, to settle for headlines, popular imagery and mythology; to forget individual sacrifices made in our name, devotion to duty and to Australia.

This generation of Australians now leaving us, whose sacrifices we honour today, is the greatest generation this nation has produced.

Born in the aftermath of the war that was, growing up through the Great Depression and coming to adulthood under the shadows of the war that was coming, they mobilised to defend our nation, its values and vital interests.

They would then undertake the economic and social reconstruction of Australia, laying the foundations for the prosperity enjoyed by subsequent generations.

In 1998 I was the member for Bradfield, representing the people of Sydney's upper north shore in the federal parliament.

Three men of advancing years came to see me. Each was a veteran and member of the 2/30th Battalion Association and survived the brutality of imprisonment described by Stan Arneil.

They came with concern for the difficulties faced by young Australians. These men had learned much in their lives and wanted to pass their reflections and wisdom on to the next generation. I agreed to help them apply for a small amount of funding from the Department of Veterans' Affairs to produce a publication.

A year later, a booklet by the 2nd/30th Battalion Association arrived in my office entitled, 'Getting On With It'.

Two reflections stood out:

> *You might want to hate the Japanese for what they did.*
> *You might never be able to forget. But I can't hate another human being, I can't.*
> *I need to forgive and it is the hardest test of all – but it's worth it because I believe in myself and I value others.*

Another:

I suppose compassion means being prepared to listen to other people's point of view and respecting those.

Their Australia is one to which we should recommit ourselves – an Australia that enshrines principle above position and values before value; one in which our responsibilities to one another, our nation and its future, transcend and define our rights.

We will be at our best in facing different, threatening horizons, if we triumph as they did – over fear. Fear not only of an enemy in war, but in peace – prejudicial fear of the unfamiliar and the unknown.

The second paradox is that the most fragile yet powerful of human emotions is – hope.

It is the belief in a better future – for ourselves, our families and our nation.

It is helping – and being helped in shaping that future, as individuals and as a people that most inspires and sustains hope. Men and women reaching out in selfless support of one another in the face of unimaginable adversity is why we pause here today.

Let us inspire the next generation to embrace the world as confident, compassionate people, imbued with this legacy. It is one of endurance, courage and understanding that in facing new and emerging horizons, what they will need most is – one another.

For we are young and we are free.

Lest we forget.

Bangka Day 75th Anniversary Memorial Service, 16 February 2017

> Addressing an anniversary memorial, Dr Nelson pays tribute to the massacre of 22 Australian army nurses on Bangka Island 75 years ago. He recalls these women who, "in the face of unimaginable adversity", sustained hope and love.

… Beneath the Byzantine inspired dome of the Hall of Memory at the Australian War Memorial is interred the Unknown Australian Soldier. Standing silent sentinel above him are fifteen stained glass windows. The most prominent image chosen in the centre facing Anzac Parade across the lake to the parliament is neither the light horseman nor a Naval Officer. It is a nurse. In her hands is a basin containing instruments. Immediately above her head is the Red Cross – universal symbol of charity. Further above it is a pelican feeding her young directly from her bleeding heart, the ultimate symbol of the quality named below – Devotion.

To completely subsume yourself into the people and the cause to which you have committed. Straddling Anzac Parade are our nation's sacred Memorials. The nurses' memorial simply says, Beyond all praise. With a sense of awkward humility, abiding reverence infused with overwhelming pride, we pause here to remember and honour. We honour sacrifices made, suffering endured and lives given for the truths by which we live. We do so as free and confident heirs to a legacy born of idealism, forged in bloody self-sacrifice and passed now to our generation. We recommit ourselves here to one another, our nation and the ideals of mankind. We are free, with a greater belief in ourselves and what it means to be an Australian in no small way as a consequence of the events that bring us here today.

The massacre of 22 young Australian Army nurses on Radji Beach, Banka Island 75 years ago, survived by only one of them. The most important year in Australia's history was 1788. The next was

1942. The Second World War was no mere extension of the First World War, nor was it about Australia's place in the world. Our vital interests were at stake and one million Australians, including 70,000 women would mobilise in defence of all we hold dear.

As the Japanese bombed the US Naval base at Pearl Harbour on 7 December 1941, they landed on the Malay Peninsula. The sweeping advance of militarist, Imperial Japan on Singapore was swift, crushing the courageous but inadequate British and allied defence of the Island. On surrender, twenty two thousand Australian troops went into captivity. Eight thousand would not survive their brutal incarceration. Although they protested leaving their patients, 65 Australian Army Nurses were embarked on *SS Vyner Brooke* on 12 February 1942. Two days later, the desperately overloaded ship was attacked and bombed by Japanese planes, sinking within half an hour of Sumatra. Twelve nurses were killed or drowned in the water. Desperately clinging to debris and determined to support one another, especially the injured, 22 would spend from 8 to 65 hours in the water before stepping onto the sand of Radji beach, Banka Island. Some were badly injured. All wore their uniforms and Red Cross armbands. The Japanese found them on 16 February.

The only survivor of what would follow was Vivian Bullwinkel who described what happened after the war:

> *About 10 o'clock on the 16th of February the ship's officer returned with a party of about 20 Japanese (soldiers). They lined us up – the men, of whom there were about 50, on one side and the 22 nurses and one civilian woman on the other. They then took the men away down the beach behind a bluff they came back and cleaned their rifles in front of us, and then signed us to march into the sea. They then started machine-gunning from behind. The bullet that hit me struck at the waistline and just went straight through. The waves washed me back into the sand … all was quiet … the Japanese had disappeared.*

Prior to their execution, tending the wounded on the beach, the nurses contemplated escape.

Matron Irene Drummond spoke softly. She reminded everyone that they could not abandon their remaining patients saying, "Where there is life there is hope". When the Japanese set up the machine guns facing the water, their fate was clear. No order was given – the nurses just started shuffling forward into the sea. There was no shouting, hysteria or panic. Sister Florence Casson had been severely wounded in the bombing, her leg broken. Unable to walk, she was helped into the sea by her friends. Aware of what was about to happen to them as they walked to the water's edge, Drummond said to her sisters, "Chins up, girls. I'm proud of you … I love you all". Three died on the beach before reaching the water, clumped together in death as they had been in life. Irene Drummond was hit with machine gun fire close to the water's edge, killed instantly by the second bullet. Vivian Bullwinkel heard some pray. Others up to their knees in the bloodstained water called the names of those they loved. But most fell silently until Vivian was hit by the bullet that would bring darkness but not death. The Japanese soldiers then bayoneted all the wounded civilians on the beach and in a fisherman's hut. Of the 65 nurses thrown into the sea in the sinking of *SS Vyner Brooke*, 34 suffered brutality, starvation and malnutrition in the women's camp. Vivian Bullwinkel and her closest friends kept her story secret.

Pat Gunther wrote to her family:

> *Dear Family, Please don't worry about me. I enlisted of my own free will, knowing I could be going into a war zone. We nurses have been interned with a lot of other women. We have always managed to stay together. I have not been raped, bashed or tortured. If I die, it will be due to malnutrition or malaria. I am still me. All my love Pat*

Such was their suffering, Pat Gunther also wrote:

> *We reached the stage where we envied those who had been lost at sea, and even the nurses who had been massacred. They had not known the misery and wretchedness of life in a Japanese internment camp. It was all over so quickly for them. Pearl Mittelheuser passed away on the 18th of August, her best friend Sylvia Muir curled in the foetal position next to her, unable to cry because of dehydration. 'Mitz' had simply whispered in dying that all she wanted was to once more hear her family call her by name. Pat Gunther had hoped to die in her sleep. She survived. Of the eight nurses who did not, all died in 1945. When Annie Sage, the Matron-in-Chief of the Australian Army Nursing Service at last located the 24 surviving nurses in September 1945 she asked, "But where are the rest?" Each of them, like each of us had only one life – only one chance to use life in a way that would serve others and our nation. They chose us.*

From the safe distance of this century, it is tempting – human beings that we are, to settle for the broad brushstrokes of history, headlines, popular imagery and mythology. Our comfortable lives breed easy indifference to individual sacrifices made in our name, devotion to duty and to Australia. This generation of Australians now leaving us, whose sacrifices bring us here today, is the greatest generation this nation has produced.

Born in the aftermath of the war that was, growing up through the Great Depression and coming to adulthood under the shadows of the war that was coming, they mobilised to defend our nation, its values and vital interests. They would then undertake the economic and social reconstruction of post war Australia, laying the foundations for the prosperity enjoyed by subsequent generations. Their Australia is one to which we should recommit ourselves – an Australia that enshrines principle above position and values before value; one in which our responsibilities to one another, our nation and its future, transcend and define our rights. We will be at our best in facing different, threatening horizons, if we triumph as these nurses did – over fear. Fear not only of an enemy in war, but in peace – prejudicial fear of the unfamiliar and the unknown.

On Radji Beach, Irene Drummond urged her friends to hope. Her last act in facing death was to offer them love. The most fragile yet powerful of human emotions is – hope. We have to believe in a better future for ourselves, our families and our nation. Hope is inspired and sustained most by reaching out in support of one another, irrespective of the cost to ourselves.

Today we honour women who did so in the face of unimaginable adversity. From this tragedy we are inspired to hope, love and friendship. Hope for – and belief in, our common future. Love for friends and between friends. Love of family and love of Australia. We honour on these playing fields women whose lives were committed not to themselves but to us, and their last moments to one another. We honour all those women who serve and have served this nation not only in its defence forces but in every field of endeavour. More than anything else, it is women who bring to leadership a heightened sensitivity to the needs of future generations. We honour them best by the way we live our lives and shape our nation. Let us inspire the next generation to embrace the world as confident, compassionate people, imbued with this legacy. It is one of courage, endurance and understanding that in facing new emerging and threatening horizons, what we will need most is – one another. For we are young and we are free. Lest we forget.

Bomber Command Commemorative Address, 4 June 2017

Speaking on the anniversary of this historical event, Dr Nelson recalls the noble sacrifice of 4,000 Australians in the Bomber Command air and ground crews.

It is a great honour for me to be invited by you to deliver this address on the occasion of the 75th anniversary of the entry of the RAAF into Bomber Command. It is also daunting …

One in five of our combat deaths were yours in bomber command.

You know why you enlisted and you did so for many reasons – patriotism, novelty, adventure and perhaps the glamour of flying.

But you were in the main, sons of those men who had fought in the First World War.

William Pearce's father had fought at Pozieres, Moquet farm, Broodseinde and the Passchendaele Ridge. He returned to Australia with a badly damaged leg and permanent limp. He told his son:

> *You can have a go at joining the air force if you like. If anything happens there it will be quick, sudden and you won't suffer at length.*

More than 27,000 Australians went through the Empire Training Scheme, supplying the 10,000 pilots, engineers, navigators, bomb aimers, wireless operators and gunners that formed the air crews.

Although we know of the RAAF heavy bomber squadrons – 460, 462, 463 and 467 squadrons, some three quarters of you served in British, Canadian or New Zealand squadrons.

You were the brightest and the best.

Selection was stringent and the training rigorous, intense and dangerous. Yet your greatest fear was being 'scrubbed' – failing exams. And 18 percent did fail the initial written tests and a further 26 percent the initial flying tests.

You adopted advanced, state of the art technology.

You served in tightly knit crews where you had utmost faith in one another, in the knowledge that a moment of inattention could result in tragedy.

You also experienced the extremes of peace and war simultaneously.

As remarkably young men you were responsible for decisions that could kill yourselves or many, many others.

You suffered the greatest battle losses of any Australian units of the Second World War. You went into your tour of 30 missions knowing the chance of survival was less than that of death. At a 3 percent loss rate on each sortie, you had a 40 percent chance of surviving the tour of 30.

In 460 Squadron alone, 11 percent of those who would be lost died on their first operation and almost half by their sixth.

From the second half of 1943 until mid-1944, the statistical chance of survival was nil.

At its end, 4,050 Australians in Bomber Command air and ground crews would be dead, 650 more again were killed in training.

There were also 1,821 awards and decorations – 98 with bar.

These included 2 Victoria Crosses, 3 Distinguished Service Orders and 6 Conspicuous Gallantry Medals.

And yet you also received 'white feathers' and suffered the insults from some back in Australia of being 'Jap dodgers'.

The power is in the story …

Kevin Dennis was a bank clerk in Adelaide when he enlisted in the Royal Australian Air Force. He trained as a wireless operator, serving in 462 Squadron.

In a Halifax bomber on a raid to Frankfurt on 13 March 1945, the aircraft was leaving the target when it was hit by heavy flak. The flight engineer was killed and the plane sustained heavy damage.

Kevin Dennis was seriously wounded – one foot was almost

completely severed and his other leg shattered. Although bleeding profusely, he refused to leave his post. He continued to send and receive messages until the aircraft's forced landing in France.

During his long hospital convalescence in England, a Conspicuous Gallantry Medal (CMG) arrived in the mail from the King.

The citation read in part, 'for courage of the highest order when he must have been experiencing extreme agony'.

Kevin Dennis is one of only ten Australians awarded the CMG for actions during the Second World War, six of which were awarded to members of Bomber Command.

Kevin Dennis never went to Anzac Day services or any other commemorative services. He never wore his medals.

Then finally, his family persuaded him to come from Adelaide to the Australian War Memorial for the Bomber Command commemorative service in 2014. Kevin Dennis' son, John, said.

> *I was over 40 before he told me anything. I said to him if you don't tell me, it's going to die with you … I have two sons and I need to pass it on to them.*

Kevin Dennis simply said,

> *I could only think of all the people I knew during the war and who aren't here.*

One hundred Australians have been awarded the Victoria Cross. From Neville House at Vedrafort in 1900 to Cameron Baird in Afghanistan in 2013, remarkable qualities and bravery beyond the comprehension of most of us gathered here.

Currently, 78 of those VCs are displayed here in the Memorial's Hall of Valour. Thanks in no small way to the passion, commitment and generosity of Mr Kerry Stokes, you – the Australian people, own 63 of those VCs and medal sets.

The bravery of these men was extraordinary. In most cases though, split second decisions were made to risk life for others and to change desperate circumstances.

But there is another kind of bravery. Decisions made over a longer period of time with the conscious, deliberate decision to certainly die.

In the same way it is dangerous to choose a favourite child, it is risky to have a favoured VC action.

However, I confess to that of Rawdon Hume Middleton being my greatest inspiration. He was one of yours.

As many of you know too well, Pilot Officer Rawdon Hume Middleton was Captain of a Stirling Bomber, 'H' for Harry of 149 Squadron.

On 28 November 1942 he was on a raid to the Fiat Aircraft factory works at Turin. It was his 29th combat sortie.

The flight had been difficult. A full bomb and fuel load through bad weather over the Alps. The Stirling of course did not have the capabilities of the Lancaster before us.

Middleton took the aircraft on three low level passes over the target for positive identification.

Suddenly they were hit with heavy anti-aircraft fire.

Both pilots and the wireless operator were wounded.

Middleton sustained grievous wounds including shrapnel wounds to his legs, arms and body. His jaw was shattered and his right eye was blown from its orbit. He passed out.

The 2nd pilot Flight Sergeant Hyder was given first aid by the crew. He managed to get control of the plummeting aircraft at 800 feet and drop the bombs.

Middleton regained consciousness. Although losing blood, he helped recover the plane. Determined to fly the aircraft home, he said repeatedly to his crew, "I'll make the English coast. I'll get you home".

They took further flak over France. More damage.

After four agonising hours they reached the coast of England.

Middleton turned the aircraft parallel with the coast and ordered the crew to bail out. Five did so and landed safely.

But two stayed – the front gunner and the flight engineer. They tried to persuade him to a forced landing on the coast.

Determined not to risk civilian casualties, Middleton turned the aircraft back out over the English Channel off Dymchurch and ordered the two crew to bail out.

Both did but did not survive the night in the water.

Middleton stayed with the aircraft, his body being washed up two months later. He was 26 years old. He is buried at Beck Row, Suffolk.

Awarded the Victoria Cross, the citation read:

> *His devotion to duty is unsurpassed in the annals of the RAF.*

Indeed it is …

The great paradox of life is that the most fragile yet powerful of human emotions is – hope.

We all have to believe in a better future.

We have to believe that tomorrow will be better than today, that next week and next year will be better, not so much for ourselves but for those whom we love, our community and our country.

Hope is most sustained by men and women reaching out in support of one another. Those – you, even when gripped by fear and knowing the risks, who support one another.

The further paradox, which I explain especially to young people, is that this place is called the Australian War Memorial.

But it's not about war.

Although it's in a context of war, it is instead about love and friendship.

Love for friends and between friends.

Love of family and love of our country.

It is about honouring and remembering men and women whose lives are devoted not to themselves, but to us – and their last moments to one another.

You are almost gone.

You were the best of the best generation this nation has ever produced.

Born in the aftermath of the war that was; you grew up through the hardships of the great depression and then came to your young adult lives under the shadows of the war that was coming.

You mobilised to defend our values and vital interests.

Then following the war you set about the economic and social reconstruction of the nation, building foundations for the prosperity enjoyed by subsequent generations.

You placed principle above position, and values before value.

Your responsibilities to one another, our nation and its future transcended and defined your rights.

At the end of the *Striking by Night* display recreating one of the raids done by 'George' here and so familiar to you, a young woman speaks.

'George' has returned again from a raid in which more than fifty bombers were lost.

As still images of crew alighting from the aircraft are displayed and a group shot of young airmen looks out at us, she says:

> *My memories are of young men, Aussie men – laughing, dancing and living for the moment … then gone, never to be heard of again. Shot down, killed in action. They were young, handsome – and so full of life.*

She is wrong about one important thing.

They *are* 'heard of'. They, their names and stories are heard, remembered and honoured here every minute of every day.

They always will be.

We will be at our best in facing new and threatening horizons if like you – we triumph over fear.

That is your legacy – your 'record'.

And here we guard it – we always will.

PER ARDUA ASTRA

For we are young and we are *free.*

Fire Support Base Coral – 50th Anniversary Commemorative Address, 12 May 2018

Speaking on this anniversary, Dr Nelson commemorates the sacrifice of those who fought at Fire Support Bases Coral and Balmoral, and who served in the Vietnam War.

... We pause here today, half a century after the heroism of those who fought at Fire Support Bases Coral and Balmoral.

We do so in honour of those who died in our name and the 61,000 Australians whom veterans here represent – young Australians who served, fought, suffered, died and were wounded in the Vietnam War.

The Vietnam War inflicted deep wounds on many of these young Australians. Many returned bearing emotional wounds denied healing by many who shunned them as reminders of war they opposed. From indifference to anger, the hurt inflicted remains the source of deep sorrows.

In this, we failed you.

Our nation emerged from the Vietnam War deeply divided, yet now determined to learn from the experiences of those who went in our name and our responses to them.

With humility, gratitude and immense pride we say to you that what you did in Vietnam – at Coral and Balmoral, is as valued by us as those who landed at Gallipoli, endured the Kokoda track, held the line at Kapyong or fought under our flag in the dust of Uruzgan.

The power is in the story – your story.

Fifty years ago today, two Australian infantry battalions, three artillery batteries and support units moved in to establish the base in an area known to the Americans as "the catcher's mit".

For the 1st Australian task Force (1 ATF), it was a leap into the unknown.

Fire Support Base Coral was just 45 km north of Saigon and 60 km north-west of the Australian Task Force base at Nui Dat. As dusk descended on the evening of 12 May 1968, so too did unease.

The Viet Cong and North Vietnamese Army had attacked Saigon a week earlier in the communist Second General Offensive. The Australians now stood at enemy infiltration routes expected to be used in withdrawing from the capital.

Intelligence warned of a likely enemy presence – small groups wishing to avoid contact.

But a brief reconnaissance by the Australians discovered 100 freshly dug enemy weapon pits close to the newly established fire support base. Ominously, enemy ground fire prevented low level air reconnaissance.

The threat had been seriously underestimated.

After a messy, disorganised insertion into the landing zone, the American company commander providing initial protection warned as he left, "You won't need to find Charlie, they'll come looking for you".

By nightfall the base defences were only partially completed with companies and support units dispersed.

Lt Colonel J. J. 'Jim' Shelton felt an enemy attack imminent. In an act that undoubtedly saved lives, he ordered his men to dig in. Most had time to dig individual 'shell scrapes' less than a metre deep. The gunners of 102 Battery had dug theirs only 15 cm when they were ordered, "stand to".

Heavy dusk rain filled the scrapes with mud, causing many weapons to later jam.

Sporadic enemy contacts began probing the base defences, marking Australian positions by return fire.

The NVA commander at Division headquarters only nine kilometres away, ordered a battalion and two infiltration groups to attack before the Australians settled. Only 250 metres from the base perimeter, the NVA dug in undetected.

Close to 3.30 in the morning, all hell broke loose.

Rocket and mortar fire fell onto the base – 102 Field Battery and 1RAR mortar platoon enduring the heaviest fire.

Five minutes of intense fire, a ten minute pause and then the North Vietnamese rushed the Australian position. One soldier shouted to Lt Tony Jensen, "There are about 400 nogs (slang for Viet Cong) 50 yards away".

Bombardier Andy Forsdike was lying with his M60 machine-gun team of seven men 20 metres out in front of 102 Field Battery:

> *VC (Viet Cong) got up from all around us … they crawled up to within four feet of the M60 and we didn't even know they were there … they were holding their AK47s up in the air spraying bullets …*
>
> *… there was yelling coming from the Mortar section – we could hear one of the Mortar Crew yelling that they were coming in, and not to fire – then we heard two Australian voices screaming 'they've got us', but because of the number of VC between us and the mortars we could not help them …*
>
> *… in the end we fired at the VC on the track and we possibly hit our two mortar men.*

The enemy assault quickly overran the mortars, moving through the position at speed.

As luck would have it, shortly before the main attack, the artillery battery had fired a mission to the north. The gunners were still standing at their posts, their guns facing directly to the assaulting enemy lines of 150 to 200 men. Gunners began firing over open sights, point blank into the waves of enemy troops.

Lieutenant Tony Jensen, second-in-command of the mortar platoon, was facing annihilation from the overwhelming force. Two men sprang from their pits and were killed. Desperate, he ordered direct fire onto his own position from the anti-tank platoon's recoilless rifles.

He screamed to his men, "Stay down … Splintex coming in!"

Thousands of Splintex darts swept across the platoon, clearing everything above ground.

Gunner David 'Thomo' Thomas of 102 Field Battery was forever haunted by this moment:

> *I will never forget carrying Splintex over the number 4 gun – Stevo's gun … I tripped and fell down and had a poncho wrapped around my ankles … I looked down and there was Bluey Sawtell. He was dead; he had been shot in the head and was under the poncho near our gun bay. I covered him up and kept going.*

One howitzer of 102 Field Battery was overrun, another damaged and abandoned. Desperate close-quarters fighting continued. Two Australian officers attacked the gun pit with grenades and regained the captured gun.

Helicopter gunships and fighter aircraft delivered support while a C-47 "Spooky" illuminated the battlefield with flares, hosing the enemy with fire from multiple mini-guns.

The enemy began a fighting withdrawal at 4.30 am, the last one found and killed in the number 6 gun emplacement just after 6 am.

The enemy had left 52 of its dead.

On a clearing patrol, several Australians were not far from the gun position when Gunner Ayson (No. 6 gun) opened fire on an NVA in the grass. On instinct the men went to ground.

Bombardier D'Arcy was now looking at an enemy soldier and into the barrel of his AK47. He pulled the trigger on his M60. It jammed:

> *All I remember was Ayson firing; I hit the ground … and seeing the barrel of an enemy gun I pulled the trigger and nothing happened. I was yelling for Burnsie to bloody well shoot him, just bloody shoot him … Burnsie assured me he was already dead and I could get up and stop shouting.*

Of the 18 men in the Australian mortar platoon, five were dead and 8 wounded.

In total, 11 Australians had been killed and 28 wounded. Their average age was 22.

This is a story of sheer courage, determination, leadership and luck.

The attack on Fire Support Base Coral was the most sustained ground attack on an Australian gun position since the Second World War …

Over almost four weeks in further actions at Coral and the near-by Fire Support Base Balmoral, Australians fought some of their largest and most sustained battles of the Vietnam War.

At its end would be 26 Australians dead and 100 wounded.

Together they had repelled a massive attack and accounted for more than 300 enemy soldiers killed.

None who survived would ever be the same again.

Robin Carbins was a member of 3RAR. On 23 May – his 23rd birthday, he inserted into Balmoral. The next day he came under heavy attack, Centurion tanks helping defend the position.

Robin completed his tour and returned to Australia ashamed to tell anyone he was a Vietnam veteran.

He had 13 jobs in two years, describing Vietnam as "the dirty war". He married, divorced and married again.

When a mate asked one day if he would march on Anzac Day, Denise, his wife of ten years said, "Why would he do that?"

Emotionally Robin turned to her, "Because I'm a Vietnam vet". He had never told her.

Years later he said:

> *It's been a long journey with PTSD … I spent 30 years trying to forget about the war, keeping myself busy.*
>
> *I still have nightmares and bad days, but I've come to terms with it.*

A Unit Citation for Gallantry has been finally awarded these men of Coral-Balmoral. Many among us will wonder what that means.

It means this.

Bob Wilson was 17 years old in 1963 when he joined the army. A boy from Oberon, he had never heard of Vietnam – "had no idea where it was". On his second tour in 1968 he fought in these actions. Of the belated award he said:

> *It feels like a great weight has been lifted off my shoulders. This is not about personal recognition, these are battle honours for our unit ... we can carry the colours on our flag and all the young blokes can wear the citation.*
>
> *When we came back, World War Two veterans didn't want to know us, they turned their backs.*
>
> *We want to make sure the young ones get proper help and are well cared for. This citation is part of that.*
>
> *I'm terrified of crowds and I can't go to the Anzac Day Dawn service, but when I'm with these blokes, it's like a pair of old slippers. I can relax.*

The wife of one veteran said this of her husband's reaction to the news:

> *It is not often that he shows his emotions like that ... he had another big cry after (speaking to you) ... and ... it was good that he was able to 'let it out' ... thank you so much for being there for him ... you always have been ...*
>
> *I think you are all ... very, very brave to have not only survived being there in Vietnam, but for all these years that have followed.*
>
> *Australia owes you a great deal.*

And we do ...

The challenge and responsibility we place at the feet of the next generation is to not allow the past to become a distant stranger.

To young Australians, these Vietnam Veterans amongst us – like you, were once young.

Yet out of a sense of duty to our country, they gave their innocent youth; 521 of their friends gave their lives, and thousands more their good health – for us.

You will honour them best by the way you live your lives and shape our nation.

To fail in this will be to diminish ourselves and demean the values that bind us for which they gave so much that is so precious.

For we are young, and we are free.

Lest we forget.

7. Leadership, Character and Public Service

Bradfield Preselection Speech, 13 May 1995

Addressing preselectors in the electorate of Bradfield, Dr Nelson makes his pitch to be the Liberal Candidate.

Today is a celebration of liberalism, as free thinkers we are here to exercise both our right and responsibility to make a choice.

Today's is a difficult decision – loyalty to a very longstanding parliamentarian, or to the best interests of our party, our country.

Today we are in the world of politics. We are here after five successive election defeats. We are here to win. Faced with a similar dilemma in 1983 our opponents put their party above Hayden and won four in a row with Hawke.

Sadly, perhaps what really counts is winning. We need to win to give effect to our ideas and policies, to those Liberal values that stem from a life spent among people. An ideal absorbed through familiarity with individual self-sacrifice and hard work in every-day life.

My family and I are here in Bradfield because I want to be here. I was asked to be here by members of the Bradfield conference.

Bradfield has enormous political and economic potential to drive the Liberal Party in New South Wales, and in Australia. In what is one of the most affluent, productive and intelligent areas of Australia, Liberal Party membership in Bradfield has declined a further 6.4 percent in the last year in contrast to neighbouring electorates.

Liberal Party support in New South Wales has further declined this week with the release of the AGB McNair poll. Bradfield no longer has a leadership role in the Party. We should have a pivotal role – it may be disruptive to some but as Peter Costello told the Sydney Institute late last year, "This is no time for complacency"

My priorities are to:

- Listen to you. Work as a team with you. Build a close relationship with the business, professional, and broader Bradfield community.

- Assist in marginal seat campaigns throughout New South Wales.
- Engender enthusiasm and financial support within the electorate for a Howard led victory.
- Support mechanisms in the non-Labor sector to train prospective Liberal candidates who are skilled in the business of politics.

The next Federal Government will determine not only the following three years but the next thirty, and set us on a course for the 21st century.

This country must have a national wealth creation strategy because it is our failure to create wealth that, more than anything else, threatens effective social reform and provision for those in genuine need.

- Our tax systems is complex.
- Industrial relations legislation is stifling growth.
- We must have a confident agenda for youth and a national office for youth affairs.
- Families and pensioners need practical support in buying private health insurance.
- We spend more money looking after prisoners than those in nursing homes whose sacrifices made us what we are.

As Australians "remember" the end of World War ll, let us remind younger generations that their responsibilities are as important as their rights.

We must demonstrate respect for our institutions and national symbols and provide vigorous resistance to those rewriting history and imposing their own divisive and opportunistic views.

Governments seem more preoccupied with minorities and the 2.5 percent at either end but what about the rest of us who work, pay taxes, raise children and generally carry the country?

These are challenging times. The country is unsure where it is going in many ways and that creates an environment where people are ready to listen if we have the right messages to give.

The Liberal Party's challenge is to see that it's influence in society is inextricably linked to the Party's willingness to confront contemporary issues in a constructive and considered manner as Liberals. To challenge the nation's thinking on a range of fundamental economic, health and social issues and to demonstrate by our actions the welfare and individualism of other human beings is foremost in our minds.

My critics accuse me of being an idealist – I hope they never stop. Young Australians and those of us who are not so young, want to see and feel idealism and passion in those who represent us but also a sense of practical urgency for achieving our economic objectives.

People, organisations and political parties who abandon idealism do so to court irrelevancy.

Within this room we are a diverse group of people with different priorities, backgrounds and experiences. We should all remember though that until wealth is created in a taxation and industrial relations climate where Australians have incentives to invest, work and pay taxes – there is nothing we can do for anyone in genuine need.

Equally, when all our economic, scientific and financial problems are solved – all important philosophical and societal questions will remain unanswered.

We are a young party founded on a philosophy that should stir hearts in both young and old. In determining this matter today, consider the words of Thomas Wolfe:

> *Man's youth is a wonderful thing*
>
> *It is so full of anguish and of magic and yet he never comes to know it as it is until it is gone from him forever.*

Let us not lose the youthful vigour and wisdom of those who founded this great party, welcoming from all walks of life and other political parties, those who knew that ours is the only philosophy that works for the common good and that of individuals.

Whatever else has been said in the past few weeks with the exchange of words and letters, you know in your hearts what needs to be done today. The nation waits a decision on our future – of how we see ourselves in contemporary Australia, of enduring Liberal values in changing times.

Let us set for ourselves in Bradfield the goal of inflaming passions in the young, and not so young, that teaches them the importance of self-reliance, independence and sympathetic generosity.

This is a defining moment in our party's history – I am privileged to be here to share it with you. Today we respect our past but embrace our future.

First Speech to Federal Parliament, 20 May 1996

Addressing the Parliament in his maiden speech, Dr Nelson shares his motivations for entering politics, and his conception of Liberalism as "about hard work, self-sacrifice and idealism in everyday life". He shares his vision of an Australia which values health and integrity of human life, as much as achieving its economic objectives.

Mr Deputy Speaker, in rising to make my first speech in the parliament, I, through you, would like to congratulate the Speaker of the House on his election to the highest office that the House can confer upon a member and wish him the courage and wisdom that the position requires. I also congratulate my friends and colleagues from both sides of the House on the quality and depth of their first speeches.

I am honoured to be here to represent the people of Bradfield – an electorate that covers what is known commonly as Sydney's Upper North Shore. Proclaimed in 1949 and named after John Bradfield, engineer and bridge designer, it follows the Pacific Highway from Chatswood West in the south to Wahroonga in the north, across to Belrose in the north-east and Castle Cove in the south-east. It is predominantly a residential area, within which live some of the most influential and resourceful people in the country. That is what makes it most special. It also contains a number of light manufacturing, service industries and commercial industries and some government administration.

From the outset, and on behalf of the people of Bradfield, I wish to acknowledge the loyal service and hard work for over two decades of my predecessor, Mr David Connolly, his wife, Monique, and their family and wish them well for the future. I would not be here now if it were not for the dedicated hard work and sacrifice of so many people, only a few of whom can I now specifically recognise. As I mention them, I am reminded of the words of Isaac Newton:

"If I could see further than others it was because I stood on the shoulders of giants."

To my father who instilled in me the value of education, decent tolerance and respect of others and a work ethic that he thought was always in the Australian Labor Party, thank you. I thank my mother, Pat, for her intelligence and her empathy and for teaching me the importance of having a passionate commitment to those things in which you believe.

My wife, Kate, married a doctor, not a politician. Yet when I told her on 7 September 1994 that I had `had enough' and would seek Liberal Party preselection, her response was, "I knew that some day you would do this. It is not something I would want for us and our children, but I will do my best to support you." In giving up what little financial security and privacy we had, moving interstate and then being indirectly subjected to some rather insensitive ridicule and denigration, she has given much more than me.

To my son, Tom, who has already told me he would "not like to be a politician", and to my daughter, Emily, who understands that I have gone into politics "to help other people", thank you …

There are others whose lives have touched me and who played a significant and critical role in making me who I am. They are people whose names I do not remember. But when you attend a cot death at 5 o'clock in the morning, or you visit a home just after midnight when parents have been informed that their teenage son has been killed in a car accident, or you sit in the kitchen of a modest home where the bank is about to foreclose due to unexpected unemployment, or you visit the home of a young girl who has been raped by her father – although nothing prepares you for these experiences as you struggle with your helplessness and your inability to provide sufficient comfort, more than anything else they are some of the experiences that will keep me true to my principles and certainly not change me by the time I finish here. Those principles are commitment, compassion and conscience instilled in me sequentially by my parents, the Jesuits and the Hippocratic principles upon which the medical profession is based.

So why am I here? What will drive me and what are some of the issues to which I commit myself? I did not plan on being a politician but there were a number of critical events that happened to me as I went along. On 2 June 1992 I spoke to the National Press Club about unemployment and the health consequences of it. When I had finished, Ian Spicer, the then Executive Director of the Australian Chamber of Commerce and Industry, was asked a question about the employment of young Australians. He got up and gave a reply that was based then on a survey that the chamber had just done of the top 200 employers in Australia. Essentially he was proposing a change to the way in which youth wages and conditions were to be negotiated.

Before he could get his backside back on the chair, Bill Mansfield, the then Vice-President of the ACTU, sprang to his feet and said, "Absolutely under no circumstances will the union movement of Australia ever talk to employers about anything like that." As I stood there listening to this, I thought, "My God, listen to this. Here are the people who create wealth in this country and who could and should employ more Australians saying, 'This is what the problem is, whatever the merits of the solution,' and then the Labor movement is saying, 'No, we're not even going to talk about it,' at a time when we have 34 percent national youth unemployment and 47 percent youth unemployment in areas like Liverpool in New South Wales."

When I was Vice-President of the AMA, I was told by the Labor health minister that I should 'not bother telling the then government what I thought it ought to do and that, if I wanted to change anything that government was doing, I would have to change the government'. I was then told by his successor that people were "wasting their money having private health insurance" and that they ought to do what she did. When I inquired what that was, it was to pay cash.

There we were representing a million families in Australia earning less than $40,000 a year, half a million people on health care cards and 800,000 pensioners who still made enormous sacrifices to care for themselves and their families, and government wasn't listening.

When I went through the preselection experience – which I know the member for Batman (Mr Martin Ferguson) found equally character building – one of my preselectors said to me, "Dr Nelson, you seem to be in a bit of a hurry. Why don't you wait until you're 40 and your wife has another baby? If you really want to be in politics, we'll find a nice place for you to go where you do not have to cause all this trouble." The lady next to me suggested that I would be more comfortable in the eastern suburbs with an earring. You are damned right I am in a hurry.

Every hour of the day our children are going into debt, with Australia's current account problem at the rate of over $2 million an hour. At the end of every day there are 48 small businesses in this country that have gone broke. There are 800 people leaving private health insurance every day to rely on public hospitals because they can no longer afford the premium. So despairing are they of the kind of future they see ahead of them that every day one young Australian between the ages of 15 and 24 commits suicide and another 50 try.

There are dozens of families who find day after day what some of us have been on about for a number of years – that is, unless we change the way that wealth is created we have absolutely no hope whatsoever of providing institutional, residential or nursing home care to the population as it ages. And we were told, "This is as good as it gets." For people in business, if you did not like it you were instructed by the previous Prime Minister to go back on to PAYE. I can tell you that that is what I am doing, but I do not think that is what he had in mind when he gave the advice.

I have surveyed the people of my electorate to find out the things that are most important to them. Apart from the aeroplanes that have been pushed over our houses day after day, the broadband cables that are being rolled out and over which we seem to have no control and telecommunications towers popping up all over the place, the things that are most important to them are essentially Australia's foreign debt, taxation reform and Australia's health care system.

There was a time when Australians and others frequently referred to us as a 'lucky country'; but you do not hear that so often these days. It seems that in many ways luck has become our problem. Over the last 13 years in particular, every year we have sold a little more of our country and we have borrowed more money from overseas to maintain an unsustainably high expectation of what government can provide. Our current account-GDP ratio, running at around 5.5 per cent, is more than twice that of any other OECD country. We have run external deficits in 28 of the last 30 years. Our net foreign debt is 40 percent of GDP. We spend four percent of GDP servicing our debt and equity obligations, and it is increasing. We have a miserable savings rate nationally of 18 percent of GDP and a disposable personal income savings rate of three per cent.

The much-touted ACTU-government accord, about which the member for Batman made great things in his maiden speech, has basically reinforced the very things that stopped job creation. It has reinforced and given support to budget deficits, which have put pressure on interest rates. It has basically supported an inefficient and inequitable taxation system. When you look at the results of the ACTU-government accord you see that in the first 10 years – from 1984 to 1994 – with an average annual growth rate of 3.5 percent, 160,000 jobs were created in the private sector. But unemployment still increased from 687,000 to 850,000.

The new 'cures' for unemployment – training, job subsidy schemes, moving widows and middle-aged people onto pensions – do not work. If you talk to people in business, including the businesses in my electorate or anywhere else, you find that they could and should employ more Australians, but they cannot and they will not because the tax system is far too complex, the industrial relations environment is far too inflexible and they are overloaded with bureaucratic and administrative burdens. These are the things that the Howard government is moving right now to address.

I believe it is time in Australia that we had a serious debate about taxation reform, which has never been a sane pursuit. The first thing we need to do is educate Australians about the language – what is sales tax, what is payroll tax, what is wholesale sales tax or FBT. The entire system needs simplification. The monumental size and complexity of the *Income Tax Assessment Act* and the entire industry which surrounds it are in themselves arguments for change.

We need to move away from a tax system which is focused on the very things we are trying to encourage – employment, productivity and savings. We cannot encourage wealth creation without simplification and we cannot sustain government spending without broadening the tax base. The looming impact of the Internet on tax avoidance completes a picture of national urgency on this issue, to which I will be the most committed during my time here …

Another area which I think more than any other during my time here will change the political, economic and social priorities of this country is the ageing of the Australian population. By the year 2001, the number of people over the age of 65 will have increased by 27 per cent. By the middle of the next century, a third of us will be over the age of 65. At present we spend more on housing criminals in Australia than we do on caring for people in nursing homes and residential institutions.

Whoever is in government, and hopefully it will be us for many years to come, there will continue to be people who are unemployed. There are serious human and health consequences of unemployment: 50 percent more doctor visits a year, 35 percent more admissions to hospital, a death rate which is 17 percent higher and a 20 percent higher death rate for the wives of unemployed men.

I believe that we ought to be considering, as the Anglican Bishop of Brisbane, Peter Hollingworth, argued unsuccessfully in 1992, that it is time in Australia that we started to pilot on a voluntary basis community development employment programs for people who are unemployed as a means of maintaining a sense of self-worth and self-esteem. Similarly, it is time that we changed the attitudes of Australians toward those who are unemployed. Most people who are unemployed are unemployed through no fault of their own. They are not dole bludgers or anything of the sort.

Over the last 13 years we have created a world in which many Australians expect that the Australian government will provide for them and we have cut a whole range of people out of the economic mainstream. I think it is time that we said to every Australian, whoever they are or wherever they were born, "There is a place for you. We will care for you, but we want you to make some kind of contribution to our future."

On average, as I said earlier, one young Australian commits suicide every day, and there are another 50 who try. There are many reasons for it. It would be wrong to say it is entirely the fault of government, but government plays a big role in determining what kinds of values and priorities we have. In looking at the problems young people have we find 30 percent of those who are looking for a job cannot find one and 60,000 young people in this country are long-term unemployed. There are 22,000 homeless children whom we know of, and we have 600,000 kids living in poverty. We have countless numbers who are remaining in the education system beyond their natural abilities for jobs that they think are not likely to exist. The threshold of resistance to despair has been lowered for a generation that have really lost confidence that we who profess to lead in public life either do not understand or perhaps do not even care about the sorts of problems they face.

Like my colleague the honourable member for Kingston (Ms Jeanes), I will be arguing for a national office for children and for youth, to put all kinds of legislation up for scrutiny in terms of what it will do for children, to give young people a political voice in the system so that they feel their future is not simply the subject of political exploitation, and to coordinate and advocate programs for young people.

One of the other issues to which I remain deeply committed is that of the health of Australia's Aboriginal and Torres Strait Islander people. Life expectancy is 15 to 20 years less than that enjoyed by non-indigenous people. We are unique amongst countries in the developed world in that we are not reducing the gap between life expectancy for indigenous and non-indigenous people. I spent time in Kenya and in Tanzania for World Vision. People asked me what it was like. Of course it was terrible, but I can tell you that, with the exception of AIDS, I did not see in those countries anything as bad as I have seen in Aboriginal Australia.

There are many reasons for it, but I think the former health minister, Graham Richardson, gave us some insight into the cause of the problem when, whilst visiting the Kimberleys – a trip for which I declined an invitation, by the way – Charles Woolley of the *60 Minutes* program asked him, "Why, Minister, after 11 years in government, is the situation still so bad?" He said, "I have spent a lifetime reading polls, and concern for Aboriginal people is not in the top million issues worrying the voters." Amongst the numerous solutions which need to be undertaken and which our government has already commenced, I think we need to work with Aboriginal people, as Noel Pearson said in 1994, to see whether in fact welfare payments can be changed in some way to provide resources to Aboriginal people in a different way which might provide better outcomes.

Yes, I am one of those people who watch *A Current Affair* at 6.30 and I am one of those people who read the *Daily Telegraph* – please don't tell Phillip Adams that – and my blood pressure goes through the roof. You ask yourself how one person can make a difference. How can any of us as individuals here, whatever side we are on, make some difference to it? I am not what you would call, I suppose, the orthodox person to be privileged to be the Liberal member for the seat of Bradfield. I did not learn Liberalism the way many of my colleagues did. But, as far as I am concerned, it is the political expression of a life that is spent amongst people. It is about familiarity with hard work, self-sacrifice and idealism in everyday life. It is about asking yourself, as Ronald Reagan used to say: is the government the problem or is the government the solution?

The real challenge for us is to see that we confront controversy in a constructive and a considered manner, to keep challenging the nation's thinking on a range of fundamental social, health and economic issues. In doing so, I think we need to question whether we are relating decisions we make to values that society has. Over the last 13 years we have become a selfish country of people who think that their rights are more important than their responsibilities and value is more important than values. The Prime Minister (Mr Howard) is here tonight and he is a man who represents what leadership is all about – not the drivel that was fed to us in the election campaign from the other side. Real leadership is about trying to evoke in people a genuine desire to overcome our own self-interest, to support things which are best for the community and for the country. Creating common ground and trying to find solutions to intractable problems are far more difficult tasks than ideological invective and party political abuse.

I want to see this country become one in which we value the health and integrity of human life, as the Prime Minister has demonstrated in the last three weeks, as much as we do achieving our economic objectives. In the end it is what we believe, our sense of values and the way we behave which will determine our destiny—not some of the things which have preoccupied this House in recent years.

Leadership in Politics and Integrity, 1996

> Speaking in 1996, Dr Nelson focuses on the importance of morality, leadership and values for politicians. He emphasises the importance of character and honesty, suggesting that "you will be remembered not for what you know, but who you are".

Several years ago, the noted criminologist, Paul Wilson, said: "there is an inherent dishonesty in politicians which makes people feel uncomfortable about them."

To this day I carry his remarks with me and thought they may be a useful point at which to begin a discussion about leadership, politics and integrity. If ever there seemed a contradiction in terms, this must be it.

The Concise Macquarie Dictionary defines integrity as: "*Soundness of moral principle and character, uprightness, honesty.*"

What is successful political leadership? Can success mean keeping one's integrity intact?

Now as a Parliamentarian and politician I frequently hear those around me using the term leadership, although few have ever had to bear the significant responsibilities of it. I have also seen otherwise inexcusable behaviour dismissed with an all too common phrase "That's politics" and "integrity" I can only recall being used in the context of maintaining the wholeness of a policy package. Then again, I have only been a politician and parliamentarian for seven months!

At the first meeting of the Parliamentary Liberal Party after the March Federal Election, I walked into the Party room and one of my colleagues (in politics, as in medicine, you lose all your friends and they become "colleagues") approached me and said "G'day Brendan. Welcome to the world of politics, but remember you don't get anywhere here unless it is at someone else's expense".

I've had to think a great deal about leadership, values, what is right and wrong, representing the views and interests of others and ensuring at the end of the day that I have no difficulty sleeping.

Several decades ago, Mohandas K. Gandhi, warned against what he called the seven social sins. The first of these he named as "politics without principle".

Late last year the Archbishop of Sydney, the Most Rev. Harry Goodhew, called upon political leaders to "represent our highest aspirations as a people" when he attacked what he saw as the "enmity, derision, and abuse" publicly offered by politicians to one another. He called on Australia's national leaders to "not be blind guides, but to represent our highest aspirations as a people".

Archbishop Goodhew's remarks were prompted by a Morgan Poll reflecting an appallingly low level of public confidence in both the political process and its participants. He advocated churches to speak to political leaders of the day, to engage in the political process.

It was a time when the Victorian Premier Mr Jeff Kennett was engaged in public conflict with church leaders in his own state over their outspoken views about the role they considered gambling to be playing in the demise of societal values. Mr Kennett had rather directly suggested to church leaders that their core business was tending to the spiritual needs of their congregations and not interfering, as he saw it, in the political process. When there are no ethics at the top of a society, it is likely there will be none throughout it either.

As John Webster's Antonio reflects in the late 16th century drama "The Duchess of Malfi", the Government …

… Is like a common fountain, whence should flow
Pure silver drops in general.
But is't chance some curs 'd example poison't near the head
Death and diseases throughout the whole land spread.

– Act 1, Scene 1

Lines 12 -15

Is it not time for us to begin to speak in terms of what is right and wrong, to relate decisions of government to a set of values that society holds dear?

In every sense there seems in political life, if nothing else, a moral vacuum that is waiting to be filled.

Churches should not be political partisan cheer-leaders if they are to be respected and credible. Most of us consider that institutional religion and the state must remain separate. However, without the neglected values of moral conscience, Australia's political life is in danger of further degeneration into public impropriety, cultural confusion and social injustice. Whilst its individual practitioners contemplate the causes and treatment of irrelevancy deprivation syndrome, Canberra's body-politic confronts a challenge of even greater proportions. Its response may have far deeper consequences for us than we imagine.

Upon hearing that the Federal Parliament would be considering a Private Members Bill on the issue of euthanasia, one of my colleagues demanded "What the hell are you on about? I've got enough to worry about in my electorate without issues like this."

What are we on about? What do Australians expect of their politicians and parliaments? Across the party-political spectrum is a view that the debate of euthanasia is "bad politics" and in an electoral sense "all downhill".

Bill Clinton succeeded in his first presidential campaign with a constant reminder "it's the economy, stupid". But is it? Do Australians work, invest and pay taxes in the expectation that their political representatives will consider only the economic and machinery issues of good government? I suspect not. If all our economic problems were solved tomorrow, would not all-important questions remain unanswered?

In the end, politics is surely about people. It is one of the essential vehicles by which each generation seeks to build a better future.

Most of us are deeply worried about our own lives and share a common concern for the legacy we leave our children. Euthanasia, illicit drug use, suicide, sexuality, emotional despair and definitional arguments surrounding the family, are not topics welcomed in the political arena. Yet if public debate and political representation is to play a catalytic role in moulding the destiny of this nation, they are issues no less important than our balance of payments, or next month's unemployment figures.

For many Australians the political process lacks relevance to their day to day lives. Our perceived obsession with economic indices, although essential, leaves an increasing number of everyday people feeling deeply alienated from the country's major institutions.

Hope is fragile, but it has always been a powerful force for change. Those who doubt this need look no further than Allan Corbett who successfully won a seat in the New South Wales Legislative Council against the major political parties. He simply registered the name A Better Future for Our Children. Most of us who enter politics do so because we believe that our service to the community makes a difference, not only to the lives of individuals but to society generally.

The way in which the Federal Parliament manages the euthanasia issue is far more important to the way we see ourselves as a nation than the count that will be taken in the final division. Are we mature enough to rise above the mediocrity that passes for political debate on a day to day basis, to cast aside ideological posturing and discuss an issue that goes to the very heart of what we believe?

In recent years, driven by polls and out of fear of adverse electoral ramifications, it seems that parliaments have failed to take seriously the fundamental question of values, a question that lies just beneath the surface of political discussion. Issues that are philosophically imprecise, not fitting comfortably into party philosophies, provide the greatest challenge.

One consequence of this is what Hugh Mackay describes as the era of "legislative morality". Whether it be euthanasia or racial vilification, much of contemporary Australia mistakenly believes that there must be a statute or law to solve our problems. In doing so, governments take from people the responsibility and skills they must have for determining the difference between right and wrong. In many ways, it is as if those who profess to lead are not willing to enunciate clearly what they consider the difference to be.

Reconnecting politics to a set of philosophical and social values is now one of the most important tasks of political life. Wider, deeper, broader and possibly more human debate in the Federal Parliament may present not only uncomfortable risks, but also an answer to the question of relevance ...

There is a forgotten ethic of public service, one of the many things which church leaders like the Anglican Archbishop of Brisbane, Peter Hollingworth, can teach our political leaders. It is an ethic of not only celebrating our rights, but also our responsibilities – to one another and our country. Archbishop Hollingworth advocated (unsuccessfully) in 1992 the implementation of community service programmes for the unemployed as a means of maintaining a sense of self-worth and self-esteem.

Behind suicide, drug use and the other problems of young people lies a profound and growing failure of our society. The problem is not that young people have not learned our values. It is that they have.

As damaging as they are, it is not the breakdown of family nor the scarcity of jobs that most threaten the future of our children. It is the disintegration of our culture. We have created a world in which young people feel they have nothing greater than themselves in which to believe. That mesh of values "God, King and Country" that held us together thirty years ago, has been dismantled to create a vacuum.

In many ways, Australia over the past 20 years has become a nation in which "anything goes", a people of cultural aimlessness and materialistic hedonism.

It may be fashionable to marginalise churches, demean the importance of community service, push children to the zenith of educational achievement and discount voluntary work as the domain of the "do-gooder", but the price of our shallowness is being paid by our children.

Leadership is still best done by example. There is a difference between right and wrong, between a life of giving rather than taking. It is a tragedy that we are losing the ability to give young people the values and skills they need to make those judgements.

Australia needs political leadership that would build a sense of community and not polarise us. Rediscovering in politics our best values is now the most important task of political life …

You come to this leadership forum in challenging times. The country is uncertain where it is going in many ways and that creates an environment where people are ready to listen if we have the right messages to give. At any turning point in the history of any country those who wish to lead have a unique opportunity and a great responsibility to see that we become a nation that values the health and integrity of human life as much as achieving our economic objectives.

My critics call me an idealist. I hope they never stop. Those who abandon their idealism and their passion do so to court irrelevancy.

Your challenge is not only to cherish and nurture your idealism but harness it to practical achievements that serve the interests of others. If you reflect on those for whom we have the highest regard, it will be those who worked to make the lives of others just a little bit better.

In order to make a difference you need courage to challenge the status quo, to confront and prod the comfortable thinking of others.

We live in world of fundamentalist intolerance and vast ignorance of the biological, ecological and political consequences of our actions. Whatever you do, seek to inflame passions in the young and not so young that teaches them to be agents of change, to challenge and change the mores of we in public life who profess to lead but all too often are led by public opinion.

In recent years Australia has become a selfish country in which people place a higher priority on rights than responsibilities, to value rather than values and a preoccupation with the here and now, rather than respect for the past and planning for the future.

I have been asked in recent years by young doctors about success. My advice to them, as it is to you, is to remember that many of the "facts" you now learn will be superseded, those that aren't you will forget. Your final achievements will eventually depend upon your continuing ability to acquire new knowledge, the inner integrity of your intellect and the humanity with which you deal with other people. Those who give in life are generally much happier than those who grab all they can get.

In the end you will be remembered not for what you know, but who you are.

Make the most of what you have and in the words of the great American poet, Thomas Wolfe:

Man's youth is a wonderful thing,
It is so full of anguish and of magic
and yet he never comes to know it as it is
until it has gone from him forever.

Budget Reply Speech, 15 May 2008

> Presenting the Opposition's Budget Reply Speech in 2008, Dr Nelson frames the new Labor Government and sets out an alternative.

Australians expected a lot with the election of a new government. Last year they listened to what the now Prime Minister and Treasurer had to say. They heard them say that they were going to be good economic managers. They heard them say that they would do something about grocery prices. They heard them say that they would do something about the price of petrol. They heard them say that they would do something about home interest rates. They heard a lot. Every Australian should now ask themselves this question: will this budget make it easier for me to keep my home, to fill my trolley with groceries, to put petrol in my car and to keep my job?

The Prime Minister and Treasurer have styled themselves as new Labor leaders, yet this is old Labor returning to haunt the Australian economic landscape again. This is an old-fashioned, high-taxing, high-spending Labor budget that seeks to punish those it does not like and discourage aspiration. The government promised to ease the pressure on working families but failed the very people they promised to help. How can any government boast of a budget that proposes to put 134,000 Australians into unemployment? Under the coalition it was "welfare to work"; under Labor, we are headed again on the road from work to welfare.

How can they boast of a budget that largely ignores the men and women whose sacrifices built this nation – seniors and retirees? How can they boast of a budget that not only leaves carers in the lurch but sells them down the river? Where were the incentives for small family business? Where was the emphasis on water, farmers and rural and regional Australians? This budget, like this government, puts media spin ahead of substance, bureaucratic doublespeak ahead of people and more than 100 reviews, inquiries and committees ahead of decisions. There is no substitute for a sound economic strategy—and Australians know it …

Today Australians are not confident about our economy. Business and consumer confidence has plunged to record-breaking lows, despite the fundamentals still being strong. Retail sales have fallen, building approvals have fallen flat, house values have fallen in many suburbs and Australians are less confident both in the economy and in their government – all this before the global liquidity crisis is yet to fully wash through the Australian economy and Labor's inflationary, job-destroying roll-back on workplace relations. Union bosses are back in town, and we have no confidence that this Prime Minister will be able to stand up to union intimidation. Why would he? After all, they invested so much money in getting him into government …

Small family businesses are the backbone of the nation. Indeed, it is one of the pillars of Liberal belief – men and women taking a risk, borrowing money to create or buy a small business and employing other Australians. Few things are more important to our way of life and our future prosperity. Get the conditions right for small business and employment will flourish and businesses will grow. We believe in encouraging and rewarding hard work. The tax system should not stifle innovation and Australians who are prepared to have a go.

Therefore, we are announcing tonight a major reduction in capital gains tax for small business. The current 15-year rule with respect to waiving capital gains tax on the sale of a small business entity on retirement from age 55 was an incentive to small business introduced by the coalition in government. To further encourage small business men and women to invest in establishing or taking over a small business, the coalition will introduce a five-year rule for capital gains tax on sale of the business for retirement. After owning and operating a small business for five years, we believe you should be entitled to capital gains tax relief should you sell your business for retirement. You will be rewarded, as you should, for your hard work, determination and sacrifice.

Education is our future. The centralised fund proposed by Labor for school infrastructure cannot replace 'parent power'. Parent groups and school principals will always know what their school needs much better than a clipboard-carrying bureaucrat who turns up from a centralised education department. The government has scrapped our Investing in Our Schools Program. These direct grants to schools made a big difference to improved buildings, classrooms, playgrounds and upgraded technology. The coalition will reinstate it. We will get them moving again. The government speaks of a so-called "education revolution" in delivering more computers to schools, while ignoring the added costs to parents and schools of connection, of maintenance and of training.

The single most important influence in the life of a child, apart from a parent, is their teacher. But no teacher can teach what they do not know. The standard of teacher training in Australia must be improved. It is unacceptably low. Higher standards in universities mean higher standards in classrooms. In this, we are failing. The coalition commits to education reform, so essential to our economic and social development. The coalition will require a number of conditions on Australian universities before they receive a dollar in public funding if they are training teachers. Entry scores to undergraduate teaching degrees at Australian universities are embarrassingly and pathetically low. The minimum university entrance score must be higher for entry to an education degree and will be formally set as a condition of funding.

Science, humanities and social science departments will be required to set and/or accredit relevant course content and assessment in education faculties. All trainee teachers will be taught how to teach children to read using proven techniques, including phonics based instruction. They must also be taught and assessed in basic sciences, mathematics, English and history. University education faculties will be required to appoint high-quality classroom teachers to their academic staff as tutors and lecturers. We need more classroom teachers teaching in our universities and fewer social engineers. This will assist in lifting the status of teaching as a profession and it will bring a greater practical focus to the training of teachers. To attract our best graduates into teaching, we must provide quality teachers with access to increased pay. Like any other profession, teachers should be rewarded and recognised on merit, as assessed by their peers. Better teachers deserve better pay. There can be no place for mediocrity when it comes to the future of the nation's teachers, yet that is tolerated in too many of our teacher training institutions. This is an education revolution.

The Prime Minister has repeatedly told the House that he would reduce the financial stress of carers by providing them with ongoing secure support. The budget has failed carers. The carers bonus, introduced by the Howard government, is only being paid this year because the Labor government was shamed into action. Devastatingly for carers, however, there is no commitment in the budget papers to pay it in future years. These men and women, these carers, are the window into our humanity. Their work is done on behalf of all Australians. What modest support they receive from government should be recognised as a wage that saves Australian taxpayers in the order of $30 billion a year. Tonight I give all Australian carers my commitment that we will use the government's inquiry to ensure equitable funding to carers in reflection of the work that they do on our behalf.

Australian seniors feel let down that the federal budget does very little to ease their cost-of-living pressures when they have done so much to build this country. That is why we will not support Labor's changes to the income test for the Commonwealth seniors health card, which will leave thousands of seniors without a health card when they need it most.

In addressing the future and the course of our nation, we need to identify and respond effectively to five key challenges. The first is the prosperity of our nation. How can we hand to the next generation a level of prosperity of which we can be proud and in which they can have confidence? This will mean taxation reform – not just simplification but lower taxes overall – and we have already begun that process. Further, how can we prosper when this budget cuts investment in research and development and swings cuts through the CSIRO?

The second challenge that we face is that of the Federation. It is very important for every one of us to ask ourselves in this the 21st century: how can we make the Federation work more effectively for our country in the interest of Australians? It will require all of us, in a mature and sober way, to examine the constitutional arrangements and responsibilities of the three tiers of government – who is responsible for what, how the money is raised and then how it is distributed.

The third challenge is that of the environment. We, as Australians and as global citizens, need to begin to live on environmental interest instead of environmental capital. It is time that we focused on water and food security as much as on anything else. Further, Australia alone cannot solve climate change, but we can do enormous environmental and economic damage to our future if we get this wrong.

The fourth challenge for us in our future is that of the security of our nation – the defence and protection not only of our country but of, increasingly, our people, our interests and the values for which we stand throughout the world.

The fifth challenge is to ensure that we are a cohesive society—to make sure that we see drug use, alcohol abuse and illiteracy not only as a human but as an economic issue. We must see the existential despair and state of 90,000 Aboriginal people living in remote parts of this country and many other things such as gambling addiction as being no less important to us in our future than getting our economic fundamentals absolutely right, upon which, ultimately, success will depend. Before the next election we will announce policy to shape the future that we want as Australians. We are an opposition, but we are also an alternative government.

Our beliefs are in the individual, in the encouragement of, and rewards for, hard work and self-sacrifice in everyday life. We believe very strongly in the family as the bedrock of Australian society, while respecting and reaching out to every other Australian, whatever their economic or personal circumstances.

We believe in choice. We believe Australians should be encouraged and supported in choice in health and education. Equally, they should be free to join a union or not to join a union.

We believe strongly in defence and security and investment in it for the protection of our nation. We believe very strongly that small family businesses are the lifeblood of our nation and its economic prosperity. We believe always in lower taxes, once our obligations to society in health, education, road infrastructure, defence and other requirements have been met.

We believe ultimately in the individual. We believe that the inherent worth of every single Australian is paramount and that our task as Liberals and as Nationals is to stand against oppressive bureaucracy and governments that too often – and under this new government – appear to think that they know what is best for Australians, instead of leaving choices and freedoms in the hands of individuals who actually make this country work.

We believe we will be at our best as a nation if we see ourselves as and strive to be an outward-looking, highly competitive and compassionate people, reconciled with our Indigenous history and imbued with fundamental values of hard work, self-sacrifice, courage, tolerance and a determination to see that we support one another, that we respect our freedoms and stand up for the rights, values and freedoms of not only all Australians but all people throughout the world.

Leave of Absence, 4 December 2008

> Addressing the Parliament in 2008, Dr Nelson reflects upon the contribution and legacy of John Howard and speaks about his decision to support the apology to the forcible removed generations of Aboriginal children.

Mr Speaker, I firstly thank you and the House for the opportunity to make some remarks during these valedictory speeches. The first thing is that we are about to celebrate Christmas, which is when Christians recognise and celebrate the birth of Christ. It is in many ways a time when we reflect on what has happened in the year that has gone and look forward to the year ahead with renewed confidence and hope, which is arguably the most fragile yet powerful of human emotions.

It has been an extraordinary year for our country. It has also been an extraordinary year for me personally and also for our party. I would like to start by thanking my wife, Gillian. A number of people on both sides of the House and around the country have said to me that perhaps I might have been more successful if they had seen and heard more of my wife, which I took as a compliment to her. There is no doubt that none of us achieves anything in our lives without people who love us and believe in us – families who make involuntary sacrifices to allow us to serve our nation, in this case through the parliament. Having said that, though, when I was asked by a young person a year or so ago when addressing a leadership conference how you stop politicians from becoming arrogant, I said, 'When you find out can you let me know?' However, I did explain that when you are my age and you have a wife you are pretty right. In explaining that, I relate that I was education minister in 2002 and I had been invited to deliver the Chapman Oration of the Institution of Engineers Australia at the Hyatt Hotel in Melbourne to a dinner audience of 500 or so engineers and their families. If you are one or you have them in your family, you know engineers are a pretty serious lot. So when I sat down, having done this, the very earnest chief executive leaned over and said, "Dr Nelson, I do apologise for continuing to eat when you began your speech, but your wife said I should enjoy something while you were talking."

That is the nature of the relationship I have with Gillian. The Leader of the House earlier today said he had observed that in the press conference I was able to do after I had lost the leadership of our party my wife had said that she was looking forward to seeing more of me, and I can report after 2½ months that just before I came down here for this sitting week she said to me, "I think I am actually going to miss you." That was reflecting on the fact that she had seen so little of me that I had been home enough for her to miss me coming down.

I would like to make some remarks, in thinking about the year that has gone, about a person of whom little, if anything, has been said over the last year. A giant of a man, not physically but politically, who cast a very long shadow over this parliament and across our country, and that is John Howard. John Howard, as we know, served the people of this country in the parliament representing Bennelong for close to 34 years. He suffered the ignominy of losing his seat of Bennelong, as we know, in the election of last year, and it is to the enormous credit of the new member for Bennelong and her party that they were able to achieve that. But John Howard has left a great lesson, I think, for all of us, and that is the importance of conviction and belief.

For our party and for me as a person who began life as a person born and bred in Labor politics and had my own personal involvement with the Crean family, whom I greatly admire, John Howard has arguably been the greatest exponent of our beliefs since Sir Robert Menzies. I made the observation when leader at one of the dinners held in tribute of John Howard that Robert Menzies in his period of having lost the prime ministership of the country and then thinking about his own political future gave a series of speeches entitled 'The forgotten people'. He spoke about the salary earners, the shopkeepers, the skilled artisans, the professional men and women and the farmers. Politically and economically, he described them as the middle class – unorganised and unselfconscious, not rich enough to wield power in its own right and too individualistic to be organised for what he described as pressure politics. And yet Menzies observed that they were the backbone of the nation. Almost as an afterthought, he further said, "It is in their children they see their greatest contribution to the country." It was for that set of beliefs and for those people that John and his wife, Janette, committed their entire lives to the service of this country. Whether you agree or disagree with John Howard and his views – and I know those on the other side certainly do not agree in almost all cases – we certainly have an enormous amount of respect for what he has given to us.

I did not participate in the so-called *The Howard Years* but there is something I would like to say which is just one small window into John Howard that I would have said in that first episode. After the Port Arthur massacre, there was enormous pressure in our country to deal with guns and gun control. Equally, there were significant sections of Australian society who felt legitimately very strongly that what was being proposed should not happen, including within my own party. I will never forget attending the first party room meeting of us in government after the Port Arthur massacre. There were many of my own colleagues who were quite opposed to the idea of us embarking on national gun control. John Howard stood before us and said, "What I am about to say to you is contrary to everything I have ever believed." He said: "We are going to have to pass rules to control the lives of people who have never done anything wrong and never will. We are going to have to tell the states what to do." That is ironic when you think of what subsequently happened in the development of the government. He said, "Never in my 23 years in public life have I been more convinced that this is the right thing to do."

Throughout his period in government as Prime Minister of the country, he showed that kind of leadership on a number of occasions. I think it is important as we finish this year that we reflect on his contribution and that made by his family to our country and in making us who we are and giving us what we have. From our side, naturally, we do argue that, amongst many things, he put this country in the strongest economic position that it could possibly be in to face the global financial crisis to which the member for North Sydney just referred.

I would also like to say that leading our party and being John Howard's immediate successor was an enormous privilege bestowed upon me by my colleagues. It was not something that I had anticipated. I had, of course, like many here – not all – quietly harboured the possibility that at some point in my political life I might take on the leadership of the party, but I did not expect that. It was genuinely a shock for me, as it was for all of us, when the member for Higgins, for whom I have the highest regard, decided for reasons I now fully understand that he would not take on the leadership of our party. And I appreciate and respect the efforts made by our now leader, Malcolm Turnbull, in contesting the leadership of the party at that time. It was extraordinarily difficult for us and obviously a new experience for me to go from government to opposition and at the same time be the leader of the party when our putative next leader had quite reasonably decided that he would prefer not to take it on. It was a major life event for many of us. We lost our leader, John Howard, we lost our putative leader, we lost our foreign minister and we effectively also lost our Deputy Prime Minister.

Whilst we were extraordinarily proud of what we had achieved, there were some things that we had to change. We had to support the ratification of the Kyoto agreement, and we made a mistake not having done that in government. I felt morally and practically that we must support the apology to the forcibly removed generations of Aboriginal children. I was ridiculed and criticised for the way in which I went about trying to make sure that the very conservative members of our party understood that I knew and respected their views. I was also criticised for the way I spoke to the apology. On those apology matters, I have yet to receive an apology from one particular person for the behaviour of some people who worked for him. I have been asked whether I regret what I said. I do not regret a single word of what I said that day – not a single word – because an atypical, more than usual number of Australians were actually tuned in to Aboriginal issues that day and if it were just about us saying sorry and being deeply sorry we would have achieved nothing. Everyday Australians who work hard and live relatively comfortable lives needed to be confronted with the state of Aboriginal Australia as it is today. Our progress as a nation, in my view, will be judged not only by the economic indices with which we are so understandably concerned but by the extent to which we lift Indigenous Australia from what is largely existential despair and appalling conditions, which still exist notwithstanding the enormous effort and goodwill of governments of all persuasions…

Finally, Mr Speaker, I meant what I said when you were appointed to that position. You are a man of extraordinary – I am not trying to get favours from you, by the way! – generosity and humility. I am a very strong believer that what goes around comes around. What went around when you sat on this side was that you were always there for all of us. It did not matter where we were – where we sat in the chamber – or whether we were gifted or not so gifted, or whether we knew standing orders or not, you were always there to lend all kinds of support and help. None of us on this side forgets it.

Valedictory (Final) Speech, 16 September 2009

Addressing the Parliament for the final time, Dr Nelson reflects on his contributions and recounts his proudest achievements.

I thank the Prime Minister, the Leader of the Opposition – my leader – and all of my colleagues who are here from this chamber and from the other place. You humble me by your presence and you honour the people I represent by being here. I thank you very much. It is with a sense of privilege, deep gratitude and team achievement that I make my final contribution to the parliament of Australia …

I begin on a serious note by thanking my children. My son, Tom, and my daughter, Emily, made the greatest involuntary sacrifices for me to serve first the medical profession through leadership of the Australian Medical Association, and then the people of Bradfield and my country, as its member. I spent more time, through their 22 years of life, travelling, at meetings, in conferences, in parliaments, at functions and on the phone than I have spent with them. And I am not alone in this place in that regard.

They were seven years old when I returned as President of the Australian Medical Association from 10 days away in remote Aboriginal communities. The self-imposed objective was to bring to the awareness of middle Australia the appalling health, premature death and existential despair of Indigenous people. Returning to Hobart late at night I went to kiss them good night. Emily roused and I apologised for my long absence. She replied: "That's all right, Daddy. You're trying to help the Aborigines." Emily and Tom, you are my greatest achievement.

It was for the Aborigines and to play a role in building a better Australia that in September 1994 I resolved to sell my home and move to Sydney. Having provided medical care to low-income families for almost a decade, I knew that the horizon of MPs in such communities is entirely consumed by life's day-to-day struggles and

I wanted to do more. But I love Tasmania and have asked that my ashes be spread at Adventure Bay, Bruny Island, 40 or 50 years from now, hopefully.

I am who I am and have done what I have only because of other people. My father died six days before the 2004 election. He did not see me go on to be defence minister and Liberal leader. That is an experience that both the Prime Minister and my leader, the opposition leader, have also had. My father was a decent, thoughtful and intelligent man possessed of deep concern for the poor, the voiceless and victims of excess. My mother taught me that life's value would ultimately be found in the people and the causes to which it was committed. My mother said that power was an instrument to be used in the service of those who had none and that in that service would be found fulfilment. I thank the Jesuits for seeking to instil in me the imaginative capacity to see the world through the eyes of other people …

I thank the Liberal Party for believing in me and for giving me extraordinary undeserved opportunities. I came to my Liberal belief through life, absorbing it through reflection upon and familiarity with the hard work, self-sacrifice and idealism of just everyday people. I am a better person and a stronger Liberal for the path that I chose.

It has been an honour to serve Bradfield, an extraordinary electorate populated by educated, hardworking people who are imbued with a deep sense of commitment to service – volunteerism, philanthropy and the best interests of Australia. These are people who give much but ask little, deserving much better than the devastating environmental vandalism being imposed upon them by the New South Wales government's rampant overdevelopment.

I arrived here in 1996 in the company of men and women who will forever be accorded a very special place in my life. Phil Barresi, Gary Nairn, Jo Gash, Danna Vale and Warren Entsch. It takes an effort to arrive in parliament as a crocodile farmer and cattle producer and leave as a gay rights activist with an earring, but that is Entschy. Amongst many others, they taught me a great deal …

Although I wanted to be a minister and to drive policy, I had all but given up believing it would ever happen when, in December 2000, John Howard asked me to be Parliamentary Secretary to the Minister for Defence. I was surprised because I sensed that John believed me risky, with an earring and a questionable background for Liberal politics. But I learned of John Howard that he respected people who challenged him provided they had an intellectually sustainable basis for their argument and refused to parade it through the media. I later learned that it was Peter Reith who convinced John Howard to give me a go. Maligned by unions, the media and their fellow travellers, Peter Reith is one of the finest men that I have met in politics. We were in Aboriginal Australia together when he was employment minister, accepting my proposal to establish an organisation to facilitate volunteerism in Aboriginal communities.

My proudest achievement as parliamentary secretary for Defence was rebuilding the propellant factory at Mulwala. Defence had planned to close it, which would have meant we would import all our ammunition and lose 750 direct and indirect jobs, creating a human and social tragedy, not to mention a strategic failure. Madness.

I relished my four years as Minister for Education, Science and Training. The then departmental secretary, Peter Shergold, wore a tie adorned with tumbling pigs – all the way through 2002 – and I was a bit too polite to ask him why. Finally he explained to a large gathering of stakeholders in the Main Committee room at the end of the consultation year on higher education reform that he called it his 'pigs might fly' tie. He considered that my chances of getting university reform through the cabinet, let alone a Senate controlled by four Independents, fell into the 'pigs might fly' category. But we did get it through: $11 billion more for the sector, with limited deregulation, governance reform, performance funding pools, scholarships, 25,000 more publicly-funded places, new medical schools, a transformational opening up of the private sector and access to income contingent loans. The 'pigs' tie is framed and it now hangs in my office.

Voluntary student unionism was delivered only by belief, persistence, negotiation and a judgment that I exercised at a critical juncture to test it in the Senate without knowing what the outcome would be. The schools agenda pursued by the current government is essentially that which we drove and legislated in 2004: national performance benchmarks in literacy and numeracy; a common school starting age; plain-language report cards; national standards for teaching; measurement and publication of school performance; principal autonomy; direct funding to schools; and the development of a national curriculum. The states had four years to comply, otherwise they would lose the Commonwealth money. That is why they are doing it. The Rudd government deserves credit for implementing the agenda, and I thank both the Prime Minister and his government for doing so and for standing up to the intransigence that I experienced from their Labor cousins in the states over the four years that I was the minister.

I also make no apology for requiring schools to fly the Australian flag and to teach values. It was right to drive values education in the knowledge that character is destiny. A values-free education risks producing values-free adults. The problem too often is not that young people have not learned our values; it is that they have.

I also believed that our nation had failed in creating a culture in which young people felt that their lives were measured by the educational choices that they made. If they did not get an outstanding university entrance score, a university degree and a BMW then, in some way, they felt they were of lesser value – lesser value to their families and lesser value to their country – than those who did. It was right to confront this orthodoxy and renew the political and policy emphasis on apprenticeships. No person's life is valued by the educational choices that they make.

We must never return to the class war in school funding. Those parents who choose to send their children to Catholic and independent schools had to be defended from those who were engaged in the politics of envy. All those children receive less public money for their education, deserving this nation's support for their education and parental sacrifice.

I thank John Howard and Peter Costello for their belief in science and research, doubling funding to the Australian Research Council and allocating an additional $8.3 billion to the nation's research and innovation agenda.

Defence remains the most demanding yet personally satisfying role that I have had in my public life. It was far more demanding than being opposition leader, which was difficult in different and less important ways. Management of the portfolio, reform of it, major procurements, intelligence, foreign policy and overseeing Australia at war – including 10 deployments – was gruelling. Acquisition of the four C-17 Globemasters, the three percent real compounding increases in Defence spending over the next decade, two additional army battalions, three F100 Aegis equipped air warfare destroyers, two 28,000-tonne LHDs and a $3 billion recruitment and retention package are the most significant legacy decisions that I leave Australia. I thank then Prime Minister John Howard and then Treasurer Peter Costello for their belief in those decisions and for their support of them. The most important, though, was de-risking the transition to the Joint Strike Fighter with the purchase of 24 FA18F Super Hornets. I drove it, I am proud of it, and I was right.

I also record my quiet admiration for a man who made mistakes and recognises them but whom I found, in my dealings with him, to be intelligent, decent, thoughtful and principled. I regard him as arguably the most misunderstood and misrepresented figure in recent history, and that is President George W. Bush. It may not be fashionable to say this, but it is true. I supported the toppling of Saddam Hussein in the post September 11 world. He may not, in hindsight, have been an immediate threat, but he was an inevitable one.

To their families, I will never forget SAS Sergeant Matthew Locke, Private Luke Worsley, SAS Signaller Sean McCarthy, Lance Corporal Jason Marks, Trooper David 'Poppy' Pearce, Captain Mark Bingley and SAS Trooper Josh Porter, who gave their lives on my watch operationally in the service of Australia as a consequence of decisions that I made, that I supported and that I administered. My life, my attitude to it and that of my country was forever changed by carrying responsibility for equipping them and placing them in harm's way. Their sacrifice transcends and endures far beyond any contribution that I have ever made or ever will. I thank every man and woman who wears the uniform of our three services for what they do in our name and under our flag, in the defence of Australia's interests and values.

I did not expect to become the leader of the parliamentary Liberal Party. I could have sat back after the election defeat in November 2007 and waited. For my own self interest, I was advised to do so. But that is not me. I knew it would be a crucial period for managing individual and collective grief at losing government and losing some of its key figures, embracing our legacy, framing the new government and setting an alternative vision for the country …

There are, in my opinion, five key challenges that face this country. The first is the prosperity that we will offer the next generation of Australians. It will require amongst other things: continuous taxation reform that is critical to incentive and Australia's international competitiveness; a flexible labour market characterised by individual choice and protection; relentless pursuit of trade liberalisation in the knowledge that isolationism will never make us safer; major reform of teacher training, which can be done without spending additional money; appointment of classroom teachers to universities as lecturers, tutors and researchers; performance benchmarks and financial rewards for teachers; and quality assurance as a prerequisite for ongoing teacher credentialling. I ask the Prime Minister also to consider implementing the 2005 report chaired by the late Dr Ken Rowe into the teaching of reading. It will do more to transform lives and lift our productivity than any other single measure in Australian schooling.

Also at the time I floated with John Howard, whose blood pressure for some inexplicable reason went up at this point, that in modern Australia, in the 21st century, the CSIRO, which had been established at a time when little research was being done in Australian universities, should be amalgamated with the ANU and that some of its regional important satellite activities amalgamated with relevant regional universities. I still believe that is the case. It would immediately give Australia a global top 10 research and teaching institution. It would drive economies of scale and it would also drive research even more effectively in regional communities relevant to the communities in which it is undertaken.

The second challenge in my view is that of the dysfunctional federation. The greatest constitutional challenge that faces this nation is the relationship between the three tiers of government, and how the money is raised. This is obviously quite a different world from that of Henry Parkes and those who gave us the Federation and the Constitution that served us so well for most of the 20th century. It is now failing us. It will require bipartisan leadership in a process to develop options for reform and to put them to the Australian people. Whatever the differences between us politically, it is obvious wherever you live in Australia, whatever your politics, that the relationship between the three tiers of government is at the heart of many of the issues that we debate here on a day-to-day basis.

The third key challenge is that of the environment. It is time for our generation to begin to live on environmental interest instead of the environmental capital that has sustained us since the industrial revolution. On climate change, let us not be a nation of intellectual lemmings. Why introduce the biggest change to the economic architecture in this nation in my lifetime with a tax on everything – massive churning of money through the economy as we emerge from the deepest economic downturn in 80 years – for no environmental gain in the absence of a global agreement? To legislate an emissions trading scheme in a country responsible for 1.4 percent of global emissions before knowing what the three major emitters will do defies not only logic; it also violates Australia's best interests. The dictum in medicine is *uberrima fides* – to always act in the utmost good faith. The interests of everyday Australians who want action on climate change but are ignorant of the cost to be imposed on them by those who do know what those costs are must surely be placed ahead of political advantage by both sides of politics.

The fourth challenge is that of the defence of Australia and, increasingly, our interests and values throughout the world. To those Australians who question our deployment to Afghanistan, please understand that our generation is engaged in an epic struggle against resurgent totalitarianism. This is a global insurgency driven by disparate groups. They have hijacked the good name of Islam to build a violent political utopia. More than 100 innocent Australians have already been murdered in Bali, Jakarta and New York at the hands of these people. They were murdered by people whose attitude to religious freedom, the rights of women and the liberating power of education violates everything for which this country has stood in its short history. We cannot leave our children held hostage to a force that they may never control. That is why it is so important that the political will be maintained in the leadership of the country from both sides of the political divide.

The fifth challenge, as I see it, is the cohesion of our society. Whether it is drug use, gambling, homelessness or the plight of Indigenous Australia, Liberals should be no less concerned for these issues than economic fundamentals. If we are falsely perceived as accountants aspiring to run an economy rather than men and women committed to building a better society we will be harshly judged. If all economic and scientific questions were ever solved, all important problems would remain still unanswered.

I also caution the nation's leadership as I leave. We have to be very clear about our values and our beliefs, never allowing Australia to become a country of cultural aimlessness. Whether by birth or by migration, we are Australians defined as we are by our institutions, triumphs, failures, heroes, villains, adversities, literature and culture. We cannot ever abandon what Arthur Schlesinger described as 'historic purpose' in building the future that we want.

The Liberal Party's future lies in its past, never forgetting from where we come, who we are and for whom we exist. Liberals gave Australia its first refugee, its first woman and its first Aborigine as members of parliament. Neville Bonner's life of grace, humility and principle in the face of extraordinary adversity has been an inspiration to me personally. As the first Aboriginal Australian elected to the parliament, he considered his greatest achievement as being there. When Robin the Hughes asked him in 1992, he said:

They no longer spoke of boongs or blacks. They spoke instead of Aboriginal people.

Robert Menzies, in 1942, arguably the most important year in Australia's history since 1788 – a seminal year for the Liberal Party – spoke and wrote of the forgotten people. I have said this to my colleagues before and I will say it again today. He wrote:

> *Salary earners, shopkeepers, skilled artisans, professional men and women ... farmers ... politically and economically they are the middle class. Unorganised and unselfconscious, not rich enough to wield power in its own right and too individualistic for pressure politics, and yet,* [he observed] ... *they are the backbone of the nation ... and in their children they see their greatest contribution to it.*

Two years later in 1944, again Sir Robert, to those who had come to Canberra to form what would become the Liberal Party emerging from the political dramas of the UAP, said:

> *What we must look for is a revival of true liberal thought, one that will work for social justice and security. True liberals have great and imperative obligations to the weak, sick and unfortunate.*

In his vision of Australia, this country would owe to 'every good citizen, not only a chance in life – but a self-respecting life.' As Liberals we must always place our principles and Australia's best interests ahead of what we think are our political interests. In my opinion and experience, one follows the other.

Thank you to my many friends and colleagues with whom I have worked, past and present. Tony Smith, Bruce Billson, Bob Baldwin and Mitch Fifield, you are men of courage and character. I will never forget it. Thank you, Peter Costello, to you and your family. Thank you for the central role that you have played in making this a more confident, prosperous and stronger country. I thank you for your support of me and I will never forget it. I wish my leader, Malcolm Turnbull, every well-deserved success for the future that will come through perseverance. To my Liberal colleagues, that future is in our hands. It is entirely in our hands.

I also thank Prime Minister Rudd for the considerable courtesies shown to me since we ended hostilities as political leaders. I thank the Prime Minister also for his commitment to screen every newborn baby for deafness. If we choose to do so, we can set a vision for our country where every child born profoundly deaf can, with a cochlear implant – if that is what their parents choose – and an appropriate program be able to hear, speak and be fully integrated into a normal school by the time they start at the age of five. A previous prime minister once said 'no child would live in poverty'. All of us support that aspiration but, as Christ himself recognised, there would always be poor. But this is something that we can do. There is not a lot of money involved. Most of it is already in the system. It requires political will and it also requires a good heart. I know on this issue especially you have both.

I am asked at the moment – and, Peter Costello, you would be asked the same – whether I would encourage young people to go into politics. To young Australians, I say never abandon your idealism. Never give up believing that you can make a difference to your community, your country and the world. The way each of us lives affects our world. You can make a decision early in your life to live in a way which changes the world. Never confuse position with principle and power. Arguably the most significant backbencher in history was William Wilberforce, who 200 years ago eschewed position to successfully challenge the repugnant economic orthodoxy of human slavery.

Success, in my experience, relies on three things. The first is to keep an open mind to other people and other ideas. None of us is right about everything, which is part of what is wrong with our system. Those who close their minds set themselves up for failure. The second is to constantly nurture and protect the inner integrity of your intellect: your ability to formulate ideas and express them to challenge and change the attitudes and opinions of other people. The third criterion for success is ultimately about the respect that we show to one another, whether in our community, the parliament or, indeed, our world.

To all Australians I say: never lose your sceptical attitude to political figures who think themselves better than others or who exploit your hard work. But I also say, as I leave, that this country is extraordinarily well-served by the men and women across the spectrum that are here: Liberal, National, Labor, Independent, Greens and a variety of other parties. I came in with a degree of cynicism; I leave with great confidence that our country is well served by what happens here – as hard as it may be to see it, at times, on the evening news. Though some are occasionally worthy of scorn, relentless attacks on politicians' remuneration diminishes the nation that they serve.

I will continue to pursue my vision of the Australia that I believe in. It should be one in which we value the health and integrity of human life as much as we do achieving our economic objectives. We should see that the barriers to the creation of wealth are the real enemy of equitable and fair social policy. We should nurture the idealism of young people. We should urge them always to embrace values for the world that they want and not just to accept values for the world they think that they are going to get.

Every Australian should know that he or she will be cared for, but in return we expect every Australian to make a contribution to this society from which we all derive a benefit. Ultimately, we should strive to be an outward-looking, intensely competitive, compassionate country, reconciled with its Indigenous history and imbued with values of hard work, self-sacrifice, tolerance and courage.

Finally – I know you are thinking it: he hasn't mentioned his wife! – I thank my wife, Gillian, and my daughter, Rebecca. Gillian endured much on my behalf in the service of my electorate and of Australia. After losing the Liberal leadership last year, she remarked in a typically understated way, "It's not a positive working environment." Gillian, for your support, encouragement, love, belief and balanced wisdom, I thank you. Whatever people think of me – and I know it was harsh – Gillian Adamson would have made an outstanding first lady. Thank you.

Dedication of the Sir John Monash Statue, 4 July 2018

> Speaking in 2018, Dr Nelson honours the memory of General Sir John Monash at his sculpture. He reflects on Monash's many contributions to his nation, as a soldier, scholar, professional, and more. Dr Nelson describes Monash ultimately as "a man who was devoted to every cause to which he committed his life and devoted to those with whom he served".

Charles Robb and Sarah Holland-Batt are the artists have produced this magnificent work in honour of our greatest general. And what Sarah Holland-Batt and Charles Robb, poet and sculptor, working together have done is to create an image of Monash as we requested – circa 1924.

After the war, but during one of the most significant decades during our nation's history. We wanted to depict John Monash in a civilian suit, wearing his RSL badge, his medals and holding a book. And as Sarah said, to depict him as a man in the midst of world that was in great flux.

"Every hour," he said, *"of every day and every night, I am in the midst of tremendous events."*

Today Les Carlyon AC was to have been here and to have spoken to us, and the dedication to be done of course by Lieutenant General Campbell. Les Carlyon unfortunately is ill and unfortunately is not here. It gets worse for you. Instead of him speaking, I'm going to speak to you.

We conceived the need to do this early in 2016. And as with many of these ideas – things we want to do, need to do, we had the idea but not the money.

And so we committed $100,000 from the estate of Robert and Nora Casebrook.

I thought very carefully about it and I asked three individuals if they would make a personal contribution to it in addition to a significant contribution by the Australian people through our government appropriation to the Australian War Memorial.

The first person I asked is a woman called Margaret Jack whom I have known for almost 20 years. Proud Australian, business woman, who's committed much of her life to business, trade and cultural ties between Australia and China. She simply said,

> *He's our greatest general. How much do you want?*

I then asked Zeke Solomon AM, senior partner Allen Arthur Robinson, whom I first met when I was Minister for Education. I noticed he was attending and contributing to a lot of discussion about intellectual efforts in education. A man who has given much of his life to the Australia-US alliance, support for the state of Israel and Australia's engagement in Asia. He too made a significant contribution.

The third I asked was Garry Browne AM. I met Garry when I was asked to speak to the Sydney Rotary about five years ago. And his family, his father served in the Second World War, male and female members of his family have served, and he said to me,

> *My parents impressed upon us John Monash's admonition that you should adopt as your fundamental creed to equip yourself for life – not just for your own sake but for that of the entire community.*

And so we are here today.

Albert Einstein was born fourteen years after General Sir John Monash and he outlived him by almost a quarter of a century. And unlike Monash he lived through, and was witness to, an even greater cataclysm of the Second World War and the murder of six million Jews. And Einstein said,

> *The desire for knowledge for its own sake, a love of justice which borders on fanaticism and a striving for personal independence.*

These, he said, *"are the Jewish tradition that allow me to regard belonging to it as a gift of great fortune."*

He said,

> *History has imposed on us a difficult struggle but if we remain devoted servants of truth, justice and liberty we will not only persevere as the world's oldest living peoples, but as we have done before, we will achieve through our productive labours, works that contribute to the ennoblement of humanity.*

And in those observations of the Jewish faith and the Jewish people, the oldest, longest living peoples in the world, Einstein said much about what informed the character of the man whose statue is before you.

Here at the Australian War Memorial we reveal our character.

Our character as a people.

Our soul …

We reveal ourselves as a people, not only in those whom we choose to lead, but those whom we choose to honour. John Monash is only the third person, the third individual at this institution, this sacred ground, to be honoured with a sculpture.

We have a stretcher bearer, disobeying orders with a donkey rescuing wounded soldiers at Gallipoli. We have a soldier-surgeon, wearing humility more comfortably than a stethoscope, having tended to men suffering under the Japanese brutality on the Burma-Thai railway in the Second World War.

And here we now have General Sir John Monash.

This man who is among a very small number of people. Some people lead from position. Generals, chairman of the board, captain of the team. Others eschew position and instead lead from principle. But occasionally we get someone who leads from both.

And John Monash was such a man.

A soldier, an Anzac, an officer and a general.

A consummate administrator.

An engineer, a pianist, a painter.

A man who committed to and dabbled in carpentry.

A Rotarian, a Scout Leader.

A scholar.

And then at the end of the war having commanded the Corps, he oversaw the demobilisation of 160,000 men in eight months.

By 1922, already for two years the Director of the State Electricity Commission in Victoria, he was President of Rotary in Melbourne and helped found Rotary in Australia.

He chaired the construction committee for the Shrine of Remembrance in Melbourne.

He led the Anzac Day Parade from 1925, from 1927 he organised it.

President of the Australian Association for the Advancement of Science.

President of the Zionist Federation of Australia.

And, as Colin McInnes said, John Monash made anti-Semitism as a respectable position impossible in Australia by the late 1920s.

And then his qualities.

A man whose intellect was never perhaps fully tested; resourceful, a man who focused on detail. A man who was fiercely independent but consulted widely and made those with whom he worked and those whom he led feel a reverence for themselves.

A man who was devoted to every cause to which he committed his life and devoted to those with whom he served and those he led.

He was consummately skilled in prosecuting his argument. Sir Robert Menzies said he was the most articulate man he that he had ever listened to.

He was also intensely patriotic. He was proud of his Jewish faith and ancestry. A part of the feature of his loyalty was that his personal staff were all Jewish and the men respected him for that loyalty.

But, paradoxically perhaps it might seem for a lay audience, he despised war. He despised its horror, the inefficiency which he described as "ghastly", the impossible cruelty and the misery.

Yet he, like this place, was reminded that in the end that there are truths by which we live that are worth fighting to defend – politically, diplomatically and at times militarily; when he saw it as necessary to maintain national and social order.

It's easy for us in our comfortable lives to forget that this country has never been more divided than it was in the 1920s.

We emerged from that war victorious, but inconsolably mourning 62,000 dead; we lived with *another* 60,000 who would die within ten years of returning. We divided principally but not only around the conscription referenda, those who had enlisted and those who were regarded as shirkers.

Monash was regarded as a pillar, a 'pole in the tent', of our brittle, fragile young democracy and we remained true to our democratic principles.

One of the indulgences you can have as a Director is you can actually say what's going to go on a sculpture. So I said, "*I want another steel band around the base.*"

During the Great Depression a right-wing movement, many fascists, exhorted John Monash to lead an insurrection against the Government. In repudiating them he said in part, "*The only hope for Australia is in the ballot box and an educated electorate.*"

And therein for the generations that will see, reflect upon and absorb the qualities of this man in this sculpture are three things.

First is to never take for granted the democratic principles and values upon which our nation has been built which are our primary interests – political, economic and religious freedoms.

Second the importance of egalitarianism, that we are people that do not place position above principle; we revere the idealism and the heroism of the everyday Australian.

This man in the 1920s was widely regarded as the most respected

Australian. Veterans in particular, saw him as unpretentious, not part of the establishment, honest intelligent and decent.

And finally, Monash knew that what will protect our nation most from ideas, attitudes and policies deeply rooted in ignorance and forged on an anvil of prejudice is – education.

Finally, he, like all of us, will be remembered not for what he was but for *who* he was, the character of the man.

Acknowledgements

David Furse-Roberts

I wish to acknowledge the following people for their invaluable assistance in the composition of this volume, *Speech: The Power of Persuasion: Selected Speeches of Brendan Nelson.*

First, I wish to recognise the Senior Fellow and former Executive Director of the Menzies Research Centre (MRC), Nick Cater, for providing me with the inspiration to embark on the timely project of researching and publishing a series of noteworthy speeches by Brendan Nelson.

With this publication brought to fruition, these selected speeches of Brendan Nelson can be read firsthand, and appreciated as a fascinating insight into his rich Liberal philosophy and lifelong dedication to advancing myriad causes from mental health, Indigenous welfare, and education reform, to the celebration of ANZAC and the preservation of Australia's military history.

I would like to thank the Executive Director of the MRC, David Hughes, together with Susan Nguyen and my former colleague at the MRC, Tim James MP, for their sustained encouragement and support. As the main instigator of this project, Tim was of valuable assistance in obtaining much of the source material and reviewing earlier versions of the manuscript. Susan provided great support with her oversight of the project and careful proofreading of the manuscript.

I especially appreciate the keen interest and enthusiasm of Brendan Nelson himself. At all times, I have valued his wise counsel and thoughtful feedback.

I am very grateful to Simon Berger for his Introduction. Written by a senior advisor and close confidante of Brendan Nelson, this incisive introduction helps to illuminate so much of the thought behind Dr Nelson's speeches.

With the editing and formatting of the volume, I am indebted to the invaluable assistance of Simon, together with Ziyan Tejani and Amy Roberts (neé Teakle), both of whom interned at the MRC. Their creativity, perspectives, and eye for detail have provided valuable input into the formatting and layout of the manuscript.

In bringing this volume to print, I am grateful to Dr Anthony Cappello and the team at Connor Court for overseeing the process of publication with their professionalism and precision.

I conclude by offering my profound appreciation to my family and friends who have supported me through this endeavour with their love, good humour, interest and encouragement.

David Furse-Roberts is a Research Fellow at the Menzies Research Centre

Index

www.ingramcontent.com/pod-product-compliance
Lightning Source LLC
Chambersburg PA
CBHW071525120726
47907CB00013B/653

* 9 7 8 1 9 2 3 2 2 4 1 8 6 *